PROCESS REDESIGN

PROCESS REDESIGN

The Implementation Guide for Managers

Arthur R. Tenner
Irving J. DeToro

Prentice Hall
Upper Saddle River, New Jersey 07458

Many of the designations used by manufacturers and sellers to distinguish their products
are claimed as trademarks. Where those designations appear in this book and Addison-Wesley
was aware of a trademark claim, the designations have been printed in initial caps or all caps.

The publisher offers discounts on this book when ordered in bulk quantities.
For more information, contact:

Corporate Sales Department
Prentice-Hall PTR
1 Lake Street
Upper Saddle River, NJ 07458
Phone: 800-382-3419; FAX: 201-236-7141
E-mail: corpsales@prenhall.com

Text designed by Carol Keller

© 1997 Addison Wesley Longman, Inc.
© 2000 Prentice-Hall PTR
    Prentice Hall, Inc.
    Upper Saddle River, New Jersey 07458

Library of Congress Cataloging-in-Publication Data
Tenner, Arthur R.
   Process redesign : the implementation guide for managers / Arthur
R. Tenner, Irving J. DeToro.
      p. cm. — (Engineering process improvement series)
   Includes bibliographical references and index.
   ISBN 0-201-63391-4 (hardcover : alk. paper)
   1. Reengineering (Management) 2. Total quality management.
I. DeToro, Irving J. II. Title. III. Series.
   HD58.87.T45 1996   96-18756
   658.4'063—dc20   CIP

Printed in the United States of America

10 9 8 7 6

ISBN: 0-201-63391-4

Prentice-Hall International (UK) Limited, *London*
Prentice-Hall of Australia Pty. Limited, *Sydney*
Prentice-Hall Canada Inc., *Toronto*
Prentice-Hall Hispanoamericana, S.A., *Mexico*
Prentice-Hall of India Private Limited, *New Delhi*
Prentice-Hall of Japan, Inc., *Tokyo*
Pearson Education Asia Pte. Ltd., *Singapore*
Editora Prentice-Hall do Brasil, Ltda., *Rio de Janeiro*

Engineering Process Improvement Series

Consulting Editor,
John W. Wesner, Ph.D., P.E.

Global competitiveness is of paramount concern to the engineering community worldwide. As customers demand ever-higher levels of quality in their products and services, engineers must keep pace by continually improving their processes. For decades, American business and industry have focused their quality efforts on their end products rather than on the processes used in the day-to-day operations that create these products and services. Experts across the country now agree that focusing on continuous improvements of the core business and engineering processes within an organization will lead to the most meaningful, long-term improvements and production of the highest-quality products.

Whether your title is researcher, designer, developer, manufacturer, quality or business manager, process engineer, student, or coach, you are responsible for finding innovative, practical ways to improve your processes and products in order to be successful and remain world-class competitive. The **Engineering Process Improvement Series** takes you beyond the ideas and theories, focusing in on the practical information you can apply to your job for both short-term and long-term results. These publications offer current tools and methods and useful how-to advice. This advice comes from the top names in the field; each book is both written and reviewed by the leaders themselves, and each book had earned the stamp of approval of the series consulting editor, John W. Wesner.

Key innovations by industry leaders in process improvement include work in benchmarking, concurrent engineering, robust design, customer-to-customer cycles, process management, and engineering design. Books in this series will discuss these vital issues in ways that help engineers of all levels of experience become more productive and increase quality significantly.

All of the books in the series share a unique graphic cover design. Viewing the graphic blocks descending, you see random pieces coming together to build a solid structure, signifying the ongoing effort to improve processes and produce quality products most satisfying to the customer. If you view the graphic blocks moving upward, you see them breaking through barriers—just as engineers and companies today must break through traditional, defining roles to operate more effectively with concurrent systems. Our mission for this series is to provide the tools, methods, and practical examples to help you hurdle the obstacles, so that you can perform simultaneous engineering and be successful at process and product improvement.

The series is divided into three categories:

Process Management and Improvement This includes books that take larger views of the field, including major processes and the end-to-end process for new product development.

Improving Functional Processes These are specific functional processes that are combined to form the more inclusive processes covered in the first category.

Special Process Topics and Tools These are methods and techniques that are used in support of improving the various processes covered in the first two categories.

Contents

15 REENGINEERING   229

Foreword

Robert C. Camp, Ph.D., PE

Business process management has emerged in the 1990s as the preeminent means of improving organizational performance. This approach addresses business and production processes, not people, as the key means of improvement and is built on principles put forth by such quality gurus as Crosby, Deming, Juran, and Feigenbaum. This book brings process redesign up-to-date to include the latest thinking on benchmarking and reengineering, concepts reinforced in the quality award criteria now prevalent worldwide.

Tenner and DeToro have captured the key points of these process improvement strategies and provide examples as well as step-by-step techniques for application. Their practical and proven approach to real performance problems means that individuals at any level in manufacturing, service, or the public sector can benefit from reading this book. Examples from three world-class firms illustrate the actual application of these process-improvement concepts, and additional examples from other firms are woven throughout the book. The book represents a valuable resource to managers embarking on an effort to improve organizational performance.

Preface

Total quality management was the dominant business strategy of the 1980s and reshaped many corporations around the world. In spite of the successes achieved by some, it eluded just as many, mostly because these companies were unable to tie quality to results like increased revenues, profits, or market share. The road to total quality management became littered with the companies that gave up or got lost along the way.

Similarly, reengineering, a technique for achieving quantum leaps in performance, became one of the hottest business topics of the early 1990s. But what are the results? Michael Hammer and James Champy, authors of the best-selling *Reengineering the Corporation*, estimated in early 1994 that well over half of the radical change programs they advocated faded into oblivion (Stewart, 1994, p. 106). Yet numerous CEOs continue to hoist the reengineering banner in campaigns to achieve radical improvement.

In recognition of the difficulty of leading an effective change effort, we've written a book to help increase the chances of success in improving organizationwide performance. This book is built on our experience, first as practitioners and then as consultants. It is designed for leaders at any level who are committed to drastically improving their organization's performance through redesigning its processes. This book goes beyond "the quick-read books" on total quality management and reengineering by providing a step-by-step guide on what to do.

Our principal objective is to offer specific and comprehensive guidance on how to achieve world-class performance by systematically improving processes. We set the stage with fundamental information to help you understand the concepts. We then provide details on specific techniques and share our experience with a variety of companies through extensive examples.

- Part I describes the organizational culture, leadership, and strategic elements that serve as the foundation for improvement. This section is organized as a brief text on the fundamental principles of process management and direction setting.

- Part II provides guidance on how to analyze performance. This section presents instructions and worksheets for identifying core processes and for prioritizing changes required in products, services, and processes. Tools and techniques are explained for documenting processes and measuring performance.

- Part III is the heart of the book. It describes how to improve processes, beginning with chartering improvement teams. This section details continuous improvement and two more aggressive approaches: benchmarking and reengineering. We build on our earlier book, *Total Quality Management: Three Steps to Continuous Improvement*, and explain benchmarking in accordance with that subject's leading authority and a valued associate, Robert C. Camp.

The book features extensive checklists and graphics to clarify key points. Discussion questions are offered at the end of each chapter to stimulate reader's thinking about the possible application of the tools, techniques, and approaches to their own organization.

REFERENCES

Stewart, Thomas A. 1994. "Rate Your Readiness to Change." *Fortune* (February 7) 106.

PART I | CULTURAL REQUIREMENTS

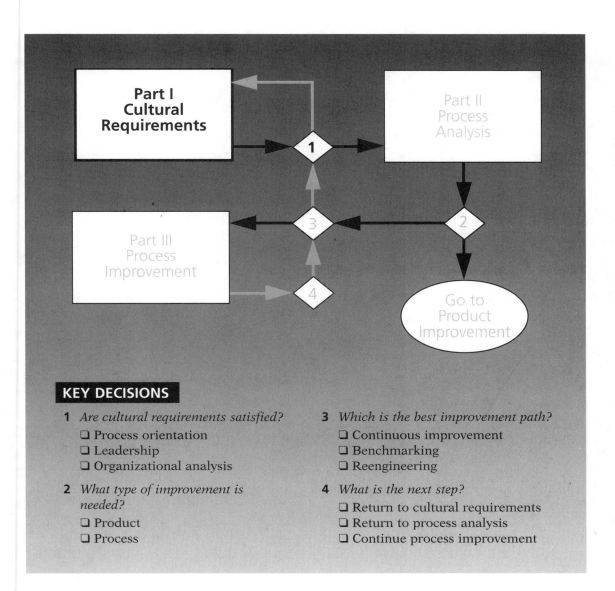

Part I Cultural Requirements	1	Part II Process Analysis
Part III Process Improvement	3 / 2	Go to Product Improvement
	4	

KEY DECISIONS

1 *Are cultural requirements satisfied?*
- ❏ Process orientation
- ❏ Leadership
- ❏ Organizational analysis

2 *What type of improvement is needed?*
- ❏ Product
- ❏ Process

3 *Which is the best improvement path?*
- ❏ Continuous improvement
- ❏ Benchmarking
- ❏ Reengineering

4 *What is the next step?*
- ❏ Return to cultural requirements
- ❏ Return to process analysis
- ❏ Continue process improvement

1 | Quick-Reference Guide to Process Redesign

This book offers a step-by-step guide for redesigning processes to improve organizationwide performance. It focuses on what to do: we don't spend a lot of time on why. Readers who require motivation need to find other sources of inspiration.

> **Genius** *is 10% inspiration and 90% perspiration.*
> THOMAS A. EDISON

This book is for leaders who know where they are going but aren't sure how to get there—leaders with or without titles, regardless of their levels in their organizations. We've designed the book to follow the sequence of steps leaders need to succeed.

This book has three main parts (see Figure 1.1). Part I establishes the cultural requirements that must be satisfied before you launch into organizationwide improvement. Part II provides the building blocks for analyzing process performance, and Part III describes three approaches to redesigning processes—continuous improvement, benchmarking, and reengineering.

Reengineering is the fundamental rethinking and the radical redesign of business processes to achieve dramatic improvements in critical measures of performance (Hammer and Champy, 1993, 32). If process improvement is like hitting a baseball, then reengineering is like hitting home runs. The stuff in between—process improvement techniques like continuous improvement and benchmarking—are the singles, doubles, and triples.

Very few players are good enough to become home-run kings without first being good hitters. This is a book on hitting—singles, doubles, triples, and homers. We explain what you need to do to be a good hitter—how to swing the bat and how to diagnose each situation to know what to do when it's your turn at the plate.

Worksheets are provided to use as you redesign your organization's processes, and the discussion questions at the end of each chapter can be used in the corporate or university classroom. Illustrations and examples are offered throughout to clarify key points.

This first chapter serves three purposes: it provides an overview of a systematic approach to organizationwide improvement; it outlines the structure of this book; and it provides checklists that serve as a quick-reference guide on how to improve organizationwide performance through process redesign.

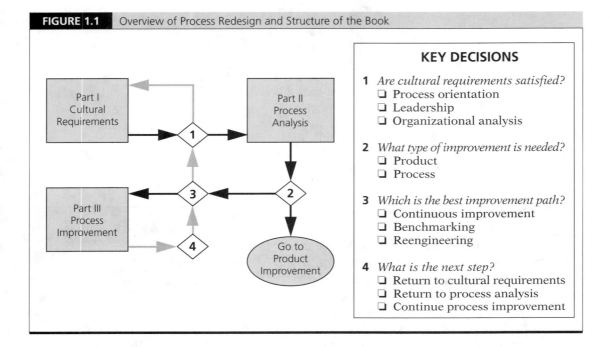

FIGURE 1.1   Overview of Process Redesign and Structure of the Book

KEY DECISIONS

1 *Are cultural requirements satisfied?*
❑ Process orientation
❑ Leadership
❑ Organizational analysis

2 *What type of improvement is needed?*
❑ Product
❑ Process

3 *Which is the best improvement path?*
❑ Continuous improvement
❑ Benchmarking
❑ Reengineering

4 *What is the next step?*
❑ Return to cultural requirements
❑ Return to process analysis
❑ Continue process improvement

CULTURAL REQUIREMENTS

Why do people fail at organizationwide improvement? The first of three primary causes is the absence of a supportive culture—the environment established by systems, style, and structure. In fact, organizations that need the greatest change are usually those that are the most deeply entrenched in nonsupportive cultures. Ensuring that the organization's culture is conducive to change—and productive change—is therefore a basic requirement.

A culture conducive to change is one that focuses on the paramount business need of understanding, anticipating, and responding to customers' demands with efficiently produced products and services. A culture conducive to such change is one that is driven by leaders who are able to develop, articulate, and inspire support for a compelling and ambitious vision. These leaders are striving for world-class excellence. They are confident and

One of the difficulties in bringing about change in an organization is that you must do so through the persons who have been most successful in that organization, no matter how faulty the system or organization is. To such a person, you see, it is the best of all possible organizations, because look who was selected by it and look who succeeded most within it. Yet these are the very people through whom we must bring about improvements.

GEORGE WASHINGTON
Second Inaugural Address

TABLE 1.1	Checklist of Cultural Requirements

PROCESS MANAGEMENT

☐ The organization is driven by the need to efficiently and effectively satisfy the customer's expectations.
☐ The organization focuses on customers and the processes that serve them and not on bosses.
☐ Process-oriented thinking is demonstrated in the organization's structure.
☐ Owners are responsible and accountable for key processes.

LEADERSHIP

☐ A compelling vision is articulated and accepted.
☐ There is a drive for achieving excellence.
☐ The means and systems are available for moving toward the stated direction.
☐ The mission is clear.
☐ Goals and objectives are clear and meaningful.

ORGANIZATIONAL ANALYSIS

☐ A formal process is used to assess the health of the organization.
☐ The health of the organization is conducive to process improvement.

willing to experiment with new ideas, especially ideas that deliberately break with tradition or bash bureaucracy.

A culture conducive to change is one that is able to select, recruit, retain, develop, and motivate a skilled and talented workforce. In this culture, everyone knows his or her mission, role, and job: goals and objectives are clear and meaningful.

A culture conducive to achieving world-class excellence is one with a process-oriented management team. In such an organization, core processes have been identified. Improvement is not confined to specific tasks or organizational boundaries. Instead, processes are addressed in their entirety, across conventional boundaries, with the specific intent of improving products and services delivered to customers. In this culture, participants are encouraged not only to achieve results but also to improve the processes by which results are achieved.

Cultural requirements needed to support organizationwide improvement are summarized in Table 1.1.

PROCESS ANALYSIS

Poor planning is the second primary cause of failure of organizationwide improvement. Significant resources are required to redesign core processes, and implementing the ensuing changes disrupts the organization. Neither long-term transformation through continuous improvement nor radical change through reengineering should be attempted without adequate preparation, planning, and senior management involvement. This usually requires that improvement is vital to the business success of the organization and the value of improvement opportunities clearly outweighs the risks and efforts required to reach the objective.

Analyzing the performance of key processes is required to ensure proper planning and prioritizing. Elements include the creation of a process inventory, the documentation of key processes, the measurement of performance, and the development of an improvement strategy. Refer to Table 1.2 for a listing of the key elements of process analysis.

Think of a process inventory as an alternative to the organizational chart. Instead of looking at a business as a tabulation of departments and people, consider it to be a set of maps that shows the sequence of steps of how things get done. The process inventory is built by defining and documenting the organization's key processes—called *core processes* by some practitioners.

The performance of each process in the inventory needs to be measured against two sets of criteria: one set quantifies effectiveness, and another set quantifies efficiency (see Figure 1.2). These measures enable the development of an improvement strategy and help set priorities, define targets, and monitor progress. These measures help make the key decision: should you focus efforts on redesigning your product or service (effectiveness) or on your process (efficiency)?

TABLE 1.2	Checklist of Process Analysis

PROCESS INVENTORY

❏ All core processes have been identified and documented.
❏ All subprocesses have been identified and documented.

MEASUREMENT

❏ *Outcome:* The performance levels for products and services that are expected by customers have been quantified and verified by testing customer satisfaction.
❏ *Output:* The expectations of customers have been translated into specifications against which process performance is compared.
❏ *Process:* The resources that are required to operate the process are known, and they have been compared to the theoretical minimum.

ANALYSIS

❏ *Improvement targets:* Competitors' capabilities, including what they might be in the future, are known.
Improvement strategy: Where should efforts be focused? *(Choose one.)*
❏ *Output*: Improve the design of products or services.
❏ *Outcome:* Improve the capability of the process to deliver outputs as designed.
❏ *Process:* Reduce resource consumption, variation, and/or cycle time.

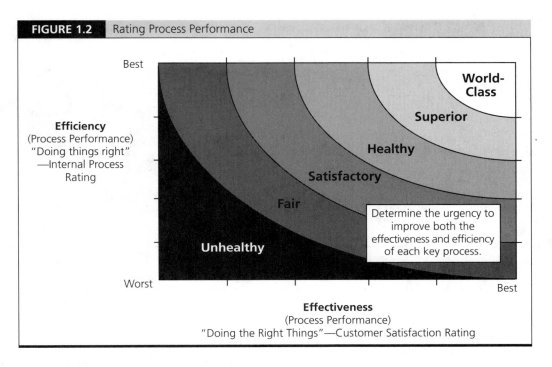

FIGURE 1.2   Rating Process Performance

> Determine the urgency to improve both the effectiveness and efficiency of each key process.

(Figure labels: Best, Worst; Efficiency (Process Performance) "Doing things right" —Internal Process Rating; Effectiveness (Process Performance) "Doing the Right Things"—Customer Satisfaction Rating; World-Class, Superior, Healthy, Satisfactory, Fair, Unhealthy)

EFFECTIVENESS describes *what* is produced in relation to what the customers need or expect. You increase effectiveness by improving the products or services (outputs) you deliver. Depending on the situation, improvement may be achieved through redesigning the process *or* redesigning the product or service.

EFFICIENCY describes *how well* the process performs. Increasing efficiency can be achieved *only* through process improvement. You increase efficiency by eliminating waste—typically through reduced costs, reduced variability, and reduced cycle time.

PROCESS IMPROVEMENT

Lack of skills or competence in systematic improvement is the third primary cause of failure of organizationwide improvement. Part III addresses this deficiency by designing improvement through the repeated cycle of plan-do-study-act. You apply this cycle through one of three approaches (see Figure 1.3):

- *Continuous improvement* on an ongoing basis for incremental gains,
- *Benchmarking* periodically for larger gains, or
- *Reengineering* selectively to achieve dramatic breakthroughs.

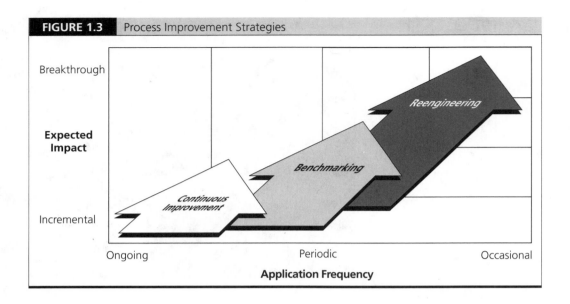

| FIGURE 1.3 | Process Improvement Strategies |

Selection of the improvement approach that is appropriate for each process at any given time is based on three factors: the *importance* and *opportunity* associated with closing a performance gap and the *feasibility* of the improvement effort. Refer to Figure 1.4 for an overview of process improvement and to Table 1.3 for a checklist to be used for planning improvement efforts.

| TABLE 1.3 | Checklist for Planning Improvement |

PLAN IMPROVEMENT

- ❏ Performance gaps have been identified for each process.
- ❏ The magnitude of improvement that is expected to be achievable has been quantified.
- ❏ The process owner understands his/her role.
- ❏ All *Cultural Requirements* are satisfied.
- ❏ The level of resources required has been estimated.
- ❏ Priorities have been determined.
- ❏ Team charters are clear and complete.
- ❏ *Process Analysis* (documentation, performance measurement, and improvement strategy) is complete.

SELECT PATH

Improvement path: considering importance, opportunity, and feasibility, which is best? *(Choose one.)*
- ❏ Is incremental improvement sufficient? If yes, go to *continuous improvement.*
- ❏ Is a step-change needed to leap-frog ahead? If yes, go to *benchmarking.*
- ❏ Is dramatic breakthrough required? If yes, go to *reengineering.*

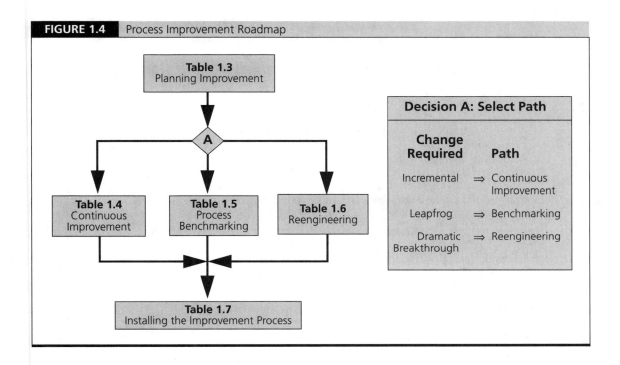

FIGURE 1.4 Process Improvement Roadmap

CONTINUOUS IMPROVEMENT

Continuous improvement is also known by the Japanese term *kaizen*. It relies on building a fundamental understanding of the customer's requirements, process capability, and the root cause for any gaps between them. Hypotheses are developed and tested, and improvement gained through the cycle of plan-do-study-act. This is a systematic approach as opposed to the classic short-cut of problem detection and subsequent solving—an approach resembling plan-do-plan-do instead of plan-do-study-act.

We provide a universal improvement model that can be applied to manufacturing as well as service and information processes in our book *Total Quality Management: Three Steps to Continuous Improvement* (Tenner and DeToro, 1992, 122). That model serves as the foundation for the continuous improvement checklist shown in Table 1.4.

BENCHMARKING

Benchmarking helps you look for and emulate the best available practices and processes. Benchmarking generally requires more resources than continuous improvement but is likely to provide larger gains. Benchmarking advocates encourage repeating benchmarking projects periodically to close gaps between "what is" and "what could be."

Robert Camp (1989, 259) offers an authoritative description of the subject in his book *Benchmarking: The Search for Industry Best Practices That Lead to Superior Performance*. His approach serves as our model for benchmarking and is summarized in Table 1.5.

TABLE 1.4	Checklist for Continuous Improvement

PLAN

❏ Continuous improvement rather than benchmarking or reengineering, is the correct approach for this process at this time.
❏ A hypothesis for the underlying root causes of the primary performance gaps has been developed.
❏ A distinction has been made between addressing common causes and special causes of variation.
❏ A plan for testing the hypothesis has been prepared.

DO

❏ The validity of the hypothesis has been tested and confirmed.

STUDY AND ACT

❏ The proposed solutions address all root causes of the deficiencies.
❏ We are ready to install improvements.

TABLE 1.5	Checklist for Benchmarking

PLANNING

❏ Benchmarking rather than continuous improvement or reengineering, is the correct approach for this process at this time.
❏ We know what we are benchmarking.
❏ Comparative companies have been identified.
❏ We understand how we are currently performing our work.
❏ Data collection has been planned.

ANALYSIS

❏ The performance gap has been analyzed.
❏ Performance of the current process has been projected into the future.
❏ We can project future performance needed.

INTEGRATION

❏ Findings have been communicated and accepted.
❏ An action plan has been prepared.

ACTION

❏ Changes have been implemented, and progress is monitored.
❏ Improvement targets have been recalibrated.
❏ We are ready to install improvements.

REENGINEERING

Unlike continuous improvement or benchmarking, reengineering is intended to drastically change the process and to do so quickly. Rather than incremental gains measured

TABLE 1.6	Checklist for Reengineering

PLANNING

❑ Reengineering rather than continuous improvement or benchmarking, is the correct approach for this process at this time.
❑ We have built a full-time team with members who have the required skills and knowledge.
❑ Impacts of current and anticipated regulations are understood.
❑ Competitors, including emerging competitors, have been examined, and their strengths and weaknesses identified.
❑ Customers and their needs have been identified.
❑ Performance gaps have been determined, and targets and time frames for closing them have been established and documented in the reengineering plan.
❑ We have aligned commitment, prepared a mandate for change, and confirmed the organization's readiness.

DESIGN

❑ Alternative scenarios have been generated that challenged the status quo, broke rules, disrupted organizational boundaries, *and* employed information technology.
❑ Proposed designs meet or exceed practices used by industry benchmarks and world-class performers.
❑ Proposed designs combine several jobs into one, locate and sequence work so it makes the most sense, reduce checks and controls, reduce the number of hand offs, *and* simplify decision making.
❑ We are ready to deploy (install) improvements.

in percentage points, reengineering breaks through to new levels of performance—an order of magnitude improvement. However, changes of this magnitude are not easily obtained. Embarking on reengineering requires justification, determination, commitment, and competence. Refer to Hammer and Champy's (1993) *Reengineering the Corporation* for comprehensive background on the subject. Their work forms the basis for our approach to reengineering and is summarized in Table 1.6.

INSTALLING THE IMPROVED PROCESS

Subsequent steps common to any improvement effort—continuous improvement, benchmarking, or reengineering—are to implement the changes, evaluate the results, and determine your next steps. Successful benchmarking or reengineering initiatives will likely lead to continuous improvement. However, what if the initiative falls short of its objectives or is abandoned? No evaluation can be complete without identifying the cause of the failure. Was the improvement effort poorly planned, misguided, or understaffed? Were process performance problems incorrectly analyzed at the outset, or were certain cultural requirements missing?

Table 1.7 provides a checklist for implementing changes and evaluating the results of process improvement. This checklist is equally applicable to continuous improvement, benchmarking, and reengineering.

TABLE 1.7	Checklist for Installing Improvements

INTEGRATION

❑ Recommended changes have been communicated and approved.
❑ A pilot has been planned and conducted.
❑ Lessons learned from the pilot have been incorporated into plans for installing improvements.
❑ The impact of the changes has been assessed.

ACTION

❑ An implementation team has been identified.
❑ The new process has been documented.
❑ Plans to manage the change have been prepared.

EVALUATION

❑ The improvement process has been evaluated.
❑ Participants have been rewarded and recognized.
❑ Results have been evaluated, and new performance targets have been established.
   What is the next step for improvement? *(Choose one.)*
❑ *Cultural requirements* were not satisfied.
❑ *Process analysis* was incomplete.
❑ *Process improvement* should continue.

REFERENCES

Camp, Robert C. 1989. *Benchmarking: The Search for Industry Best Practices That Lead to Superior Performance.* Milwaukee: Quality Press.

Hammer, M., and J. Champy. 1993. *Reengineering the Corporation.* New York: HarperBusiness.

Tenner, A. R., and I. J. DeToro. 1992. *Total Quality Management: Three Steps to Continuous Improvement.* Reading, MA: Addison-Wesley.

2 | Process Management

TRADITIONAL VIEW OF ORGANIZATIONS

If asked to describe their organization, most people would draw a chart showing at the top the senior positions with names and titles and then the reporting positions cascading down through the organization. Most people would identify the individuals occupying the boxes in the chart and their areas of responsibility.

This type of description is useful for explaining the players in an organization, their roles, and their level within the hierarchy. This *traditional* (Rummier and Brache, 1991, 5) way of describing an organization is patterned on the classical military model in which thousands of soldiers are under the command of one leader (see Figure 2.1). The traditional view accurately reflects how work *used* to be done.

FIGURE 2.1 Traditional View of Organizations

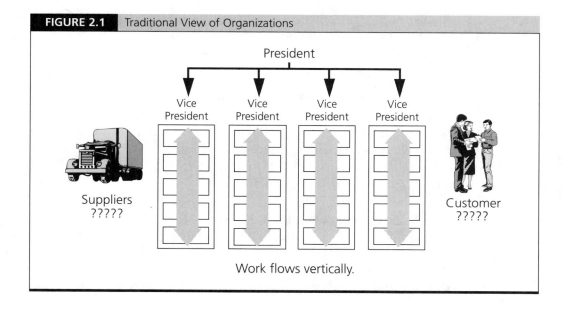

Work flows vertically.

The military uses the hierarchical structure to organize the massive number of soldiers required for tactical ground warfare. A typical army is constructed with corps, divisions, brigades, regiments, battalions, companies, platoons, and squads, which are the smallest units, and consist of nine soldiers. A general working with the corps commanders directs division commanders, who in turn direct brigade commanders, who ultimately issue orders down through a chain of command that eventually are implemented by 15,500 soldiers (U.S. Army Forces, 1989).

Similarly, laborers laying track for the railroads that opened the Western frontiers of the United States in the nineteenth century were organized in gangs, consisting of a dozen or so workers and a crew chief. An overseer or superintendent was placed on top of every dozen crew chiefs. Thousands of laborers were observed and directly supervised (Stein, 1983, 19).

At the turn of the century, this same hierarchical structure was applied to industry because its masses of uneducated and unskilled workers required direct supervision to ensure that their work was performed correctly. Many jobs were menial and involved physical labor and tools to leverage human strength. It made sense for businesses to be designed like the military or like the railroad gangs, so that direction could cascade from the senior managers to the workers. Workers, like soldiers, were grouped in small units so they could be observed and directed by a supervisor as they performed their tasks.

The decision-making and direction-setting roles of traditional organizations were concentrated among the leaders at the top. These were the *thinkers*, whereas those at the bottom were the *doers*. This type of organization responded to problems in three steps:

1. Communicate information up the chain of command.

2. Analyze information and set direction at the top.

3. Issue orders down the chain of command for deployment at the bottom.

Unfortunately, the traditional chart no longer portrays how work is performed today. An alternative chart is needed to describe how organizations perform key tasks, such as developing new products, filling customers' orders, servicing customers, or collaborating with suppliers.

PROCESS VIEW

Today's work differs from the traditional model in three significant ways. First, employees are better informed, better educated, and less tolerant of work for the sake of work. Most people are not satisfied with merely being employed: they want meaningful productive work. When people see problems today, they want to be able to correct them. Second, work itself has changed: physical labor has been replaced by information and knowledge work, supervision by direct observation is often impossible, and the service sector has supplanted manufacturing as the dominant employer. Third, expectations are different: the rapid pace of change now demands that decisions must be made at the working level. Competition kills organizations that think they have the luxury of communicating information and decisions through a multilayered hierarchy.

Another key difference today is that competition is not between people, products, or companies: it is between processes. This point is illustrated by the personal computer industry, which introduces new models with increased capability every several months. Computer manufacturers can no longer expect the market life of an individual computer product to extend over several years. Instead manufacturers engage in a frantic effort to introduce new capabilities at ever lower costs in shorter time.

The issue is less the appeal of a single new computer model than the ability to constantly generate new models that embody the latest technology at lowest costs. The manufacturer that possesses such a process can produce a stream of new products on a timely basis that satisfy market demands. Such a firm should be able to compete successfully in this industry.

Industries in which product life cycles are shrinking demand an increasing number of new products in a firm's pipeline merely to maintain revenue levels and market share. The products or services that some organizations sell today may not be the same in five years. Therefore, today's sales may be less important than the processes that yield new products or services. Becoming wedded to one product or technology is potentially dangerous, since the firm may be selling different products or services within a few years or may even migrate to a completely different business.

Similarly, industries in which products enjoy long life cycles demand an increasing capability to effectively and efficiently deliver these products to the marketplace. How is this accomplished? Sustained improvement is realized through the systematic improvement of the processes that produce these products and services.

Because of the fundamental changes that are occurring in how work is performed, the type of structure depicted by the traditional organization chart fails to offer an accurate description of contemporary businesses:

- The traditional view perpetuates the incorrect impression that individuals need to be directed and supervised as they perform their jobs.

- The traditional chart does not acknowledge customers, suppliers, or how work flows horizontally across the organization. It fails to show the relationships among individuals in the same function, between different functions, or with customers.

- The traditional view focuses on the *boss*, whereas today's leading organizations are striving to focus on the *customer*.

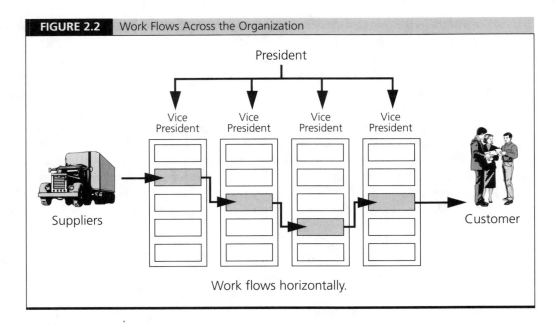

FIGURE 2.2   Work Flows Across the Organization

President

Vice President Vice President Vice President Vice President

Suppliers

Customer

Work flows horizontally.

In short, running an enterprise as described by the traditional organization chart fails to acknowledge modern realities. New structures are needed to capture the relationships among individuals in today's organizations. Figure 2.2 shows the horizontal flow of work as it cuts across the various functions depicted on the traditional, hierarchical organization chart. Although this traditional system works, it doesn't work very well.

BENEFITS OF PROCESS VIEW

Understanding the flow of work is essential, since the problems that today's organization encounters are usually *between* functions and not *within* them. For example, employees in finance departments usually have educational and business backgrounds in finance. They understand their own function and what the chief financial officer expects. These employees may tend to have relatively few problems within their own function but may begin to have problems when they prepare budgets or financial forecasts for other groups outside of finance.

Cross-functional problems are not limited to finance but commonly are found when any department depicted by the traditional organization chart interacts with other units: product development with manufacturing, manufacturing with distribution, distribution with sales, and so on throughout a traditional organization.

These problems are overcome by taking a different view of organizational structures—one that focuses on customers and processes instead of bosses. Figure 2.3 identifies the customer-supplier chain along which products and services are produced and delivered. This view is instructive because it follows work as it proceeds

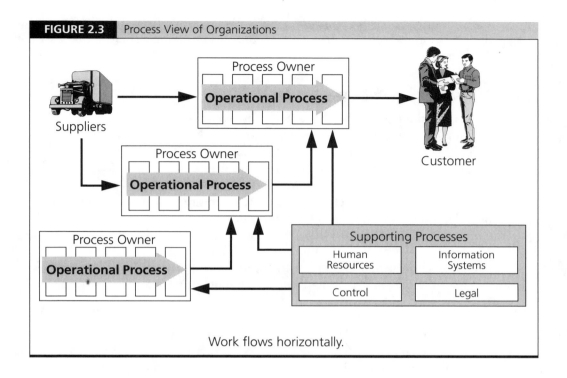

FIGURE 2.3   Process View of Organizations

Work flows horizontally.

across the organization. Perhaps even more important, functional roles and titles reflecting the traditional hierarchical structure are replaced by process owners—leaders who are responsible and accountable for the operation and improvement of the core processes.

Businesses can be described as a *network* of processes that can be identified, documented, controlled, and improved. This *process* orientation overcomes the problem in traditional organizations where information flows up the chain of command so that decisions can be made at the top. In the environment represented by the traditional view, problems between organizations are usually resolved at the highest levels. Since senior managers may lack the specific information to solve the problem correctly, their decisions may not be timely or appropriate. In addition, individuals escalating issues to senior managers tend to become defensive about their involvement and protective of their turf.

"Taking a process approach implies taking the customer point of view, since processes are the means by which an organization does what is necessary to produce value for its customers" (Davenport, 1993, 7). Thus, viewing organizations as a network of processes identifies the internal as well as external supplier-customer relationships that generate products or services.

Since the traditional organization picture simply shows individuals in various boxes and silos, a natural response to performance problems is to ask, "Who screwed up?" Focusing on processes avoids the bunker mentality that accompanies the traditional view. The process view focuses on fixing deficient processes and not deficient people.

EXAMPLES OF PROCESS VIEW

The Pool Products Division of Olin redrew its organization chart in 1994 "so flat that you could stick it under the door. Fourteen departments became eight process teams with names like *fulfillment, new products* and *resources*." The teams were arranged in a doughnut around the customer. The new structure included only two titles, coach and teammate. "By eliminating titles and departments, General Manager Doug Cahill wanted to force people to be responsible for their work, not for their jobs. As long as work got done, any teammate was free to pitch in wherever he could. Bonuses would be based on division profit, not departmental goals. Only the customer had to be satisfied, not the boss" (Stewart, 1994, 48).

Ford's 6,200-employee customer service division offers a second example of a company that ripped up its organization chart to focus on increasing customer satisfaction. Ford found that it trailed not only its Japanese competitors but even its archrival, General Motors, in this measure of performance. Ford announced the reorganization of its service division in late 1994 around four core processes (Jacob, 1995, 94):

- Fixing it right the first time,
- Supporting dealers and handling customers,
- Engineering cars with ease of service in mind, and
- Developing service fixes quicker.

It explained this reorganization as follows (Jacob, 1995, 94):

> THE DIVISION *has stopped selling parts to independent repair shops directly, even though this was profitable, because it didn't contribute to customer satisfaction and customer retention, the new touchstones.*
>
> *That's the right way to think about something as fundamental as the transition from a functional organization to a horizontal one, says McKinsey's [consultant Frank] Ostroff: "This is not just about efficiency. It starts from 'Where do we want to be in ten years? What business do we want to be in? What are the processes that drive that?' " Ford made building easy-to-repair cars one of its core processes, and so rather than pinching pennies, it has doubled staffing in upstream engineering.*
>
> *Dealer support is a second core process. Dealers are independent businessmen, but obviously Ford's effort to improve service would be a nonstarter without their cooperation. To enlist it, Ford is simplifying the way it works with dealers by reducing the battery of functional experts—parts specialists, marketing incentive specialists, and many, many more—dealers routinely dealt with.*

THE HYBRID REALITY

Like many companies advancing to the process view of an organization's structure, Ford's service division did not totally abandon the classical organization chart. Refer back to the structure portrayed in Figure 2.3, and observe that it combines a number of operational building blocks with several functional ones. This graphic represents a hybrid of the functional and process-oriented structures.

This hybrid offers the best of both worlds. Functional structures can be retained where specialized expertise is of paramount importance. At the same time, the responsiveness of the flatter, process-oriented structure can be tapped "wherever you can perform better by having real-time, integrated, parallel work—for example, developing new product or account-management teams" (Jacob, 1995, 96).

When asked by *Fortune* to offer a road map for getting from a functional organization to a horizontal one, McKinsey's Ostroff replied, "You must first do the analytical homework to understand what it takes to achieve competitive advantage [Chapter 4]. Then you must determine what core processes [Chapter 6] drive that and whether a cross-functional, process-based organization will get you there. You don't just redesign work; you design an enabling organization that goes with it. You get that one-time improvement from redesigning work. And you get coherent goals from strategically defining core processes" (Jacob, 1995, 96).

SUMMARY

Business performance is merely the result of the sum total of all processes being employed by the firm. Improving performance requires focusing on and improving the major processes by which a firm conducts its business. Trying to manage a business by reacting to results is like driving a car by looking only in the rear-view mirror. Results or outcomes are an after-the-fact measure of performance—a rear-view mirror. Accepting a process orientation provides an opportunity to improve performances before inferior products or services are produced or delivered. Improving the process instead of fixing the results ensures lasting progress.

Acceptance of a process orientation means rethinking where and how senior managers should devote their attention. If new-product development is a distinguishing capability, then the process for developing new products must be the focus of attention. This key process must be understood, documented, measured, and benchmarked against others to ensure that it is world-class. Only a small process advantage of 5 to 10 percent is required for a firm to dominate the market. To support this point of view, General Electric has defined a "world-class organization"— a goal they are pursuing—"as an organization that knows its processes better than its competitors know their processes" (Watson, 1992, 34).

A willingness to restructure the organization and redraw the organization chart to represent a process view instead of a hierarchical one is the first step toward accepting a process orientation.

DISCUSSION QUESTIONS

1. Table 2.1 compares the attributes of traditional and process views. Fill in the blanks that best describe your organization's views.

TABLE 2.1	Attributes of Traditional and Process Views		
	TRADITIONAL VIEW	**PROCESS VIEW**	**YOUR ORGANIZATION**
A. **FOCUS**	Boss	Customer	
B. **PRIMARY RELATIONSHIPS**	Chain of command	Customer-supplier	
C. **ORIENTATION**	Hierarchical	Process	
D. **DECISION MAKER**	Management	All employees	
E. **STYLE**	Authoritarian	Participative	

2. Based on your answers to question 1, draw a chart that best portrays the elements and relationships in your organization.

3. Compare your answer from question 2 to your official organization chart, and identify the barriers that prevent replacing that official chart with your picture.

REFERENCES

Davenport, T. H. 1993. *Process Innovation, Reengineering Work Through Information Technology.* Cambridge, MA: Harvard Business School Press.

Jacob, Rahul. 1995. "The Struggle to Create an Organization for the Twenty-first Century." *Fortune* (April 3), 94.

Rummier, G. A., and A. P. Brache. 1991. *Improving Performance: How to Manage the White Space on the Organization Chart.* San Francisco: Jossey-Bass.

Stein, Barry. 1983. *Quality of Worklife in Action.* New York: American Management Association.

Stewart, Thomas A. 1994. "How to Lead a Revolution." *Fortune* (November 28), 48.

U.S. Army Forces. 1989. *Your Army Today: America's Landpower in Transition.* Maxwell Air Force Base, AL: Air University Press.

Watson, Gregory H. 1992. *The Benchmarking Workbook: Adapting Best Practices for Performance Improvement.* New York: Productivity Press.

3 | Leadership

The redesign of an organization's processes cannot be successful if the organization is unclear about the direction in which it wants to progress, if it lacks objective measures of progress toward its goals, or if its systems and culture push employees

> *If you don't know where you're going, any road will do.*
> **WILL ROGERS**

in the wrong direction. This chapter explains how members of a senior management team can define and then articulate the right direction for their organization.

The demand for rapid and sweeping change by corporations became rampant by the late 1980s. Change for change's sake, however, can be counterproductive. Members of the organization need to know what must be changed and what must be retained. James Collins (1995, 141) paints an absurd picture to illustrate this point:

> IMAGINE A PRESIDENT of the United States wrestling with challenges of a rapidly changing and increasingly chaotic world and handing his top advisors a memo that begins: "We no longer hold these truths to be self-evident. We can no longer afford to hold the belief that all men are created equal."
>
> The Commander-in-chief then speaks: "We need to take a hard look at the Bill of Rights. We certainly can't let those out-dated values get in our way. Nothing is sacred anymore—not freedom of religion, not freedom of the press, not the right to trial by jury. We're in the third wave now. We must change."
>
> Of course, this is an absurd scenario. But I've created it to drive home a point: reengineering and other prevailing management fads that urge dramatic change and fundamental transformation on all fronts are not only wrong; they are dangerous. Any great enduring human institution must have an underpinning of core values and sense of timeless purpose that should never change. Give up the bedrock principles—the "what we stand for" and "why we exist"—of a great nation, and it will eventually cease to be great.

ROLE OF LEADERS

Making significant changes to an existing organization—whether through long-term and sustained continuous improvement or short-term and dramatic reengineering—requires skill, determination, and good judgment. This combination of abilities is often referred to as effective leadership. The elements and characteristics of leadership have been described and defined many times in many ways but can be distilled to three essential qualities that are common among all great leaders:

- Great leaders have a vision of creating something new, different, and better—whether it is a new product or a better service or a new national priority. Regardless of the specific goal, the vision of great leaders can be characterized as challenging, with results representing excellence or having lasting value.

- Great leaders have the abilty to identify and align resources to share their vision, build commitment, and work toward achieving it. No matter how beneficial or how important the vision might be, it is worthless if people do not recognize its value and contribute toward its achievement.

- Great leaders' visions are fundamentally correct. The difference between famous and infamous hinges on the difference between right and wrong. Leadership manifests itself by getting people to march to the music, but marching in the wrong direction can have worse consequences than not marching at all.

SETTING A DIRECTION

Setting the direction to improve all products, services, and processes is accelerated if everyone challenges the status quo every day. Leaders can set the stage for this challenge by developing answers to six fundamental questions:

- *Mission:* Why do we exist? What is our purpose?
- *Vision:* What will we look like in the future? What do we want to become?
- *Values:* What do we believe in? What do we want everyone to abide by?
- *Goals and objectives:* What are the long- and short-term accomplishments that will enable us to fulfill our mission and attain our vision?
- *Policy:* What guidance will we provide to the many individuals in our organization as to how they should provide products and services to our customers?
- *Methodology:* How are we going to move toward our vision and accomplish our goals and objectives?

Answers to the first three questions form the cornerstones of the leadership framework. The mission defines why the organization exists. The vision shows what the organization's aspirations are, and the core values explain how people are expected to behave. Answers to the remaining three questions fill in the details and build on these cornerstones. The relationship among these building blocks is shown graphically in Figure 3.1.

These questions, while seemingly simple and obvious, are enormously complex and difficult to answer, especially when an organization's traditional products and

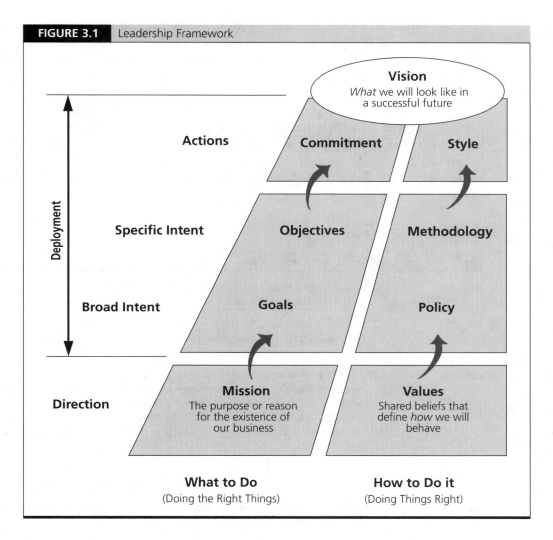

FIGURE 3.1   Leadership Framework

services are buffeted by new technologies, by competent and aggressive competitors, or by changes in customers' expectations. Nonetheless, failure to respond to each of these questions renders an organization incapable of understanding and meeting its customers' demands, allocating its resources effectively and efficiently, and capitalizing on the talents of its people.

MISSION

The question of why an organization exists is answered in the *mission statement.* This statement is comprehensive, easy to understand, usually one paragraph in length, and describes the purpose served by the organization. When published and disseminated within the organization, a well-articulated mission provides a clear statement of purpose to all employees as they perform their daily tasks. When it is widely communicated to the public at large, the mission statement sets expectations among customers as to what they should receive from this organization.

Careful balance is required in defining the scope of the mission. If it is too narrow, it could focus attention incorrectly, miss opportunities, or alienate employees who contribute in areas that are not covered. On the other hand, if it is too broad, it could be uselessly vague or result in wasting resources by trying to do everything. Table 3.1 lists eight criteria for drafting effective mission statements.

TABLE 3.1	Mission Statement Criteria
ACCURATE	Explicitly state the organization's purpose—why it exists and for whom. Cover its major activities.
PRECISE	The mission statement identifies boundaries and limits. Clearly state what the organization does, so that customers and employees can accurately infer what it does not do.
UNIQUE	The product or service produced may give the organization uniqueness. If not, does it use a unique technology or distinctive competency? Is work performed for a particular customer set or specific geographic area? If the product or service is above or below a certain cost or performed only within a specified time interval, then the cost and/or time required may be unique.
UNAMBIGUOUS	Choose words for their precision. Look for words that have a common context for the entire population that will be reading the statement.
SUCCINCT	Brevity is a key objective. After accuracy, the primary goal is ease of understanding and remembering.
STABLE	Missions should not change with the wind. An organization that is constantly "remissioning" is still searching for its purpose.
COMPREHENSIVE	Cover the entire span of products or services that are vital to the organization's success. Combine affiliated products and services into common terms. If you end up with a string of seemingly unconnected items, maybe they should not be part of your business in the first place.
CONSISTENT	Does the mission of the organization match the realities of its competitive climate? Do the mission statements of internal functions align with the overall mission and mesh with each other?

SOURCE: Adapted from Tolle (1988, 15).

Cascading the Mission Downward Through the Organization

Just as a corporate-level mission statement defines the purpose of the overall organization, functional-level statements clarify how subordinate units contribute to the whole. Continue the missioning process downward through divisions, plants, laboratories, product groups, supporting functions, and projects (Tolle, 1988, 15):

> PROBLEMS *such as interdepartmental rivalry, lack of cooperative efforts, loss of team work, hostile feelings among organizations, and excessive resource requirements are often traced to nonexistent, inaccurate, poorly written, or unpublished mission statements. In many instances, mission ambiguity is a contributing factor of failure to meet objectives and commitments, failure to meet others' expectations, efforts to suboptimize one unit at the expense of the whole, and a variety of internal unit conflicts.*

Ernest F. Tolle lists four sets of terms to avoid when drafting functional-level statements. His caveats apply equally to the corporate-level mission:

- *Quantity:* Quantities and volumes change almost daily in many organizations. The element of quantity is neither precise nor stable and does not belong in mission statements.
- *Quality:* United States industry is acutely aware of the quality issue. Quality and quantity are conditional outcomes and are more appropriate in goals and objectives statements than in mission statements.
- *Cost and time:* Unless these elements meet the mission statement criterion for uniqueness (see Table 3.1), they are unnecessary and will only clutter the mission statement without adding value.
- *"Support," "help," "assist":* These are imprecise and vague words. They neither describe the task to be done, nor do they suggest any limits or boundaries. Whenever these words show up in a draft mission statement, identify and use the tasks that constitute the *support* or *help* instead of using these words (Tolle, 1988, 15).

Example Mission Statements

The following mission statements are offered as illustrative examples. Does each one satisfy the criteria listed in Table 3.1? Does each avoid the four caveats?

> FORD MOTOR COMPANY *is a worldwide leader in automotive and automotive-related products and services as well as in newer industries such as aerospace, communications, and financial services. Our mission is to improve continually our products and services to meet our customer's needs, allowing us to prosper as a business and to provide a reasonable return to our shareholders, the owners of our business.*
> (FORD MOTOR COMPANY, 1991)

> IMPERIAL OIL *is a responsible and efficient developer of the country's natural resources and supplies a wide range of quality products and services, primarily under the ESSO brand.*
> (IMPERIAL OIL, LTD., 1991, A-2)

> TO PROVIDE *our customers distribution and transportation services for their goods in a commercial, safe, and damage-free manner.*
> (CANADIAN NATIONAL RAILWAY, 1990)

VISION

The *vision statement* provides a description of what the future organization will evolve into and, like the mission statement, guides employees at every level as to how they should manage their respective responsibilities. Usually the vision statement is drafted as soon as the mission statement is completed and is developed through the same collaborative process.

The vision statement need not use precise financial or market terms. Rather, the intent is to provide a broad description of what an organization can become, if everyone's efforts are focused and successful. The vision is not a dream, or soft expectation of what is desirable but rather a realistic picture of what is possible. The vision statement states what the organization wants to become and where it wants to go. This direction may be based on data about what is being achieved by others and what is possible for this organization.

Avoiding Fatal Flaws

Any of three flaws can be fatal to the process for building an inspirational vision: failure to have a genuine vision that is important, challenging, and at the same time realistic; failure to communicate the vision; and failure to rally everyone's genuine support. In his book *The Fifth Discipline*, Peter Senge (1990, 9, 206, 217–218) summarizes these fatal flaws:

IF ANY ONE IDEA about leadership has inspired organizations for thousands of years, it's the capacity to hold a shared picture of the future we seek to create. One is hard pressed to think of any organization that has sustained some measure of greatness in the absence of goals, values, and missions that become deeply shared throughout the organization. IBM had "service"; Polaroid had instant photography; Ford had public transportation for the masses; and Apple had computing power for the masses. Though radically different in content and kind, all these organizations managed to bind people together around a common identity and sense of destiny.

When there is a genuine vision (as opposed to the all-too-familiar "vision statement"), people excel and learn, not because they are told to, but because they want to. But too many leaders have personal visions that never get translated into shared visions that galvanize an organization. All too often, a company's shared vision has revolved around the charisma of a leader, or around a crisis that galvanizes everyone temporarily. But, given the choice, most people opt for pursuing a lofty goal, not only in times of crisis but at all times. What has been lacking is a discipline for translating individual vision into shared vision—not a "cookbook" but a set of principles and guiding practices.

A vision is truly shared when you and I have a similar picture and are committed to one another having it, not just to each of us, individually, having it. When people truly share a vision they are connected, bound together by a common aspiration. Personal visions derive their power from an individual's deep caring for the vision. Shared visions derive their power from a common caring. In fact, we have come to believe that one of the reasons people seek to build shared visions is their desire to be connected in an important undertaking.

Visions that are truly shared take time to emerge. They grow as a by-product of inter-actions of individual visions. Experience suggests that visions that are genuinely shared require ongoing conversation where individuals not only feel free to express their dreams, but learn how to listen to each other's dreams. Out of this listening, new insights into what is possible gradually emerge.

Tom Peters (1987, 482) urges, "Develop and live an enabling and empowering vision. Ensure that the vision is at once (1) specific enough to act as a 'tie breaker' (e.g., quality is more important than volume) and (2) general enough to leave room for the taking of bold initiatives in today's ever-changing environment." To help in this endeavor, examine the following two examples and the eight traits for effective vision statements offered in Table 3.2.

TABLE 3.2	Develop an Enabling and Empowering Vision

1. *Effective visions are inspiring.* Steve Jobs at Apple wanted no less than to start a revolu-tion in the way the average person processed information. Fred Smith, founder of Federal Express, had a vision of truly reliable mail service. The Nordstrom family seeks to create "an experience" with their stores. These leaders were not simply engaged in "market creation," as important as that is. They were engaged in a crusade and asked employees, customers, and suppliers to join them.

2. *Effective visions are clear and challenging—and about excellence.* The visions of various leaders seem to bring about a confidence on the part of employees that instills in them a belief that they are capable of performing the necessary acts. These leaders are chal-lengers and not coddlers.

3. *Effective visions make sense in the marketplace and, by stressing flexibility and execution, stand the test of time.* The vision is paradoxical: It is relatively *stable*—focusing on supe-rior quality and service, for instance. But it is *dynamic* in that it underscores constant improvement. The vision positions the company by defining how the company makes itself distinctly different from all its competitors.

4. *Effective visions must be stable but constantly challenged—and changed at the margin.* The vision must act as a compass in a wild and stormy sea, and, like a compass, it loses its value if it's not adjusted to take account of its surroundings.

5. *Effective visions are beacons and controls when all else is up for grabs.* To turn the vision into a beacon, leaders at all levels must model behaviors consistent with the vision at all times.

6. *Effective visions are aimed at empowering our own people first and customers second.*

7. *Effective visions prepare for the future but honor the past.*

8. *Effective visions are lived in details and not broad strokes.* A vision is concise, encompass-ing, a picture of sustaining excellence in a major market.

SOURCE: Adapted from Peters (1987, 486–490).

Example Visions

> *AS WE ACCOMPLISH our mission, CN Rail will be a long term business success by being:*
> - *Close to our customer*
> - *First in service*
> - *First in quality*
> - *First in safety*
> - *Environmentally responsible*
> - *Cost competitive and financially sound*
> - *A challenging place to work*
>
> CANADIAN NATIONAL RAILWAY, 1991

> *WE WILL BE the preferred provider of safe, reliable, and cost-effective products and services that satisfy the electricity-related needs of all customer segments.*
> (FLORIDA POWER AND LIGHT COMPANY) (DECARLO, 1991)

VALUES

Every organization operates with certain behaviors being understood without ever being said. But why leave these things unstated, if they are important to running the business? Why not provide clear definitions of those important things, so everyone has a clear sense of the *values* of the organization?

But be careful. State your true shared values, not a set of ideals that looks good on posters and on wallet-sized laminated cards. In fact, if stated values are inconsistent with realities, their posting will be a hindrance and will reveal the hypocrisy of the leadership team. Values cannot merely be proclaimed; they need to be lived convincingly. To understand the power of consistency and credibility, consider the example of Levi Strauss & Co. (Mitchell and Oneal, 1994, 46):

> *TALK, TALK TALK. As a black mid-level executive in the early 1980s, that's all Louis Kirtman got from the white men above him in top management. Levi's had long enjoyed a reputation as a socially responsible employer. But that didn't mean much to Kirtman as he watched black executives he thought were highly qualified passed over for plum jobs, while his own career seemed stalled on a lonely plateau. Top management always mouthed diversity, Kirtman says, "but in the end, they chose people they were comfortable with" for key positions.*
>
> *Fast forward to 1994, and Kirtman is a much happier man. As president of Levi's Britannia Sportswear division, the 48-year old executive is a step away from joining the company's senior management ranks. Life changed for him in 1985, when senior executives began feeling heavy pressure from above to make "workplace diversity" a reality rather than a topic of conversation.*

The transformation at Levi's is attributable to Chairman and Chief Executive Robert D. Haas, the great-great-grandnephew of founder Levi Strauss (Mitchell and Oneal, 1994, 46) (see Table 3.3):

HASS BELIEVES THE corporation should be an ethical creature—an organism capable of both reaping profits and making the world a better place to live. Creating tangible opportunities for minority employees is only one part of the equation. Haas is out to make each of his workers, from the factory floor on up, feel as if they are an integral part of making and selling blue jeans. He wants to ensure that all views on all issues— no matter how controversial—are heard and respected. The chairman won't tolerate harassment of any kind. He won't do business with suppliers who violate Levi's strict standards regarding work environment and ethics. A set of corporate "aspirations," written by top management, is to guide all major decisions.

Another example of credible corporate values is offered by a major worldwide manufacturer (Ford Motor Company, 1991):

PEOPLE: Our people are the source of our strength. They provide our corporate intelligence and determine our reputation and vitality. Involvement and teamwork are core human values.

PRODUCTS: Our products are the end result of our efforts, and they should be the best in serving customers worldwide. As our products are viewed, so are we viewed.

PROFITS: Profits are the ultimate measure of how efficiently we provide customers with the best products for their needs. Profits are required to survive and grow.

TABLE 3.3	What Levi's Aspires To
NEW BEHAVIORS	Management must exemplify "directness, openness to influence, commitment to the success of others, and willingness to acknowledge our own contributions to problems."
DIVERSITY	Levi's "values a diverse workforce (age, sex, ethnic group, etc.) at all levels of the organization. . . Differing points of view will be sought; diversity will be valued and honesty will be rewarded, not suppressed."
RECOGNITION	Levi's will "provide greater recognition—both financial and psychic—for individuals and teams that contribute to our success. . . those who create and innovate and those who continually support our day-to-day business requirements."
ETHICAL MANAGEMENT PRACTICES	Management should epitomize "the stated standards of ethical behavior. We must provide clarity about our expectations and must enforce these standards throughout the corporation."
COMMUNICATIONS	Management must be "clear about company, unit, and individual goals and performance. People must know what is expected of them and receive timely, honest feedback."
EMPOWERMENT	Management must "increase the authority and responsibility of those closest to our products and customers. By actively pushing the responsibility, trust, and recognition into the organization, we can harness and release the capabilities of all our people."

SOURCE: Mitchell and Oneal (1994, 47).

How Do We Set Direction?

Statements of mission, vision, and values that are developed behind closed doors by a single executive or by just a few top-level managers in isolation serve a useful purpose but are limited in impact. Here, the key advantage of developing these statements quickly is lost once the task is completed.

The advantage of securing ownership, commitment, and involvement will accrue to organizations that use a collaborative process to forge these key statements. Further, benefits will last for an extended period of time. A senior manager who either establishes a new vision or reaffirms an existing mission by involving others in a participative manner garners ownership and commitment from all those who were involved in the process. Table 3.4 offers guidelines on how to develop your organization's direction-setting statements.

TABLE 3.4	Step-by-Step Guide for Setting Direction

1. *Look to your prior experiences.* You don't come to the table cold. You've been part of the organization (or some organization) for years. What have you learned? What really bugs you? What's been memorable? What seems to have been going on at work when people are really soaring? When they are at each other's throats?

2. *Fiddle around, but make haste.* Make lists. Doodle. Write ideas on index cards. Talk with others—from all walks of life—and seek their advice. Reflect on all such numerous inputs—but move fast.

3. *Engage participants.* After doodling a bit, you might schedule fifteen meetings in the next thirty days with disparate groups—first-line people from each function, first-line supervisors, suppliers, customers, wholesalers, community leaders. Chat about your ideas. Seek their list of top-ten irritants—their ten best experiences in the company or function—and keep on scratching away.

4. *Clarify over time.* Perhaps a two- or three-day session with those who report directly to you is in order. Again, swap stories, dreams, and precise internal and market assessments. Wallow in the data (mainly anecdotes). Ask them to come to the party with lots of data, gathered by doing their own smaller-scale version of what you've been up to. Maybe the result will be a formal declaration, maybe not. Maybe it will be two flip charts' worth of handwritten ideas that everybody sticks up in his or her own office. Perhaps it will eventually be turned over to a printer and circulated to everyone on wallet-sized cards and posters alike. But then again, maybe it never will.

5. *Remember, listening is basic.* Leaders must be superb listeners, particularly with those advocating new or different images of the emerging reality. Successful leaders, we have found, are *great askers*, and they do pay attention.

6. *Draft and revise.* Integrate the information that has been gathered and prepare draft statements. Carefully review the drafts with all participants for content—accuracy, precision, clarity—and for style. Revise, revise, revise.

7. *Examine and adjust.* Periodically critique your direction-setting statements. Test their relevance and accuracy in light of strategic changes and make appropriate adjustments.

SOURCE: Adapted from Peters (1987, 490–492).

Three potential pitfalls need to be guarded against. First, managers often are more preoccupied with completing the task of establishing these statements and moving on to new activity than using this exercise as a means of securing support from key managers, employees, and departments. Be aware of the task-oriented mentality, and recognize the value of the process itself.

Second, using a participative decision-making process to develop fundamental statements does not imply democracy or a need for total consensus. When making a major change in the organization's culture, some individuals invariably disagree with the new direction. Determine which views represent added value and which ones represent anchors holding the organization to past practices that are inconsistent with the new vision. "An unconscious conspiracy in contemporary society prevents leaders—no matter what their original vision—from making changes. Within any organization, an entrenched bureaucracy with a commitment to the status quo undermines the unwary leader" (Bennis, 1990, 18).

Third, having stated that participation is important, be careful not to cross the fine line that separates participation from abdication. Senior management is responsible for the direction of the organization and for developing the enabling strategies. Participation is one way to accomplish this task, but ultimate responsibility for deciding which course to take cannot be delegated.

GOALS AND OBJECTIVES

Leaders must next move from the broad direction provided by their mission, vision, and values to declare what actually must be accomplished. Unless these statements are translated into measurable performance targets, they will be little more than nice sets of words. Goals and objectives form the vital link between direction setting and deployment. Goals and objectives represent the cornerstones for deployment, just as mission, vision, and values represented the cornerstones for setting direction.

- *Goals* cover the organization's broad intent by defining what is to be attained through sustained effort over the long term.
- By contrast, *objectives* specify what is to be achieved in a scheduled period of time in order to progress toward each goal.

The following example goals are for one company whose vision was presented earlier in this chapter (Florida Power and Light Company, 1989, 10). This set is comprised of three main goals and two or three clarifying points for each of the main goals. These clarifying points should not be confused with objectives. Separate sets of specific objectives are required to ensure progress toward each goal. Consider how these goals contribute toward that company's vision, how progress toward the goals might be measured, and how the goals might challenge the organization:

1. *Improve customer satisfaction with sales and service quality:*
   a. *by reducing customer complaints to be among the lowest in the electric utility industry,*
   b. *by having adequate capacity to meet the needs of existing and future customers, and*
   c. *by having service unavailability to be among the lowest in the industry.*
2. *Strengthen effectiveness in nuclear plant operation and regulatory performance:*
   a. *by achieving nuclear plant availability to be among the highest in the industry, and*
   b. *by improving nuclear safety through the achievement of reduced automatic plant shutdowns to be among the lowest in the industry.*
3. *Improve utilization of resources to stabilize costs:*
   a. *by improving quality,*
   b. *by maintaining stable and reasonable prices, as compared to the CPI, while maintaining a fair rate of return for stockholders, and*
   c. *by securing the safety of our employees and community.*

Clear-cut measurable objectives help spur everyone in the right direction and serve as mileposts to gauge progress in the pursuit of longer-term goals. Objectives should be established for each goal. Five criteria help in framing effective objectives. In their textbook *Strategy Formulation and Implementation*, A. A. Thompson and A. J. Strickland (1989, 31) present example objective statements that illustrate use of five criteria (see Table 3.5):

1. *Objectives should be definitive and specific.*
2. *Objectives should describe accomplishments or results, not activities or behaviors.*
3. *Objectives should be measurable (quantifiable).*
4. *Objectives should delineate a time frame or deadline.*
5. *Objectives should be challenging yet achievable (they should be within the control of the responsible business unit and not rely on what might be accomplished by other organizations).*

Just as the missioning process was cascaded downward through the organization, corporate goals and objectives should also be cascaded downward through divisions and work groups. The direct linkage offered by this approach enables everyone to see how their efforts contribute toward organizationwide objectives.

DEPLOYMENT

The last four elements of the leadership framework (see Figure 3.1) enable deployment of the direction-setting decisions. Two of these elements—policy and methodology—define how work is performed by *everyone*. The other two—commitment and style—define what and how *management* acts on a day-to-day basis. Commitment relates to *what* is done by managers themselves and in collaboration with other resources. Style relates to *how* they do things.

TABLE 3.5	Stating Objectives: "Good" Versus "Bad" Examples
Poor:	Our objective is to maximize profits.
Remarks:	How much is "maximum"? The statement is not subject to measurement. What criterion or yardstick will management use to determine if and when actual profits are equal to maximum profits? No deadline is specified.
Better:	Our total profit target in the next fiscal year is $1 million.
Poor:	Our objective is to increase sales revenue and unit volume.
Remarks:	How much increase is expected? Also, because the statement relates to two topics, it may be inconsistent. Increasing unit volume may require a price cut; and if demand is price inelastic, sales revenue would fall as unit volume rises. No time frame for achievement is indicated.
Better:	Our objective this calendar year is to increase sales revenues from $30 million to $35 million; we expect this will be accomplished by selling 1 million units at an average price of $35.
Poor:	Our objective next year is to boost advertising expenditures by 15 percent.
Remarks:	Advertising is an activity and not a result. The real objective is what result the extra advertising is intended to produce.
Better:	Our objective is to boost our market share from 8 percent to 10 percent next year with the help of a 15 percent increase in advertising expenditures.
Poor:	Our objective is to be a pioneer in research and development and become the technology leader in the industry.
Remarks:	This objective is very sweeping and ambitious, especially if the industry is one with a wide range of technological frontiers.
Better:	During the 1990s our objective is to continue as a leader in introducing new technologies and new devices that will allow buyers of electrically powered equipment to conserve energy usage.
Poor:	Our objective is to be the most profitable company in our industry.
Remarks:	This objective is not specific enough. What are the measures of profit—total dollars or earnings per share, unit profit margin, or return on equity investment, or all of these? Also, because the objective concerns how well other companies will perform, the objective, while challenging, may not be achievable.
Better:	We will strive to lead the industry in rate of return on equity investment by earning 25 percent after-tax return on equity investment in the next fiscal year.

SOURCE: Adapted from Thompson and Strickland (1989, 31).

A full exploration of these elements is beyond the scope of this book. They are listed here simply for completeness. Components within these elements include organizational structure, performance measurement, work practices, business planning, human resource systems, and communications. Organizational structure was touched on briefly in Chapter 2, and performance measurement is explained in Chapter 7.

Making significant changes to an existing organization—whether through long-term and sustained continuous improvement or short-term and dramatic reengineering—requires skills in both leadership and management. The difference between these two skill sets is stated succinctly by Warren Bennis (1990, 18):

> LEADERS *are people who do the right thing; managers are people who do things right. . . Americans (and probably those in much of the rest of the world) are underled and over-managed. They do not pay enough attention to doing the right things, while paying too much attention to doing things right.*

Life isn't fair. In addition to what you do, how you do it counts with equal importance. Plan to lead by example; serve as the role model. Become the foremost spokesperson of your own vision, but also be a living, walking, talking replica. Reallocate how you spend your time. For example, as CEO of his Malcolm Baldrige National Quality Award-winning company, Roger Milliken devoted fully one-half of his time to quality improvement. To emphasize his priority, the subject of quality was the first agenda item at Milliken's staff meetings (Bennis, 1990, 492):

> THE PRINTING *of cards and slogans is the least important part. If you began with a formal declaration, you are probably doomed. You don't know what it really means, let alone anyone else. You are likely to be continually trapped by a thousand tiny inconsistencies as you wobble toward clarity. That is, some small personnel decision or some small customer decision requires you to do the thinking you should have done before turning on the printing press. Such inconsistencies, after a formal declaration, convict you of hypocrisy and set the process back, perhaps derailing it forever.*

SUMMARY

Organizationwide improvement through the redesign of key processes requires management and leadership from the executive suite. This work cannot be delegated, and the process of *how* things are done is equally important to *what* is actually accomplished.

Leaders need to begin by addressing basic questions about what their organization is and what it is to become. Through a collaborative process, they will secure the cornerstones of the organization's foundation: mission, vision, and core values.

With this foundation, leaders can galvanize commitment by all members of the organization. They can establish relevant goals and objectives and provide an environment within which the details can be built. The clarity, accuracy, and precision of these statements sets the direction of improvement efforts. The level of ambition and acceptance controls the speed.

Finally, don't underestimate the impact of your personal actions. Use your own style to reinforce the crusade toward your vision. On the other hand, if you are not committed to the fundamental statements that you have had printed, laminated, and posted, recognize that your style will betray you and reveal your true beliefs. If this is the case, rip down the false statements, go back to the beginning of this chapter, and start over.

DISCUSSION QUESTIONS

1. In your own words, briefly answer the following questions for your organization:

    a. What is the purpose of your organization?

    b. What do you want the organization to become in the future?

    c. What are the long-term accomplishments needed to fulfill your answers to a and b?

    d. What are the short-term accomplishments needed for each answer to c?

2. Compare each answer from question 1 to the organization's official statements:

    a. Mission

    b. Vision

    c. Goals

    d. Objectives

3. Where answers in question 2 are missing or deficient, what action do you need to take?

ACKNOWLEDGMENT

Much of this chapter is adapted from pages 159–176 of A. R. Tenner and I. J. DeToro, *Total Quality Management: Three Steps to Continuous Improvement*. Copyright © 1992, Addison-Wesley Publishing Company, Inc. Reprinted by permission of the publisher.

REFERENCES

Bennis, Warren. 1990. *Why Leaders Can't Lead*. San Francisco: Jossey-Bass.

Canadian National Railway. 1990. June. Reprinted by permission.

Canadian National Railway. 1991. June 13. Reprinted by permission.

Collins, James. 1995. "Change Is Good—But First, Know What Should Never Change." *Fortune* (May 29), 141.

DeCarlo, Neil. 1991. Corporate Communications Department, Florida Power and Light Company, Miami, FL. Telephone interview with Arthur R. Tenner, June 28.

Florida Power and Light Co. 1989. "Summary Description of FPL's Quality Improvement Program." Miami, FL: Florida Power and Light Company. Reprinted with permission.

Ford Motor Company. 1991. June 14. Reprinted by permission.

Imperial Oil, Ltd. 1991. *Outline of the Organization*. Toronto: Imperial Oil, Ltd.

Mitchell, Russell, and Michael Oneal. 1994. "Managing by Values." *Business Week* (August 1), 46.

Peters, Tom. 1989. *Thriving on Chaos*. New York: Knopf.

Senge, Peter M. 1990. *The Fifth Discipline*. New York: Doubleday. Copyright © 1990 by Peter M. Senge. Used by permission of Doubleday, a division of Doubleday Dell Publishing Group, Inc.

Thompson, A. A., and A. J. Strickland. 1989. *Strategy Formulation and Implementation*. 4th ed. Homewood, IL: Irwin.

Tolle, Ernest F., Jr. 1988. "Developing the Mission Statement: Why, What, When, and How." *Organization Development Journal* (Spring), 15.

4 | Organizational Assessment

Every manager engages in some form of organizational assessment every day. By asking for information, reading reports, observing job performance, or attending formal presentations, managers are continuously assessing what's happening in their area of responsibility. These *informal* assessments proceed through various activities:

- Attending meetings and presentations,
- Discussing project progress and status with subordinates,
- Reviewing project reports and checking mileposts, and
- Comparing progress with peers.

These activities allow managers to understand what employees are working on, to communicate expectations of what they should be working on, to understand the skills and tools that are being employed, and to suggest, and possibly offer training on, those skills and tools that should be employed. Stated differently, assessment is required to find out what is going on, to change what is going wrong, and to support what is going correctly.

Informal assessments are often ad hoc, arising out of the normal interaction between managers and employees. But is this form of assessment sufficient to drive the performance improvement that is required today? In our view, it is not.

USING THE MALCOLM BALDRIGE NATIONAL QUALITY AWARD CRITERIA AS AN ASSESSMENT TOOL

The United States Congress established the Malcolm Baldrige National Quality Award (MBNQA) in 1987 to "stem the eroding leadership of American products and services as well as assist in the nation's productivity growth" (Heaphy and Gruska, 1995, xvii). The award recognizes companies that have made substantial progress and achieved a high degree of excellence in improving quality and productivity.

> *If you measure yourself against the criteria laid out by the Baldrige award, you have a blueprint for a better company.*
> **JERRY JUNKINS**
> CEO Texas Instruments
> (Main, 1990, 101)

More important, the MBNQA is structured as an educational tool and is tuned and improved annually to capture new learnings. Many organizations have applied for the award, and many others have obtained the application brochure simply to use its guidelines as a self-assessment tool. We support this tactic and offer in this chapter a concise introduction to the award criteria to provide organizations with a *formal* means of self-assessing their own health.

The award is currently managed by the National Institute of Standards and Technology (NIST) and administered by the American Society of Quality Control (ASQC). For a comprehensive picture of the award, refer to *The Malcolm Baldrige National Quality Award: A Yardstick for Growth* by Maureen Heaphy and Gregory Gruska (1995).

RATIONALE FOR USING THIS ASSESSMENT TOOL

The award's criteria attempt to address every key aspect of business performance, from business processes to business results. Its criteria have been selected because they relate to items that lead to improvement in business performance and not because they sound good at an awards ceremony. They cover the complete range of business activities "starting from the customer—and market related performance, productivity in the use of all assets, speed and flexibility, product and service quality, cost reduction, and overall financial performance" (NIST, 1995, 2). These criteria are designed to facilitate a diagnosis of business processes and business results, both of which are critical to improving business performance while achieving outstanding customer satisfaction. NIST (1995, 2) attributes the following benefits to using the MBNQA criteria:

- A realistic assessment by an external examiner (when assessment is conducted by MBNQA examiners),
- An accelerated pace of performance improvement,
- New ways to evaluate interactions with suppliers, customers, partners, and competitors,
- Means of integrating and aligning disparate activities into a focus on achieving organization goals,
- An understanding of when and which improvement tool (continuous improvement, benchmarking, reengineering) is most appropriate,
- A scoring system that provides a clear means of distinguishing between typical and world-class performance, and
- Enhanced opportunities to network and learn from others pursuing organizational improvement.

As testimony to the widespread acceptance of the MBNQA criteria, they have been used as a model for the U.S. government operations, the President's Quality Award

Program (Federal Quality Institute, 1995), and by twenty-seven of thirty-nine states that offer quality awards (Bernowski, 1993, 27).

SCORING CRITERIA

In addition to offering instructive criteria, the MBNQA provides a scoring system that also helps an organization to gain insight into its performance. The award covers seven categories, and the 1996 guidelines divide these categories into twenty-four requirements with fifty-two areas to address.

Performance is evaluated three ways: *approach, deployment*, and *results*. Approach and deployment are scored for items in all seven categories and account for two-thirds of the total score. Thus MBNQA evaluates the processes employed by a company to achieve superior performance and not the quality of the products or services themselves:

- *Approach* refers to the *method* used to address each area. The emphasis is on establishing a fact-based improvement process.

- *Deployment* refers to the *extent* to which the approach is applied. The emphasis is on eliminating gaps between plans and implementation. After all, an excellent approach yields no value if it is not deployed.

- *Results* refer to the *outcomes* achieved compared to those desired by their stated criteria. Here, current performance levels are compared to benchmarks or to other relative measures. Scoring of results also considers trends and the "breath and importance of the performance improvement" (Bernowski, 1993, 27). Results are scored for items in categories 6 and 7 and account for one-third of the total score.

The relative importance of each of the fifty-two items is reflected by weighting it with a certain number of points. A perfect score for every item yields a total score of 1,000 points. As a point of reference, MBNQA assessors' scores *prior to site visits* for the period 1988 through 1994 ranked the majority of applicants in the 250- to 600-point range, with no applicant receiving a score higher than 875 points (Heaphy and Gruska, 1995, 329).

Although the point scores are used for determining an overall assessment, many criteria are interrelated, and a deficiency in one may negatively affect performance in another. Scoring guidelines from the 1996 MBNQA application are summarized in Table 4.1.

MBNQA PERFORMANCE CATEGORIES

The following sections summarize the categories, requirements, and areas that organizations need to address for the 1996 MBNQA.

TABLE 4.1	Scoring Guidelines for the Malcolm Baldrige National Quality Award		
SCORE	**APPROACH**	**DEPLOYMENT**	**RESULTS**
0–30%	None to a small systematic approach in primary areas Transition from reacting to problems to a general improvement orientation	Major gaps in deployment that prevent achievement of primary purpose	No or poor results in the early stages of improving trends or good performance in a few areas Results not available for many to most areas of importance
40–60%	Sound systematic approach, responsive to primary purpose of area Fact-based improvement process in place	Early stages of deployment	Trends improving in key areas No pattern of adverse trends Some areas compare favorably to benchmarks
70–90%	Sound systematic approach, responsive to overall purpose of area Fact-based improvement process a key management tool	Approach well deployed, no major gaps, but may vary by unit	Performance good to excellent in most areas Most improvement trends sustained Good leadership and good relative performance levels in many to most performance levels
100%	Sound systematic approach, fully responsive to all requirements of area Strong fact-based improvement process, strong refinement and integration, excellent analysis	Approach fully deployed, without gaps or weaknesses	Performance excellent in most areas of importance Excellent improvement trends and/or performance levels sustained Strong evidence of benchmarking leadership demonstrated in many areas

SOURCE: Adapted from NIST (1995, 25).

1.0 LEADERSHIP

1.1 Senior Executive Leadership

This category covers senior management's personal involvement in setting direction and leading a performance-focused management system. Areas addressed include the following:

- The setting by leaders of the values and high expectations for the organization, and
- The ability of those in senior management to evaluate and improve the organization's business management system, including their own individual leadership skills.

1.2 Leadership Systems

This category covers how the organization integrates customers' expectations and the organization's performance indicators into the business management system. Areas addressed include the following:

- How the organization's values and expectations are integrated into the business management system, including the roles and responsibilities of all managers, and how these expectations are communicated and reinforced throughout the organization, and
- How financial and nonfinancial performance is reviewed, how these measures relate to stakeholder's interests, and how this information is used to create improvement actions.

1.3 Public Responsibility and Corporate Citizenship

This section covers the responsibility that the firm has in its management practices to the communities in which it works and to the public in general. It addresses these areas:

- How the organization ethically and legally complies with the regulations and laws, and how it considers the public good in its actions, and
- How the organization is involved in the communities in which it works.

The leadership category is not the heaviest in weight (90 points), but it clearly is the most significant because it is the "driver." Nothing happens without the active involvement and leadership of senior executives.

Heaphy and Gruska (1995, 24–25) have developed a management grid that can be used in assessing progress in each category as the organization moves from a traditional internally focused reactive organization to one that is increasingly aware of what needs to be done, to one that is improving, and finally to an outstanding organization characterized by sustained performance improvement and satisfied customers. See Table 4.2 for an application of their grid to leadership items.

TABLE 4.2	MBNQA Management Grid: Indicators of Progress in Improving Leadership		
TRADITIONAL	**AWARENESS**	**IMPROVING**	**OUTSTANDING**
Lofty goals are stated. Motivating people is the solution. Quality is delegated. Business units compete with each other.	The mission and vision statements include all stakeholders. It is recognized that procedures and practices cause most variation.	Management is open to new ideas from others, including other companies. Leaders consider the whole system. Barriers that rob people of their pride in work are removed.	Leadership is highly visible and active in quality activities. Leaders act as coaches. Communications of quality values inside and outside the company are ongoing. Leadership considers the total system.
		EQUIVALENT MBNQA SCORE	
0–30%	40–50%	60–70%	80–100%

SOURCE: Heaphy and Gruska (1995, 24–25).

2.0 INFORMATION AND ANALYSIS

2.1 Management of Information and Data

This category covers the effective use of data and information to support satisfying customers and securing marketplace success. Areas addressed include the following:

- How critical data are selected and managed, and
- How the selection of data is improved and how data are used to support process management and performance improvement.

2.2 Competitive Comparisons and Benchmarking

This grouping covers the use of external comparative data to drive organizational performance improvement and better competitive positioning. Areas addressed include the following:

- How comparative and benchmark data are selected and used to drive improvement, and
- How the firm evaluates and improves the process for collecting benchmarking and other comparative data used to improve the business management system.

2.3 Analysis and Use of Company-Level Data

This category covers how relevant data from external customers, internal operations, and financial performance are analyzed to support the business management system. Areas addressed include the following:

TABLE 4.3	MBNQA Management Grid: Indicators of Progress in Improving Information Analysis		
TRADITIONAL	**AWARENESS**	**IMPROVING**	**OUTSTANDING**
Employees and managers fight fires. Most data regarding quality are for key products and services. Employees have lots of data but little information.	Root-cause analysis prevents reoccurrence. Some useful visual displays of data are used. Analysis is switched from opportunities per 100 to opportunities per 1,000.	Valued-added reports and graphs are used. Data are collected from design and support areas (accounting, purchasing, personnel, computer services). Opportunities are tracked per million. Managers are aware of best practices globally.	Information of extensive depth and breadth is available. Information is readily accessible throughout the organization. There is a positive correlation between internal measures and customer satisfaction. Employees understand why best practices have worked at other companies.
EQUIVALENT MBNQA SCORE			
0–30%	40–50%	60–70%	80–100%

SOURCE: Heaphy and Gruska (1995, 24–25).

- How data from all parts of the organization are used to support operational decision making and planning, and

- How the firm relates all data—customer, market, product quality, operational performance—to financial or market indicators of performance.

As with leadership, this category has a relatively low weight (75 points), but the information collected here is linked to a number of other categories and therefore has more impact than its weighting implies. The progress that would be evident as a firm moves from traditional to outstanding in this category is illustrated in Table 4.3.

3.0 STRATEGIC PLANNING

3.1 Strategy Development

This group covers how an organization establishes its strategic direction and how it translates that direction into its business management system. Areas addressed include the following:

- How strategies are developed and used to improve organizational performance relative to competition,

- How strategies are translated into actionable activities, and
- How the strategic planning process itself is improved.

3.2 Strategy Deployment

Examines how the firm manages the key business projects into the future, especially relative to competitors and achieving benchmarks. Areas addressed include the following:

- How the firm develops its key business drivers and how these drivers are translated into actions, and
- Two- to five-year projection of the firm's key operational performance measures.

This category is weighted at 55 points, and progress of organizations can be tracked using the indicators in Table 4.4.

4.0 HUMAN RESOURCE DEVELOPMENT AND MANAGEMENT

4.1 Human Resource Planning and Evaluation

This section covers how the planning for human resources is aligned with the organization's business plans and the development of the workforce. Areas addressed include the following:

TABLE 4.4	MBNQA Management Grid: Indicators of Progress in Improving Strategic Planning		
TRADITIONAL	**AWARENESS**	**IMPROVING**	**OUTSTANDING**
There is a business plan (no quality plan). Optimization occurs within a department.	Progress to the business plan is reviewed. The business plan is updated annually. There is a quality plan.	The business plan and quality plan are one. The plan includes quality goals. The plan covers a one- to two-year horizon. There is cross-functional input to plan, but it is limited in scope.	The business plan includes quality goals and strategies. Customers, suppliers, and employees provide input into the plan. Resources are provided to achieve goals. Short- and long-term views are taken. The plan includes products and services. The total system is optimized.
EQUIVALENT MBNQA SCORE			
0–30%	40–50%	60–70%	80–100%

SOURCE: Heaphy and Gruska (1995, 24–25).

- How the firm translates requirements from the business plan into detailed human resource plans, and
- How the firm improves its human resource planning and aligns its plans with the strategic business plans.

4.2 High-Performance Work System

This section examines how work is designed and whether the supporting recognition and rewards systems are structured to encourage employees to contribute effectively to the high expectations set by management. Areas addressed include the following:

- How the firm has designed work to achieve high-performance work units, and
- How the supporting systems—recognition and rewards—are structured to support high-performing employees.

4.3 Employee Education, Training, and Development

This section describes how the firm's education and training programs contribute to its plans by strengthening employees' capabilities. Areas addressed include the following:

- How the firm's education programs serve to build employees' capacity to respond to customers, to work in high-performance units, and to progress and advance within the organization, and
- How training is developed, delivered, reinforced, evaluated, and improved.

4.4 Employee Well-Being and Satisfaction

This section examines how an organization develops and maintains a work climate that is conducive and supportive to employees. Areas addressed include the following:

- How the organization maintains a safe, healthful environment,
- What services, facilities, and activities the firm makes available to all employees, and
- How the firm monitors employee well-being, motivation, and employee satisfaction.

This category is weighted at 140 points, and progress can be monitored by comparing an organization's characteristics to the indicators in Table 4.5.

5.0 PROCESS MANAGEMENT

This category covers the key aspects of process management that are included in all core processes and their related subprocesses. Typically, these core processes involve operational and supporting processes that cover key systems within an organization, including how they are designed, managed, and improved.

TABLE 4.5	MBNQA Management Grid: Indicators of Progress in Improving Human Resource Management

TRADITIONAL	AWARENESS	IMPROVING	OUTSTANDING
Training is offered to employees. A suggestion box is available.	Employees are on problem-solving teams. There is increased focus on getting more suggestions. Mass training occurs.	Employees are told they are empowered. Training is just-in-time. Employees are involved in process analysis and improvement. Opportunities are provided for teams and individuals to contribute. Employee satisfaction levels show positive trends.	There are internal supplier-customer relations. Employees feel and act empowered. The culture supports the use of new skills. Employees feel their opinions are important. Employee satisfaction, attendance, and turnover rate are outstanding.

		EQUIVALENT MBNQA SCORE	
0–30%	40–50%	60–70%	80–100%

SOURCE: Heaphy and Gruska (1995, 24–25).

5.1 Design and Introduction of Products and Services

This category covers how new or modified products or services are developed and introduced. Areas addressed include the following:

- How processes are designed, including the understanding of customer's requirements, the translation of those requirements into process metrics, and how suppliers are involved,

- How processes are reviewed and tested to ensure defect-free performance, and

- How processes are evaluated and improved.

5.2 Process Management: Product and Service Production and Delivery

This section examines how the firm's key delivery processes are managed to ensure that all design and service requirements are met. Areas addressed include the following:

- How an organization maintains the performance of key processes so that they meet all process goals, and

- How these processes are evaluated and improved to achieve reduced cycle time.

5.3 Process Management: Support Services

This category assesses how well the firm's supporting processes are designed, managed, and improved. Areas addressed include the following:

- How supporting processes are designed to meet their specific process goals,
- How the firm maintains the performance of these supporting processes, and
- How these processes are evaluated and improved to provide superior performance.

5.4 Management of Supplier Performance

This category examines how the organization ensures that all inputs provided by suppliers meet the organization's requirements. Areas addressed include the following:

- How the firm communicates its requirements to suppliers, and
- How the firm manages and improves supplier relationships.

This category is weighted at 140 points, and progress in this category can be monitored by comparing an organization to the indicators in Table 4.6.

TABLE 4.6	MBNQA Management Grid: Indicators of Progress in Improving Process Management

TRADITIONAL	AWARENESS	IMPROVING	OUTSTANDING
Quality effort is focused on manufacture of product or delivery of service. Company employs incoming parts and materials inspection.	Quality is owned by manufacturing. Control charts are used to monitor some processes. End-of-line assessment is the safety net. Skip-lot sampling is used.	Some prevention activities are in place. Key core processes are identified, studied, and improved. The motto is "if it ain't broke, improve it." Process control and improvement activities are in place in support areas. Suppliers are part of the team.	Prevention is the philosophy. Robust designs are implemented. Process control and improvement are widespread. Cycle time is reduced. Suppliers are certified. Assessments are done on processes and systems.

EQUIVALENT MBNQA SCORE			
0–30%	40–50%	60–70%	80–100%

SOURCE: Heaphy and Gruska (1995, 24–25).

6.0 BUSINESS RESULTS

This category covers the firm's performance in every key business area. It examines current performance levels as well as sustained improvement trends.

6.1 Product and Service Quality Results

This section assesses performance results for all products and services offered by the firm, as well as efforts to continuously improve. Areas assessed include current levels of performance in products and services offered based on key metrics.

6.2 Company Operational and Financial Results

This category assesses all operational and financial performance results for all products and services offered by the firm as well as the efforts to improve. Areas assessed include current levels as well as trends in operational and financial performance.

6.3 Human Resource Results

This category assesses the firm's results in maintaining and improving employee development and well-being. Areas assessed include current levels as well as trends of employee satisfaction, well-being, and involvement in self-directed responsibility.

6.4 Supplier Performance Results

This category assesses results of supplier performance and performance improvement. Areas assessed include current levels as well as trends of supplier performance.

This category is weighted at 250 points, and progress can be monitored by comparing an organization to the indicators in Table 4.7.

TABLE 4.7	MBNQA Management Grid: Indicators of Progress in Improving Business Results
TRADITIONAL	**AWARENESS**	**IMPROVING**	**OUTSTANDING**
Data are available to quantify quality of product or service.	Some data are tracked in support areas.	Data on key core processes throughout the organization show mostly positive trends. Some comparisons are made to industry norms.	The three- to five-year trend shows continual improvement. The company is one of the leaders according to the data for product, services, and response time throughout the organization.
EQUIVALENT MBNQA SCORE			
0–30%	40–50%	60–70%	80–100%

SOURCE: Heaphy and Gruska (1995, 24–25).

7.0 CUSTOMER FOCUS AND SATISFACTION

Category 7.0 assesses the organization's ability to understand, assess customer's requirements, and maintain customer relationships as evidenced by retention and market share—all relative to competitors.

7.1 Customer and Market Knowledge

This category examines how a firm determines short- and long-term customer's requirements. Areas addressed include the following:

- How customer's requirements and related information are gathered and utilized to both provide and improve the delivery of products and services,
- How the firm addresses future customer's requirements and expectations, and
- How the firm evaluates and improves these critical data-gathering and customer-sensing processes.

7.2 Customer Relationship Management

This category covers the response mechanisms that manage the interactions with customers. Areas addressed include the following:

- How the firm provides access to customers to facilitate their being able to collect information and provide data on products or services provided,
- How the firm resolves customer dissatisfaction,
- How the firm follows up to determine customer satisfaction and secure feedback, and
- How the firm evaluates and improves customer relationship management.

7.3 Customer Satisfaction Determination

This category examines, relative to competitors, how a firm determines customer satisfaction and intention to repurchase. Areas addressed include the following:

- How the firm's processes determine customer's level of satisfaction,
- How well customers are satisfied compared to competitors, and
- How the firm evaluates and improves these critical processes.

7.4 Customer Satisfaction Results

This category assesses the firm's customer's satisfaction or dissatisfaction results, compared to competitor's levels of performance and results. Areas addressed include the following:

- Current levels of customer satisfaction, and
- Current levels of customer satisfaction relative to competitors.

TABLE 4.8	MBNQA Management Grid: Indicators of Progress in Improving Satisfaction		
TRADITIONAL	**AWARENESS**	**IMPROVING**	**OUTSTANDING**
Employees take care of customer problems. The company tracks customer satisfaction with lagging indicators by "looking in the rear-view mirror" (e.g., market share). The company assumes silence means satisfaction.	The company's warranty is typical for industry. A customer satisfaction survey is conducted.	Employees listen to the customer. Employees satisfy the customer. The company has service standards. Customers have easy access to the company. Front-line employees have current information and are empowered to make things right for the customers. There is a positive trend in customer satisfaction.	The company leads the customer regarding the art of the possible. Commitments to the customer lead the industry. The company delights the customer. Customer problems are rare. The company is one of the leaders in customer satisfaction, loyalty, and market share niche.
EQUIVALENT MBNQA SCORE			
0–30%	40–50%	60–70%	80–100%

SOURCE: Heaphy and Gruska (1995, 24–25).

This category is also weighted at 250 points, and progress can be monitored by comparing an organization to the indicators in Table 4.8.

OVERALL ASSESSMENT

The MBNQA serves as a tool that any organization can use to assess its health with respect to criteria that are widely accepted as being crucial for an organization to excel in business performance and customer satisfaction. Various approaches can be taken to apply it, including using external consultants and attending commercial training programs.

Most important, the tool can be used to help prioritize improvement opportunities and to measure progress. Table 4.9 is provided as a self-assessment worksheet.

TABLE 4.9	Malcolm Baldrige National Quality Award Self-Assessment Worksheet

INSTRUCTIONS

1. **Score** % Use *Scoring Guidelines* (below) to assess your performance for each item on the worksheet (next page).
2. **Points** Multiply the *Weight* for each item by your *Score* percentage.
3. **Gaps** Subtract *Points* from *Weight* to determine the improvement opportunity for each item.
4. **Total** Assess your organization's overall health by adding your *Points*.

SCORING GUIDELINES

SCORE	APPROACH	DEPLOYMENT	RESULTS
0–30%	None a small systematic approach in primary areas Transition from reacting to problems to a general improvement orientation	Major gaps in deployment that prevent achieving primary purpose	No or poor results in the early stages of improving trends or good performance in a few areas Results not available for many to most areas of importance
40–60%	Sound systematic approach, responsive to primary purpose of area Fact-based improvement process in place	Early stages of deployment	Trends improving in key areas No pattern of adverse trends Some areas compare favorably to benchmarks
70–90%	Sound systematic approach, responsive to overall purpose of area Fact-based improvement process a key management tool	Approach well deployed, no major gaps, but may vary by unit	Performance good to excellent in most areas Most improvement trends sustained Good leadership and good relative performance levels in many to most areas
100%	Sound systematic approach, fully responsive to all requirements of area Strong fact-based improvement process, strong refinement and integration, excellent analysis	Approach fully deployed, without gaps or weaknesses	Performance excellent in most areas of importance Excellent improvement trends and/or performance levels sustained Strong evidence of benchmarking leadership demonstrated in many areas

CRITERIA	WEIGHT	SCORE%	POINTS	GAPS
1.0 Leadership	**90**			
1.1 Senior executive leadership	45			
1.2 Leadership systems	25			
1.3 Public responsibility and corporate citizenship	20			
2.0 Information and Analysis	**75**			
2.1 Management of information and data	20			
2.2 Competitive comparisons and benchmarking	15			
2.3 Analysis and use of company-level data	40			
3.0 Strategic Planning	**55**			
3.1 Strategy development	35			
3.2 Strategy deployment	20			
4.0 Human Resource Development and Management	**140**			
4.1 Human resource planning and evaluation	20			
4.2 High-performance work systems	45			
4.3 Education, training, and development	50			
4.4 Employee well-being and satisfaction	25			
5.0 Process Management	**140**			
5.1 Design and introduction of products and services	20			
5.2 Process management: product and service production and delivery	45			
5.3 Process management: support services	50			
5.4 Management of supplier performance	25			
6.0 Business Results	**250**			
6.1 Product and service quality results	75			
6.2 Company operational and financial results	110			
6.3 Human resource results	35			
6.4 Supplier performance results	30			
7.0 Customer Focus and Satisfaction	**250**			
7.1 Customer and market knowledge	30			
7.2 Customer relationship management	30			
7.3 Customer satisfaction determination	30			
7.4 Customer satisfaction results	160			
Total	**1,000**			

TABLE 4.9 — SELF-ASSESSMENT WORKSHEET — continued

SUMMARY

Quality consultants subscribe to the axiom often quoted in medicine, "Prescription without diagnosis is malpractice." The *Malcolm Baldrige National Quality Award* provides a useful methodology and a set of criteria by which any organization can diagnose the gap between its current and future states. Only then should its improvement strategies be developed and deployed. This chapter provides individuals pursuing the means to self-assess their organization and avoid charges of malpractice.

DISCUSSION QUESTIONS

1. Explain how the Malcolm Baldrige National Quality Award criteria might serve as a tool for assessing your own organization's health.

2. Answer item a or b depending on your answer to question 1:

   a. If the MBNQA is not a useful tool, describe what you would use in its place.

   b. If the MBNQA is a useful tool for assessing your organization, explain how you would use it. Is any guidance or training in its application needed? Would you need external expertise to implement it, or is your organization self-sufficient?

REFRENCES

1996 Application, Federal Quality Institute, United States Office of Personnel Management. *The President's Quality Award, 1996.* Washington, DC: U.S. Government Printing Office.

Bernowski, K. 1923. "The State of the States." *Quality Progress* (May), 27.

Heaphy, M. S., and G. F. Gruska. 1995. *The Malcolm Baldrige National Quality Award: A Yardstick for Growth.* Reading, MA: Addison-Wesley.

Main, J. 1990. "How to Win the Baldrige Award." *Fortune* (April 23), 101.

National Institute of Standards and Technology (NIST), U.S. Department of Commerce. 1995. *Malcolm Baldrige National Quality Award, 1996 Criteria.* Gaithersburg, MD.

PART II | PROCESS ANALYSIS

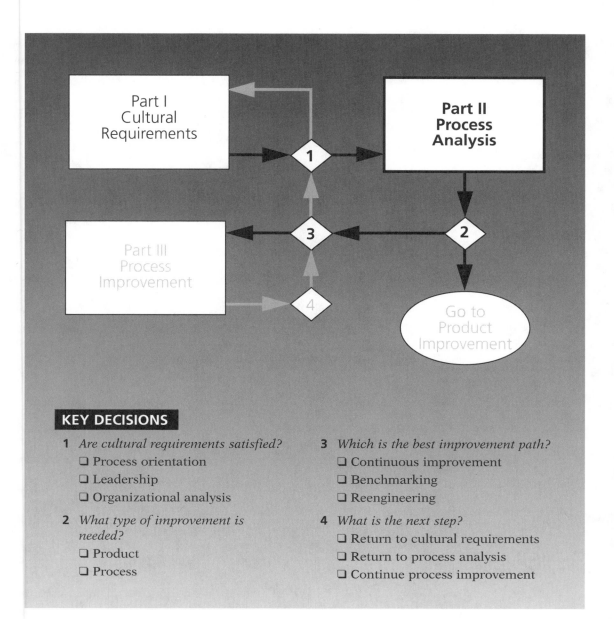

KEY DECISIONS

1 *Are cultural requirements satisfied?*
- ❏ Process orientation
- ❏ Leadership
- ❏ Organizational analysis

2 *What type of improvement is needed?*
- ❏ Product
- ❏ Process

3 *Which is the best improvement path?*
- ❏ Continuous improvement
- ❏ Benchmarking
- ❏ Reengineering

4 *What is the next step?*
- ❏ Return to cultural requirements
- ❏ Return to process analysis
- ❏ Continue process improvement

5 | Define and Classify Processes

If process mastery is an essential building block for gaining a competitive advantage (see Chapter 2), then the foundation for business success includes understanding how to identify, classify, and assess processes. This chapter helps you to build that understanding by defining the elements of a process and the relationship among the elements. The chapter then offers a choice of techniques that can be used for compiling an inventory of the processes that are employed by any organization.

Chapter 6 continues laying the foundation for process mastery by providing tools, guidelines, and examples for identifying which processes deserve special attention because of their critical impact on an organization's success. Certain processes represent the means by which an organization will achieve its goals and earn the distinction of being called *core processes*.

DEFINING *PROCESS*

What is a process? The conventional response might be that a process is "a series of actions, changes or functions that bring about an end or result" (*American Heritage*, 1978, 1043). This definition is useful but incomplete for the purpose of systematic improvement and redesign.

Wesner, Hiatt, and Trimble (1994, 38) offer another definition that is more suitable for businesses: "Process is defined as one or more tasks that transform a set of inputs into a specified set of outputs (goods or services) for another person [customer] or process via a combination of people, procedures, and tools."

E. H. Melan (1993, 15) contributes to this definition by stating that a process must provide an output of greater value than the inputs by means of one or more transformations. By integrating Melan's contribution with Wesner, Hiatt, and Trimble's definition, a more robust explanation is established:

PROCESS: One or more tasks that add value by transforming a set of inputs into a specified set of outputs (goods or services) for another person [customer] by a combination of people, methods, and tools.

This definition, combined with an understanding of the terminology and a model to portray their relationships (see Figure 5.1), offers a firm foundation for understanding even the most complex processes. In essence, providers work within a process to transform materials from suppliers into value-added outputs for customers.

DISTINGUISHING BETWEEN PROCESSES AND OUTPUTS

It is fascinating to observe bright, energetic, highly paid executives get completely twisted around as they embark on improvement efforts when they have confused outputs and processes. One source of confusion stems from the term process being commonly used as either a verb or a noun. Using the verb transform as a synonym for the verb process helps with the clarification because it is hard to confuse transform as a noun.

Another technique that helps to distinguish between processes and outputs is to use a noun to describe the output, and a verb to describe the process. Confusion can be avoided by stating the process as a gerund—a verbal noun form ending in -ing. Consider these simple examples where the term *bill* can be either the input, the process, or the output.

The process for *paying* bills	Pay*ing* is the process (verb), bills (noun) are inputs from suppliers, and checks (noun) are the outputs.
The process for *billing* customers	Bill*ing* is the process (verb), and the bills (noun) are the outputs to customers.

The act of delivering an output to another person helps to distinguish between what is *transformed* within a process and what is *transferred* to a customer. The former remains internal to the process and is not an output. On the other hand, the goods or services represented by the latter are the result of the process and are outputs. As a test, if you find that you are your own customer, then you are still within the process and you are not yet producing an output. Outputs can be further clarified by describing what outputs are not (seeTable 5.1).

FIGURE 5.1	Process Model

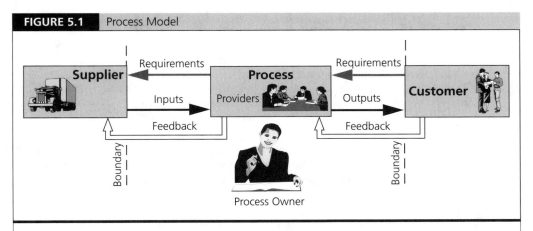

Terminology

Customers: Customers are the *individuals* to whom the products, services, or outputs are delivered. To the extent possible, customers should be identified as people and not as organizations. Organizations cannot be interviewed and questioned as to their requirements and expectations. If it is not possible to identify a customer for an output, beware: you may be producing scrap.

Outputs: Outputs are the goods or services produced by a process that are provided to another individual, the customer. Customers, in turn, use, consume, or transform these outputs in their own processes.

Transform: The tasks, activities, and procedures inside of the process add value to inputs by transforming them into value-added outputs for customers. Transformations can be physical, locational, transactional, or informational (Melan, 1993, 15).

Inputs: Inputs are the goods or services that are provided by suppliers and transformed by the process into outputs.

Providers: Individuals who work within a process and are involved in the transformation of inputs into outputs. Providers are also referred to as *participants*.

Suppliers: Suppliers are the individuals who provide inputs.

Requirements: Requirements describe the outputs expected by customers. Similarly, requirements are also the description of inputs expected from suppliers.

Feedback: Feedback is a statement of satisfaction—or dissatisfaction—from customers regarding the performance of outputs.

Boundaries: Process boundaries delineate the tasks, activities, and procedures that comprise the process. Processes are bounded upstream at the interface where suppliers provide inputs, and downstream at the interface where outputs are transferred to customers.

Process owner: The process owner is the person who has responsibility and authority for the operation and improvement of the process. The process owner is *not* an organization or a group. The process owner *is* an individual.

TABLE 5.1	Outputs Are Not . . .

- *Things that you supervise or approve but are actually produced by others*. An example is a report developed by a member of the staff and approved by a senior manager. The report is the output of the individual on the staff and not that of the senior manager. The senior manager has outputs, but this report is not one of them. The senior manager may be better described as a cosupplier of the report. This distinction is important since it would be a mistake to try to improve the report by examining the process of the senior manager when, in fact, that is not the process that produced the report.

- *Goals or outcomes for the organization*. Examples are profits, customer satisfaction, revenues, and market share. Like morale, these are outcomes that are the result of not one but a series of individual outputs produced by a number of people. Therefore, if the objective is to improve an outcome, it is necessary to identify every output involved and improve the performance of the processes that produced these outputs.

- *Steps in a work process*. Things that are produced in a work process for internal use and not passed to others are not outputs. Examples are work plans or calendars that are maintained for an employee's own use but not passed to others.

- *The overall function described by an individual's job title or responsibility*. The service manager of a computer service department, in all likelihood, does not actually repair computers; therefore, computers repaired are not his or her outputs. Even though the manager is surely responsible for the timely repair of malfunctioning computers, the servicing of the computer is the output of the person who performs that specific work. The service manager generates outputs as well, but they are more likely to be staffing plans, forecasts, training plans, budgets, and others that he or she produces and passes on.

CLASSIFYING PROCESSES

Having defined *processes*, the next task is to understand where to find them and where to draw their boundaries in the organization.

Everyone who produces a product or provides a service obviously uses a process by which inputs are transformed into outputs. Sometimes, as in professional services practiced by attorneys or accountants, the processes are invisible, since they may have never been documented. Sometimes processes are formally and completely documented and are constantly refined, as in manufacturing, medicine, and piloting aircraft. Regardless of the level of process visibility, in every case in which an output has been generated, a process or series of processes was employed to produce that product or to deliver that service.

Processes have historically been identified by their association with functions or departments, and one technique to identify processes is to first identify the functions that exist within an organization. A typical listing of business functions might include the following (Harrington, 1991, 10–13):

Accounting	Information systems	Purchasing
Distribution	Legal	Research and development
Engineering	Marketing	Sales
Finance	Product design	Shareholder relations
Human resources	Production	

Some processes are so well known and clearly bounded that the group performing the work takes on the name of the process. In finance, for example, groups are commonly named after processes, such as accounts payable, accounts receivable, invoicing, payroll, and credit.

PROCESS LEVELS

After identifying a process—payroll, for example—the series of subprocesses within the payroll process must be identified in order to understand how the work is performed with sufficient clarity to improve performance. For example, subprocesses in preparing payroll checks or electronic payment transfers include creating and updating employee records, time reporting, job reporting, creating and updating tax records, exception-time reporting, vacation reporting, and check or electronic transfer processing.

With very little effort, the analysis of process levels can be made as complex as nuclear physics. As an analogy, consider that the authors attended high school when life was relatively simple and when matter was known to be composed of elements and compounds. These were constructed from groups of atoms, and everyone knew that atoms were built with protons, neutrons, and electrons. The discovery of subatomic particles has made life appear to be more complicated but has improved scientists' fundamental understanding of physical phenomena.

Defining atomic particles is analogous to defining and understanding processes. Organizations can dig deeper and deeper inside any process to discover its basic building blocks. In general, digging deeper requires more work and yields better understanding. The key to effective improvement efforts is to recognize the point of diminishing returns. The number of levels of processes and subprocesses that is appropriate to penetrate will vary from one organization to another. In general, the number of levels will increase in proportion to the size of the organization.

Several techniques have been developed for classifying processes. Each technique provides the flexibility for digging to whatever depth is appropriate for any specific organization.

PROCESS CATEGORIES

One technique for identifying processes is to categorize processes according to the type of work being performed, as opposed to the function in which it is performed.

This may be more pertinent to emerging organizations that structure the business as a series of interconnected processes as opposed to a hierarchy of individuals.

G. Watson (1992, 18–19) in his *Benchmarking Workbook* identifies eight categories of processes that most organizations use to run their business. Within each of these eight categories are hundreds if not thousands of subprocesses. Here are the typical major groupings identified by Watson:

> *DESIGN AND DEVELOPMENT: Usually includes processes that collect customer needs, requirements, and expectations and that develop products and services to meet those identified needs.*
>
> *MARKETING AND SALES: Develops advertising literature and other product promotion activities, as well as pricing, packaging, and documentation. Sales processes include acquiring new customers, serving existing customers, and all processes related to selling.*
>
> *PURCHASING: Includes the acquisition of services as well as raw materials.*
>
> *PRODUCTION: Includes the processes that transform the inputs acquired by purchasing into finished products that are offered for sale. In service organizations, includes the processes by which services are provided to the client.*
>
> *SERVICE: Includes those after-sale activities that are performed to maintain, repair, refurbish, and upgrade products sold previously.*
>
> *DISTRIBUTION: Includes processes involved in transporting and physically delivering products to customers.*
>
> *CONTROL: Includes processes involved in strategic planning, business planning, and financial oversight.*
>
> *SUPPORT: Includes processes that provide human resource assistance, legal guidance, environmental, health and safety direction as well as facility management, training, and other similar internal services.*

DECIMAL NUMBERING SYSTEM

A decimal numbering system is a technique to delineate among subprocesses that nest one within another. A major process is designated as 1.0, with each of its subsequent subprocesses numbered as 1.1, 1.2, and so forth. Further layers of subprocess 1.1 are designated as 1.1.1, 1.1.2, and so forth. For example,

> *1.1 Determine customer needs and wants*
> > *1.1.1 Conduct qualitative assessments*
> > > *1.1.1.1 Conduct customer interviews*
> > > *1.1.1.2 Conduct focus groups*
> > *1.1.2 Conduct quantitative assessments*
> > > *1.1.2.1 Develop and implement surveys*

The *International Benchmarking Clearinghouse* at the American Productivity and Quality Center (APQC) has applied the decimal numbering system to thirteen categories of operational, management, and supporting processes that can be found in most organizations. This classification system (see Appendix A) can be used as a checklist against which organizations can compare their own processes to assure that none have been overlooked.

CREATING A PROCESS INVENTORY

Watson's process categories, the decimal numbering system, and APQC's process classification system are merely examples of techniques for completing the task at hand—compiling an accurate and comprehensive inventory of the processes and subprocesses used by the organization to produce its outputs. The technique selected is simply a matter of preference for any organization.

Two questions are helpful to ensure that the inventory is complete. These might be asked when a draft of the inventory has been compiled and is circulated within the organization for comment. Negative answers to either question represent opportunities to discover processes that were omitted from the inventory:

- Are any outputs produced that are unaccounted for in the draft inventory?
- Are any tasks or activities performed that are unaccounted for in the inventory?

SUMMARY

Developing an understanding of your organization's processes is a fundamental but underappreciated management responsibility. Often managers perceive working with processes as bureaucratic, cumbersome, and of little practical value. Yet without this approach, permanent improvement can rarely be secured.

During a 1982 visit to several Deming Prize winners in Japan, a senior officer at one firm heard of our interest in business process management and commented, "Of course process management is the only way to secure permanent business improvement. But you will have a hard time convincing your business associates in the U.S. because they probably perceive this type of work as too detailed, boring, and not the basis on which people get promoted." For a number of years, this observation about the U.S. was accurate; but that view is now outdated.

DISCUSSION QUESTIONS

1. Do you have sufficient information to compile a process inventory? If not, do you know where to obtain the required information?
2. How would you begin to create an inventory of processes used by your organization? Would you use Watson's process categories, a decimal numbering system, the APQC process classification system, or another approach?

3. Use the approach identified in question 2 to define the main processes of your organization.

4. List the subprocesses associated with one of the main processes identified in question 3.

REFERENCES

The American Heritage Dictionary of the English Language. Boston: Houghton Mifflin.

Harrington, H. J. 1991. *Business Process Improvement: The Breakthrough Strategy for Total Quality, Productivity, and Competitiveness*. New York: McGraw-Hill.

Melan, E. H. 1993. *Process Management: Methods for Improving Products and Services*. New York: McGraw-Hill.

Watson, Gregory H. 1992. *The Benchmarking Workbook: Adapting Best Practices for Performance Improvement*. New York: Productivity Press.

Wesner, J. W., J. M. Hiatt, and D. C. Trimble. 1994. *Winning with Quality*. Reading, MA: Addison-Wesley.

6 | Identify Core Processes

The techniques for classifying processes and for compiling a process inventory that were described in Chapter 5 are mechanistic and do not by themselves differentiate the relative importance among processes. All processes do not have equal value. Some processes are more important than others because of their critical impact on an organization. Certain processes represent the means by which an organization will achieve its *goals* and *objectives*, fulfill its *mission*, and attain its *vision*.

The term *core* is used to distinguish those processes that are essential to the organization's success. *Core, key, macro, systems-level*, and *level 1* are synonyms that various practitioners use to describe the same thing. Any of these terms can be selected, as long as it is consistent throughout the organization and over time. An organization's ability to clearly define, understand, and improve its core processes represents a strategic weapon in a competitive marketplace.

A RATIONALE FOR CORE PROCESSES

Identifying core processes can satisfy a number of needs. First, core processes can serve as strategic weapons in the battle to achieve the organization's mission and vision by focusing on crucially important business drivers (see Chapters 3 and 4). Second, the identification of core processes can serve to clarify inefficiencies in the organizational structure. Third, the identification of core processes can serve to redeploy improvement efforts that were previously launched against relatively unimportant targets.

CORE PROCESSES AS STRATEGIC WEAPONS

In the pharmaceutical industry, for example, the pipeline of new products is critical to maintaining and increasing market share and revenues. Therefore, *new-product development* is a core process for pharmaceutical companies.

The treatment of new-product development differentiates pharmaceutical companies at a strategic level. This core process has become so expensive and difficult that the pharmaceutical industry essentially segments itself. Companies that focus on new-product development as a core process are referred to as research-focused companies. Pfizer, for example, is focusing on the discovery of novel therapeutics to maintain its competitive advantage. Other companies, such as Merck, SmithKline Beecham, and Eli Lilly have chosen a different route for competitiveness. By acquiring companies known as pharmacy benefit managers in the mid-1990s, they entered the low-cost, high-volume managed-care markets. This strategic decision enabled them to reduce their dependence on the new-product development process (Beach, 1994).

CUTTING THROUGH FUNCTIONAL BARRIERS

The new-product development core process integrates certain subprocesses: research, development, purchasing, marketing, sales, production-design, and finance. In traditional, hierarchical organizations, the new-product development process would cut across a half dozen or so functions with a different executive responsible for each functional subprocess. Who then owns new-product development in the traditional organization? Organizationally every one of the functions with a role in developing new products is a partial owner, but effectively no one has overall ownership.

To work around this lack of ownership and accountability, traditional organizations will often designate a senior manager as the *process champion*. This executive usually will be the one whose function has the greatest stake or share in the core process. The champion, in turn, will appoint a full-time *process owner* who will direct improvement efforts. The owner may not necessarily have the resources or authority required to redesign the process and will need to negotiate with other executives who control the functions through which the core process passes for resources and support.

Alternatively, organizations that adopt a process orientation (see Figure 2.3) can command a strategic advantage by clearly assigning ownership of core processes. By redefining organizational boundaries to correspond to core processes, the process owner will have both the responsibility and the authority to improve his or her core process. Employees no longer report to managers of functional silos but to owners of operational processes.

REDEPLOYING IMPROVEMENT TEAMS

The identification of core processes can be used to redeploy underachieving quality improvement teams. Many organizations launched these types of teams only to be disappointed by the lack of success or in the negligible bottom-line impact.

Numerous organizations unleashed teams that were empowered to work on projects of their own choosing. While many contributed to the organization by attacking important problems, some teams targeted relatively unimportant objectives.

Many quality circles started with the notion that management was not to interfere with them. As with some quality improvement teams, some of these circles yielded results of marginal value. Some circles tended to work on "hygienic" issues and rightfully ran out of steam. Empowerment was sometimes abused and misused in the absence of cohesive direction.

Contrast these approaches with one by which senior managers identify core processes, assign ownership, and then commission improvement teams to reduce costs or cycle time or to improve quality. This latter approach puts management back in charge of the organization's improvement efforts and directs the activities to those areas with maximum impact.

IDENTIFYING CORE PROCESSES

Senior managers are usually the best positioned to identify those processes that are core because only senior managers have a broad organizational perspective. Because of their work, they have an overall view of how the organization operates; they decide on the direction that the organization will take, and they know how well the organization is doing. With this information, senior management has the opportunity and the responsibility to select those processes that are of critical importance and deserve special attention.

> *You can't redesign processes unless you know what you're trying to do. What you're after is congruence among strategic direction, organizational design, staff capabilities, and the processes you use to ensure that people are working together to meet the company's goals.*
>
> **PAUL ALLAIRE**
> *Chair and CEO of Xerox*
> *(Garvin, 1995, 78)*

The identification of core processes begins with documenting the organization's goals (see Chapter 3), such as increased market share, improved customer satisfaction, increased return on assets, enhanced value to the shareholder, and involvement and support to the community. But what do these type of goals mean to assembly workers on the plant floor, to sales representatives in the regional offices, or to middle managers at the corporate office? The task is then for senior managers to connect the work that people do to the goals that the organization wants to achieve.

This task progresses by linking each goal to all applicable processes in the organization's inventory of processes (see Chapter 5). The main process represents a core process, and the subordinate—or lower-level—processes can be termed subprocesses.

The assumption in this identification process is that the goals clearly state what is to be accomplished over the long term (five years), and that each goal is associated with a subset of objectives that must be accomplished in the short term (one to two years). With this clarity of purpose, it becomes possible to identify the processes through which goals will be achieved. Similarly, process improvement initiatives can be coupled to specific objectives.

TREE DIAGRAM AND SELECTION MATRIX TOOLS

The *tree diagram* serves as a tool to help in visualizing the linkages between processes and goals. A simplified example in Figure 6.1 links a typical corporate goal to a small sample of the processes that enable the organization to achieve its goal.

Linking goals to processes becomes more complicated as the number of goals increases. The preceding example showed a single goal. When working with multiple goals, a matrix analysis is usually the preferred technique. Table 6.1 shows the skeleton of such a matrix, with goals listed across the top, and the inventory of processes listed down the page. The matrix is completed by marking the degree by which each process contributes to each goal.

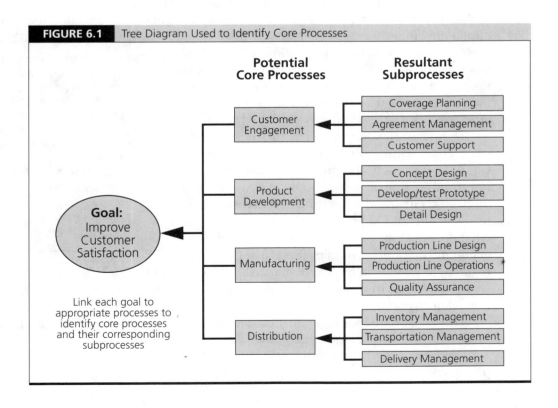

FIGURE 6.1   Tree Diagram Used to Identify Core Processes

TABLE 6.1	Sample Core Process Selection Matrix

Instructions: List goals across the top, and processes down the side of the matrix. Mark the impact of each process on each goal: (H) = High; (M) = Moderate; (L) = Low; (Blank) = None

	GOAL 1	GOAL 2	GOAL 3	GOAL . . .
Process 1.0				
1.1				
1.2				
1.2.1				
1.2.2				
1.3				
1.3.1				
1.3.2				
Process 2.0				
2.1, etc.				

A common approach is simply to mark H, M, or L for high, moderate, or low impact, respectively, in each cell of the matrix. Examination of the completed matrix reveals the array of processes associated with each goal. Core processes and subprocesses attached to each goal can then be identified. Additionally, the completed selection matrix shows goals that are linked to each other through shared processes. In such cases the goals should be reviewed to determine whether they are complementary or conflicting.

ATTRIBUTES OF CORE PROCESSES

Consider the following attributes when deciding on whether or not a particular process should be classified as a core process:

- *Strategic importance:* Processes that qualify to be classified as core processes have a major impact on the organization and are crucial to its success. Candidate processes should be strategically relevant to the organization's mission and goals. Core processes may provide a competitive advantage if they perform properly. Conversely, core processes pose a major competitive weakness if they are ineffective, inefficient, or remain unimproved.

- *Customer impact:* Processes that directly affect customers are always worthy of consideration as candidates and might be designated as *operational* core processes. Examples include order fulfillment and after-sales service. Internal processes—such as financial control, facilities management, and human resources—are called *supporting* or *resource* processes and are sometimes considered core processes.

- *Cross-functional:* Core processes frequently cut across organizational boundaries and involve numerous functional, departmental, or even divisional units.

Note, however, that process-oriented organizations that are structured along process lines will likely find that their core processes are contained within their respective organizational units (see Chapter 2).

PROCESS HIERARCHY

The preceding discussion of attributes will probably raise more questions about core processes than provide answers. These questions prompt offering further clarification on the classification of different types of processes. Commonly used terms to classify processes typically account for three factors:

- *Size: Core processes* tend to be large and complex systems. These systems generally comprise a number of functional processes, which, in turn are constructed from a series of *subprocesses*. Practices, procedures, tasks, and activities represent the basic building blocks of subprocesses (see Figure 6.2). Each building block transforms inputs into outputs through the integration of people, methods, and tools.

> **Helpful Hint**
> Consider constructing your process inventory around your core processes.

- *Importance:* Major, large, complex processes that are critically important to the organization earn the distinction of being named core processes. However, size is not the determining factor: importance is the determinant. Organizations also will find large complex processes that are not critically important. These subordinate processes do not warrant being distinguished as core processes, in spite of their size.

- *Jurisdiction:* Core processes will tend to be cross-functional in traditional, hierarchical organizations that are structured around areas of specialization. Core processes in these types of organizations will include one or more *functional processes*.

SAMPLE CORE PROCESSES

How many core processes should a company have? The answer is that it depends on the size and scope of the organization. The number of core processes could be as few as one or two for a small business or as many as a dozen in a large organization. Examples of core processes selected by two major international manufacturers—Xerox and General Electric (GE)—are listed in Table 6.2 (Ramaharandas, 1994, 4–10; Tichy and Sherman, 1993, 84–94). Xerox identifies the first four of its processes listed in Table 6.2 as operational and the last two as supporting. Similarly, GE divides its core processes into five operational and one supporting process.

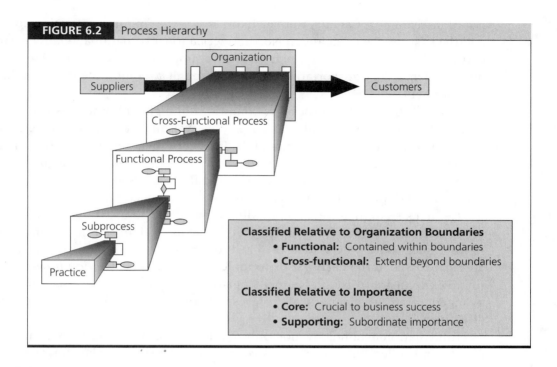

FIGURE 6.2   Process Hierarchy

Classified Relative to Organization Boundaries
- **Functional:** Contained within boundaries
- **Cross-functional:** Extend beyond boundaries

Classified Relative to Importance
- **Core:** Crucial to business success
- **Supporting:** Subordinate importance

TABLE 6.2   Example Core Processes of Leading Manufacturers

XEROX	GENERAL ELECTRIC
1. Market to collection	1. Advanced technology
2. Integrated supply chain	2. Offering development
3. Time to market	3. Go-to-market
4. Customer service	4. Order-to-remittance
5. Corporate governance	5. Service delivery
6. Infrastructure	6. Support

CORE PROCESSES AT REIMER EXPRESS

In our experience, Reimer Express Lines, Ltd. represents the epitome of simplified process management (Tenner and DeToro, 1992, 102–103). In the late 1980s, Reimer defined its business as being dependent on two core processes—one that delivers freight for customers and the other that collects money from customers. These came to be termed *freight flow* and *money flow*. John Perry, vice president for quality, helped shape Reimer's approach, and the authors gratefully acknowledge his contributions.

Based in Winnipeg, Canada, Reimer Express was the first transportation company and the first service company in North America to win a national quality award. It earned this recognition from the federal government of Canada in 1989 for achieving excellence in transportation services through a commitment to continuous improvement.

Reimer's freight-flow process is comprised of eight subprocesses (Figure 6.3). Reimer believes it is critical that employees working in each subprocess of the freight-flow service chain understand the impact of their activities on the other elements. This understanding is achieved by training employees in all eight elements. Employees identify *roadblocks to quality* and thereby assist the company in managing the total process for increasing customers' satisfaction.

Reimer's sustained focus on quality service earned a strong reputation that propelled the company beyond merely moving freight on roads in Canada. Reimer successfully expanded into rail and air transportation. A rethinking of core processes in the early 1990s to include a third—*information flow*—enabled further expansion through Reimer Logistics. Perry (1995) explains, "The three-pronged focus was a natural progression to make the overall system work effectively."

Information technology not only made a positive impact on transporting freight and collecting money, but it represented the strategic key for moving into new business arenas to capture a larger piece of the shipping pie. Reimer recognized the importance of the linkages across its core processes and assembled a broader range of services under one umbrella to provide one-stop shopping for shippers as an integrated system. Reimer Logistics serves all of North America and boasts the inclusion of several large U.S.-based corporations on its list of customers.

ERICSSON OFFERS SUBPROCESS EXAMPLE

The next step is to identify the subprocesses that comprise each core process. These subprocesses will likely include various functional processes that when connected together form the core process. As an example, Table 6.3 lists core and subprocesses for Ericsson.

Based in Sweden, Ericsson doubled its sales of mobile telephone systems from 1992 to 1994. It led the industry outside of North America in 1994 with 56 percent of the market—well ahead of AT&T (20 percent) and Motorola (13 percent). In the North American market, Ericsson ranked second with its 31 percent share, behind AT&T (34 percent). Working to sustain the trend, Ericsson modified its organizational structure in 1995 to support its two core processes—*customer order flow* and *product development flow*. Ericsson (1995) also defined a third main supporting area—*business development flow*.

FIGURE 6.3	Freight-Flow at Reimer Express

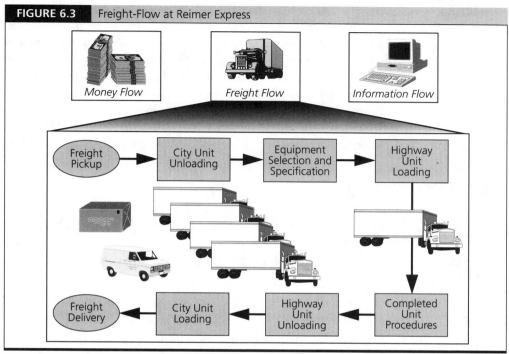

SOURCE: Adapted from Perry (1995).

TABLE 6.3	Core and Subprocesses at Ericsson

CUSTOMER ORDER FLOW

Customer order flow planning
  Tactical market planning
  Tactical material planning
  Tactical resource planning
Product introduction
  Market introduction
  Product deployment
Sales to order
  Sales
  Proposal preparation
  Contract and order
Delivery
  Project definition
  Business fulfillment
  Invoicing and payment collection
  Engineering
  Supply
  Installation and test
  Customer support services
  Training and professional services

PRODUCT DEVELOPMENT FLOW

Product concept development
  Product concept study
Product provisioning
  Service provisioning
  System provisioning
  Sourcing
  In-service provisioning

BUSINESS DEVELOPMENT FLOW

Business planning
  Business plan preparation
  Business plan creation
  Business plan presentation
  Ericsson strategic plan creation
Continuous improvement planning process
  Self-assessment
  Continuous improvement directives preparation
  Continuous improvement directives creation
  Continuous improvement directives plan creation

SOURCE: Adapted from Ericsson (1995, 1–6).

SUMMARY

The preceding tools, guidelines, and examples are offered to help organizations begin the task of identifying the specific systems or processes that deserve special attention. Some are obvious—new-product development in the pharmaceutical industry, order-to-remittance in the mail-order PC business, market-to-collection in the copier business. The point is that the list of core processes varies both by organization and by the strategic direction set by senior managers.

Identify those few key processes that are vital to your organization's business drivers and strategy, and then identify their respective subprocess building blocks.

DISCUSSION QUESTIONS

1. Use the tree diagram or selection matrix to identify one or more core processes within your organization. These tools help to link goals (Chapter 3) to your process inventory (Chapter 5).

2. Identify the subprocesses that comprise one of the core processes identified in question 1.

REFERENCES

Beach, C. A. 1994. Personal communications with the director of licensing and development at Pfizer, Inc., December.

Ericsson. 1995. *News Flash* 2, no. 1 (January), 1–6.

Garvin, David A. 1995. "Leveraging Processes for Strategic Advantage." *Harvard Business Review* (September-October), 78.

Perry, John. 1995. Conversations with the vice president for quality at Reimer Express, Winnipeg, Canada, April.

Ramaharandas, E. 1994. "Xerox Creates a Continuous Learning Environment for Business Transformation." *Planning and Review* (April-May), 4–10.

Tenner, A. R. and I. J. DeToro. 1992. *Total Quality Management: Three Steps to Continuous Improvement*. Section on "Core Processes at Reimer Express" adapted from pp. 102–103. Copyright © 1992 Addison-Wesley Publishing Company, Inc. Reprinted by permission of the publisher.

Tichy, N. M., and S. Sherman. 1993. *Control Your Destiny or Someone Else Will*. New York: Doubleday.

7 | Measure Performance

WHY MEASURE?

The absence of measurement limits an organization's ability to evaluate the effects of changes and therefore precludes systematic improvement. Given

> **If** you're not keeping score, then it's just practice.

that the establishment and use of performance measures are fundamental requirements for redesigning processes, the issue then becomes one of understanding *what* to measure.

Some readers may feel that their organization is already doing a great job of measuring. Indeed, some organizations have established exemplary measurement systems. Unfortunately, most have not.

The corporate world has historically measured financial performance and sales volume. Standardized procedures have evolved to ensure consistency in reporting these data, and significant resources are dedicated to their analysis. Dr. W. Edwards Deming cited excessive attention to these types of measures as one of seven deadly diseases that plague Western industry. He particularly criticized reliance on quarterly and annual financial statements as "management by use only of visible figures, with little or no consideration of figures that are unknown or unknowable" (Deming, 1986, 98).

A similar excess has been observed in the measurement of customer satisfaction, a practice that began to proliferate in the late 1980s as companies began to recognize that they needed to focus on customers. Consumers were bombarded with questionnaires from well-meaning companies. But resources were squandered by asking inappropriate questions and by not taking appropriate action once responses were returned.

Measures of financial performance, sales volume, and customer satisfaction are not wrong: they are merely insufficient. Many organizations fail to understand how these indicators fit within the comprehensive measurement strategy that is required to effectively redesign processes.

This chapter helps practitioners to overcome this deficiency by clarifying how to identify and use three types of performance measures: efficiency, process effectiveness, and outcome. Outcome is most commonly represented by customer satisfaction, and this chapter offers an alternative approach—measurement of product or service effectiveness—that reveals the cause-and-effect relationships among the processes along the customer-supplier chain.

After introducing a framework for identifying and using performance measures, this chapter then identifies key measures that can be posted on a "scoreboard" to evaluate performance improvement. Chapter 8 continues exploring the subject of measurement by describing specific sets of measures for quantifying *efficiency*. Chapter 9 completes the trilogy by explaining how to connect the customer into measurement systems by quantifying the *effectiveness* of processes and their outputs.

THREE TYPES OF MEASURES

What are measures in the context of processes? They are simply people's attempts to quantify what is happening. Understanding the performance of a process depends on defining each element in the process *and* the relationship among the elements. Furthermore, the accuracy and precision of the measurements will govern how closely models and analyses can replicate reality.

The process model that was introduced in Chapter 5 provides a basis for defining three types of measures (see Figure 7.1). The type of measure determines where in the process you can find performance indicators and collect data. The process model and its three types of measures also reveal the interrelationships of products and services throughout the customer-supplier chain.

FIGURE 7.1	Performance Measurement Framework
Terminology	**Explanation**
1. Process *or* Efficiency	Resources consumed in the process relative to minimum possible levels
2. Output *or* Effectiveness	Ability of a process to deliver products or services according to specifications
3. Outcome *or* Product/service effectiveness and customer satisfaction	Ability of outputs to satisfy the needs of customers

Process Model shows where to find each type of measurement.

Process → Output → Outcome

PROCESS

Measures of efficiency quantify the resources consumed in the process relative to minimum possible levels. These measures, such as cost, variability, and cycle time, are explained further in Chapter 8.

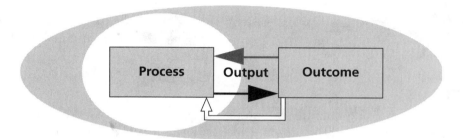

Efficiency is measured *within* the process. Efficiency is not measured by examining products after they are produced nor by surveying customers. To solidify this relationship, the terms *efficiency* and *process measure* will be used interchangeably throughout this chapter.

Process measures represent parameters that directly control the integration of people, materials, methods, machines, and the environment within the process. While frequently understood and used in manufacturing operations, process measures are often absent from service functions. Process measures also include the performance of subprocesses and inputs from suppliers.

Understanding and applying process measures helps to predict the characteristics of the outputs *before* they are delivered to customers. These measures are important for improving process performance.

OUTPUT

Measures of process effectiveness quantify the ability of a process to deliver products or services according to their specifications. These measures, which are explained further in Chapter 9, represent the specific features, values, and attributes of each product or service that are expected by customers.

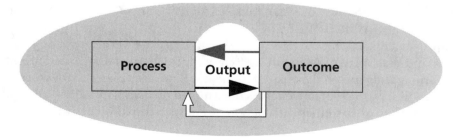

Similar to efficiency, which is quantified relative to minimum theoretical levels, effectiveness too is a relative term. Process effectiveness is calculated by a comparison of the process's ability to deliver products and services (outputs) relative to the customer's requirements. That is, process effectiveness compares the output characteristics actually delivered by the process to the corresponding characteristics specified by the customer.

Process effectiveness is measured by examining products and services when they are produced and is referred to as an *output measure*. Measurement of the output reveals what is delivered to customers.

OUTCOME

Measures of outcome quantify the ability of outputs to satisfy the needs of their customers and represent the ultimate performance measure. Outcomes are beyond the direct control of the supplier and rely on the customer's expectations and actions. Outcomes can be measured in either of two ways:

- *Product/service effectiveness:* This measure determines how well the product or service (output) performs in the customer's process. Since the determination of customer's performance can be intrusive, customer satisfaction is commonly used as a surrogate measurement.

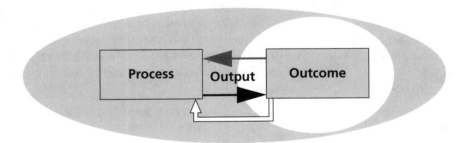

- *Customer satisfaction:* This measure determines how well each product and service satisfies the needs and expectations of the customer and recognizes that satisfaction is based on vague, idiosyncratic perceptions.

Measures at the outcome level can be determined only *after* the product has been delivered or the service provided.

Improvements in *process* effectiveness will correlate with *product/service* effectiveness and customer satisfaction as long as measurements are accurate and the specifications truly match the customer's needs. Since it is easier to measure outputs than outcomes, process effectiveness is determined on an ongoing basis. Product/service effectiveness or customer satisfaction are measured periodically for validation.

Outcome Measures Recognize Relationships Along the Process Chain

Question: if outcomes can be measured in either of two ways, then which is preferred? Answer: we suggest that both types should be used. Unfortunately, most organizations have limited their focus to merely one—customer satisfaction. To help establish a better balance, this chapter offers three examples of product/service effectiveness measures. The measurement of customer satisfaction is explained further in Chapter 9.

> ***Inability*** *to recognize the relationship among process, output, and outcome measures is symptomatic of failure to understand the process.*
>
> **(PERFORMANCE AXIOM)**

Measuring product/service effectiveness offers two advantages over the measurement of customer satisfaction. First, this measure overcomes the random error introduced by satisfaction measures that by their very nature must be based on vague, idiosyncratic perceptions of customers. Second, the validity of product/service effectiveness measures can be checked by examining the performance of each process along the customer-supplier chain.

Example 1: Measuring the Outcome of Petroleum Refining

A simplified example of a commonly used everyday product illustrates the relationship among the three types of measurements along the customer-supplier chain (see Figure 7.2). This example follows two sequential processes—refining crude oil into gasoline and burning gasoline in an automobile engine to produce power.

In making decisions as to which brand or grade of gasoline to buy, customers are concerned with how the product itself will perform in their car, the purchase price, and the attributes of service at the point of purchase, such as convenience with regard to time and location, appearance of the facilities, and behavior of the attendants.

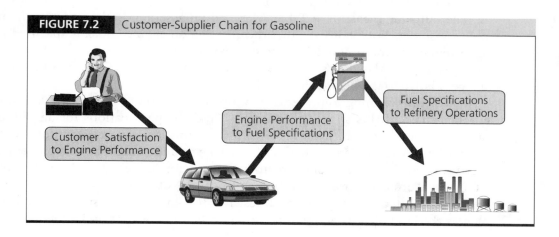

FIGURE 7.2   Customer-Supplier Chain for Gasoline

Customer Satisfaction to Engine Performance

Engine Performance to Fuel Specifications

Fuel Specifications to Refinery Operations

TABLE 7.1	Measures for Engine Performance

OUTCOME	Customer survey regarding engine knock
	  67% Pleased
	  31% Satisfied
	   2% Dissatisfied

OUTPUT	Customer wants
	  No knocking
	Process delivers
	  No knocking

PROCESS	Sample engines
	  Load range
	  Throttle positions
	  Temperatures
	  Octane = 89.3

To focus on just one characteristic for the purpose of this example, consider the performance of the product itself—the customer's need for smooth, quiet, trouble-free operation of his or her car's engine. Engines' needs have been translated by refiners into a set of product specifications for gasoline, and octane represents one such specification. Rather than asking customers or service station attendants meaningless questions like, "How do you rate the octane of our gasoline," refiners can measure performance outcomes by understanding engine performance.

One snapshot of example measures for engine performance is shown in Table 7.1. This snapshot offers one specific set of values for each type of measurement. In reality, however, the picture is complicated because the variability of the data also must be understood. Even for a single driver with one car, the required octane will vary with weather, altitude, and condition of the engine (such as wear, deposits, and intake and cooling system performance).

The outcome measure in Table 7.1 relied on assessing satisfaction of the ultimate consumer. Note, however, that the question on engine knock is specific to the performance of the product in question. Polling drivers as to how well they like your gasoline or their car's acceleration would not necessarily define the performance relative to the octane delivered.

Petroleum refining represents the upstream process along the customer-supplier chain of this simplified example. Product specifications for an output—gasoline—such as octane are translated into performance parameters for the various operations and incoming feed streams. One example might be the temperature, pressure, and flow rate of one stream into a reactor. Table 7.2 shows a simplified set of measurements for the refining process. Notice the use of an objective measure of outcome—engine knock-test results—instead of a subjective measure such as the level of satisfaction among service-station owners and attendants.

TABLE 7.2	Measures for Refinery Performance
OUTCOME	Knock test @ 89.3 octane
	86% None
	14% Incipient
	0% Yes
OUTPUT	Engine needs
	89 Octane
	Process delivers
	89.3 Octane
PROCESS	Feed to Reactor A
	Flow rate = 37k bbl/day
	Temperature = 455 F
	Pressure = 725 psi

TABLE 7.3	Relationship of Product Measurements	
	TYPE OF MEASURE FOR EACH PROCESS	
MEASURE	**ENGINE**	**REFINERY**
Customer satisfaction	Outcome	—
Engine performance	Output	Outcome
Fuel/octane	Process	Output
Reactor A operation	—	Process

So what has this example shown? It began by defining the desired outcome as the smooth, quiet, trouble-free operation of the customers' car engines. This requirement was satisfied by operations in the refinery and relied on process measures such as temperature, pressure, and flow rate into a reactor. The translation of the desired outcome through the engine and refinery processes reveals the role and relationship among the key measures. The refining process is controlled by measuring temperatures, pressures, and flow rates at the reactor, not by measuring octane in the service station tanks.

This translation was possible because the processes were described, modeled, and understood. These translations, shown in Table 7.3, follow the links in the customer-supplier chain.

Example 2: Measuring the Outcome of Training

An example of training for the customer service representatives of an appliance manufacturer helps to clarify the three types of measurement for a company's internal service division. Figure 7.3 shows the flow of service through three links of the customer-supplier chain: designing training, delivering training, and contacting customers.

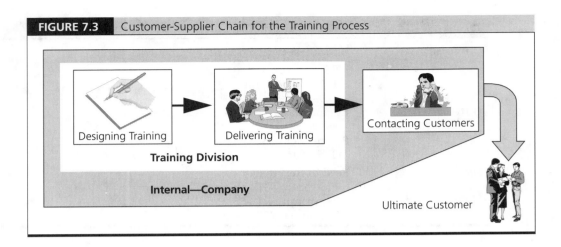

FIGURE 7.3   Customer-Supplier Chain for the Training Process

Designing Training

Delivering Training

Training Division

Contacting Customers

Internal—Company

Ultimate Customer

An instructional designer in the Training Division developed a four-hour training session to improve service representatives' ability to answer maintenance questions on a new household appliance. Activities included the identification of training needs of the service representatives, development of the required training program, preparation of an instructor's guide, and production of classroom materials.

Efficiency measures for the training design processes were only partly defined. One obvious measure is the length of time required for each activity, but the Training Division has not clarified others. Instead it focuses on output measures and develops internal process measures as needed to understand and improve performance.

Outputs from this work include the design of the four-hour course, a 72-page instructor's guide, a 26-page participant's manual, and 34 visual aids for use in the classroom. Note that these output measures (4, 72, 26, and 34) are counts of quantity and not quality or performance. The effectiveness of these outputs is characterized by attributes such as accuracy, completeness, clarity, and ease of use.

A classroom trainer delivered ten sessions of the course to 240 customer service representatives. The inputs into the delivery process included outputs from the design process. Activities within the training delivery process included lesson planning, classroom preparation, and presentation of the actual course. Outputs from training delivery are outcomes of training development.

As an outcome of the training process, service representatives now are able to answer twenty-four additional customer inquiries each week. These additional calls are outputs of the customer contacting process. One outcome of these calls is an increase in sales of the new product by $60,000 per month. Another outcome is improved customer satisfaction attributable to the new skills of the sales reps.

	TABLE 7.4	Relationship of Training Measurements		

	TYPE OF MEASURE FOR EACH PROCESS		
MEASURE	**DESIGNING TRAINING**	**DELIVERING TRAINING**	**CONTACTING CUSTOMERS**
$60,000 per month higher sales	—	—	Outcome
24 contacts added weekly	—	Outcome	Output
10 classes delivered 240 service reps trained 5 skills gained by each service rep	Outcome	Output	Process
72-page guide 26-page manual 34 visual aids 4-hour design	Output	Process	—
Time to develop new course	Process	—	—

Table 7.4 shows how the type of measurement is defined by its frame of reference. To see how this works, examine one particular measurement from three reference points. Training 240 service reps is an *outcome* of the course design process. This same measure is a direct *output* from the course delivery process. This same measure is an activity in the customer contact *process* of the sales representatives. This moving frame of reference shows how measurements are translated as products/services flow along the customer-supplier chain.

The Training Division is able to improve its performance in the development and delivery of training programs through the analysis of all three types of measurement. The objective outcome measures that are defined along the customer-supplier chain can be used as valuable supplements to course evaluation forms that are commonly given to participants at the conclusion of corporate training programs.

Example 3: Measuring the Outcome of R&D

The application of meaningful measurements to corporate research and development has been a subject of debate for decades. Acceptance and use of the three types of measurement can help to remedy this situation (see Figure 7.4).

Measurements within the process are used routinely by scientists and engineers to perform their tasks. Process measures are represented by data in their day-to-day activities and experiments. These are the data accumulated within the projects themselves, whether they are technical, administrative, or financial.

Outputs from the research process include technical reports, patents, publications, and presentations. These outputs can be measured, but as with process measures, these indicators are rarely of interest to the customers. These uninspired

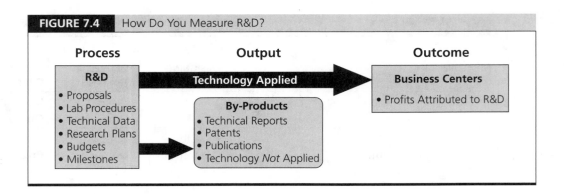

FIGURE 7.4   How Do You Measure R&D?

customers include corporate directors, as well as managers and technical staff of the manufacturing divisions who apply the results of the research. While these customers are interested in the content of the output from R&D, their operations are hardly affected by counting these outputs.

The factor that has been missing from these measures is the bottom-line impact—measurement of the outcome. How can the ultimate desired objective of corporate research functions be described? The objective is for users of technical discoveries to be "happy customers." These users represent the corporate profit centers, or the manufacturing divisions, and they are made happy through increased profits. Measuring research against this ultimate objective is fraught with problems and usually avoided.

British Petroleum (BP) is one organization that bucked the trend and measured R&D performance at the outcome level (Fishlock, 1988, 19). As director of research, John Cadogan used these data in the preparation of an annual balance sheet for the board of directors. Cadogan initiated the process in 1985 and included records for the three previous years. The value of R&D was calculated by dividing the financial benefit attributed to research for a given year by the research budget.

BP's measure of R&D outcome was based on the judgment of their business center managers, who were asked to quantify how much of their annual profits were attributable to research. Researchers developed a listing of their projects that were being implemented in each business center. Managers used the respective listings to prepare their responses.

While many shortcomings of BP's approach could be cited, it offered two distinct benefits. First, Cadogan's system was designed to be quick and simple. It discouraged "overworking the numbers." Second, the system directly asked customers for their perception of the value of specific research projects to their own operations. The impact of errors in estimating the value of R&D was minimized through this approach, since the ultimate objective is to satisfy the customer, and it was the customers' perceptions which were being measured.

A SCOREBOARD TO IMPROVE PERFORMANCE

Most people and organizations are driven by performance measurement. After all, what gets measured gets done. The absence of meaningful goals and measures can lead to useless meandering. Perhaps even worse, use of the wrong measures can drive organizations in the wrong direction.

Look at the sports world for examples: both individual and team sports are filled with key measures of performance that tie directly to the outputs delivered by their respective processes. Whether it is batting averages, service aces, birdies, or percentage of successful field goals from various yardages, certain highly visible measures relate directly to performance expectations of individual professionals. Similarly, runs scored, games won, and rushing yardage represent key measures for teams through the combination of interrelated processes of individual team members and competitors.

Whether you are striving to become a sports legend or a corporate hero, the same principle applies: identify the key measures of performance, and display them in lights on a gigantic scoreboard. The scoreboard should display the measures that are of critical importance to your customers and hence to your own success. The scoreboard should be balanced and also display measures that are important to your other vital stakeholders—shareholders, employees, and the community.

MEASURING IN FOUR DIMENSIONS

In addition to the output actually delivered to the end customer, each process generates by-products and outcomes for other "customers." One by-product is financial return for shareholders. Another is jobs for employees. A third by-product is social impact on the community.

> ***Quality Versus Quantity:*** *Measuring attributes of the output (quality) is for customers. Counting numbers of outputs (quantity) is for shareholders.*

As shown in Table 7.5, performance measures can be defined in each of these four dimensions. Each dimension corresponds to the output or outcome desired by its respective stakeholder. In general, most organizations must be responsive to four sets of stakeholders: the end-user or customer, the shareholder, the employee, and the community.

Antidote to a Deadly Disease

These four dimensions of performance measures offer an antidote to the deadly disease of running a company on visible figures alone. Deming (1986, 97–125)

TABLE 7.5	Four Dimensions of Measures	
DIMENSION	**FOCUS**	**EXAMPLE MEASURES**
Actual product or service (output)	End user or customer	• Effectiveness of processes to deliver specific features and attributes defined by customers • Customer satisfaction
Financial return	Shareholder	• Cost • Capital utilization • Prices • Return on investment • Sales volume • Productivity • Profits • Cost of quality • Throughput • Cycle time • Waste • Efficiency
Jobs	Employees	• Specific needs and values defined by employees • Employee satisfaction • Attrition
Social impact	Community	• Regulatory compliance • Pollution control, waste disposal, and recycling • Grants and contributions • Blood drives and United Way campaigns • Presentations and publications • Taxes and fines

explains in *Out of the Crisis* that this disease is the result of management's fixation on counting money. In essence, Western companies have focused on themselves and the financial markets rather than on their customers, their employees, or the community.

Organizations moving to focus on the customer can facilitate their transformation by defining and using measures that indicate customer satisfaction. Similarly, organizations striving for total involvement of their workforce need to attend to the parameters that directly relate to improving employees' satisfaction with their jobs.

A balanced approach is needed, and none of the dimensions can be ignored. To the extent that the shareholder's objectives, the customers' requirements, the employees' needs, and the community's expectations overlap with each other, the task becomes easier (see Figure 7.5). Long-term success can be ensured by selecting and leading a balanced attack to improve systematically in all dimensions.

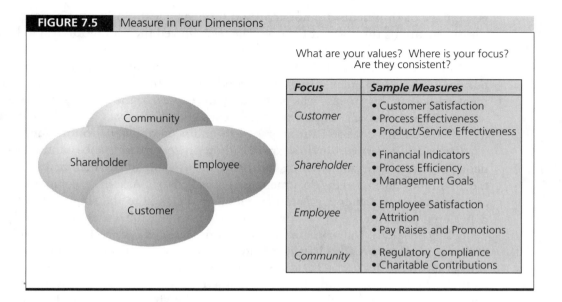

FIGURE 7.5   Measure in Four Dimensions

What are your values? Where is your focus?
Are they consistent?

Focus	Sample Measures
Customer	• Customer Satisfaction • Process Effectiveness • Product/Service Effectiveness
Shareholder	• Financial Indicators • Process Efficiency • Management Goals
Employee	• Employee Satisfaction • Attrition • Pay Raises and Promotions
Community	• Regulatory Compliance • Charitable Contributions

Example of Balanced Approach at SAS

Jan Carlzon (1987, 107–112) offers two examples in his book *Moments of Truth* that show how rebalancing the dimensions in which it measures can help an organization in refocusing its attention. As CEO of Scandinavian Airlines System (SAS), Carlzon helped move his company toward one that would focus on satisfying the customers' needs through an empowered workforce. One thing he did was replace performance measures of interest to the shareholders (sales volume and efficiency) with measures of interest to the paying customers.

SAS historically had measured the performance of its air cargo division by the amount of freight it carried and how well it used available capacity in the cargo holds of the aircraft. The logic had seemed flawless. Efficiency and profitability for a commercial airline are improved by filling the "empty bellies" of passenger planes with air freight.

However, in order to focus on the customers' needs and facilitate decision making at the working level, these measures were inadequate. How important was SAS profitability to its cargo customers? How did these historic measures help employees to do their jobs?

What mattered most to the customers was what SAS termed "precision": prompt delivery to specified locations. Furthermore, the cargo customers' defined *prompt* as "next day." Recognizing this requirement, SAS ran an experiment to measure the capability of their process to deliver the required precision.

This experiment was conducted in spite of the fact that SAS thought they were doing very well. After all, the cargo division had reported that only a small percentage of shipments did not arrive on time. As a test, SAS sent 100 packages to various locations throughout Europe. The test showed the average arrival to be four days and not the next day.

As a result of this test, SAS recognized that it was not measuring the correct parameters. It was measuring a by-product for the shareholders, instead of measuring how the process was performing in relation to the real customer's expectations. The customer's requirement for next-day delivery was beyond the capability of the existing system. Even worse, SAS had been oblivious to this gap.

In a second example, Carlzon explained how process performance parameters were defined for baggage handlers. At SAS historic measures had been defined in terms of the amount of cargo and the documentation attached to it. As long as volume remained at high levels and the documentation remained attached to the shipments, SAS had considered performance to be fine. In fact, Carlzon explained that new records were being set constantly. Unfortunately these records were self-serving for the organization and were being established in spite of late deliveries and unhappy customers.

SAS empowered its cargo handlers to define more appropriate measures. Known as their *QualiCargo* system, these data compared the various cargo terminals with each other and were published monthly. The following QualiCargo data were collected to demonstrate process performance against the criteria of greatest interest to the customers:

- Length of time to answer the telephone,
- Conformance to promised deadlines,
- Cargo arrival with intended plane, and
- Length of time from landing to availability.

SAS improved its cargo handling system and reduced late shipments from 20 percent to 8 percent. Furthermore, this success did not require adding staff or forcing the existing staff to work harder. Instead, the accurate system of measurement identified previously unrecognized problems and led to procedural changes and reallocation of resources. SAS combined financial information with data on performance relative to customer requirements provided by QualiCargo. These measurements enabled the cargo handlers to understand what was important to the customers and profitable to SAS.

QualiCargo was one of many SAS initiatives to help focus on satisfying customers' needs through an empowered workforce. All employees at SAS cargo knew that precision was important to the customers and that precision was important to SAS because this was what the customers pay for. Furthermore, employees knew exactly what components comprise precision and that top priorities were answering telephones, booking shipments, receiving them, forwarding them along with their documentation, receiving them at the other end, reconciling cargo, preparing for customer pickup, and informing customers when their shipments are ready.

This new insight also affected how the cargo division approached its daily operations. Supervisors no longer needed to direct the activities of the baggage handlers and schedule coffee breaks and work shifts. Instead everyone knew what to do, when to do it, and why it was important.

SELECTING KEY MEASURES

W. H. Davidow and B. Uttal (1989) provide excellent guidance on the subject of measurement in their book *Total Customer Service*. After examining hundreds of process and output measures, they concluded that even the best sets of measures will result in suboptimization unless they are balanced against frequent measures of customer satisfaction (Davidow and Uttal, 1989, 201). They continue to explain that employees will perform exactly as the measures tell them to, regardless of the original intent of the measures. Furthermore, the measures may serve the needs of only the shareholders and ignore the ultimate customers, employees, and community. At best, measures provide an imperfect representation of the customer's expectations. Even if they are reasonably accurate and complete, they will drift out of alignment because expectations change in response to advertising, competition, and experience.

Davidow and Uttal offer four tools for implementing measurement systems. Table 7.6 lists these along with six essential variables offered by Tom Peters (1987) in his book *Thriving on Chaos*.

TABLE 7.6	Comparing Measurement Guidelines
ESSENTIAL VARIABLES OF MEASUREMENT SYSTEMS[a]	**TOOLS FOR IMPLEMENTING MEASUREMENT SYSTEMS**[b]
• Simplicity of presentation (few and understandable variables) • Visibility • Involvement of all concerned • Undistorted collection of primary information throughout the operations area • Straightforward measurement of what's important • Achievement of an overall feeling of urgency and perpetual improvement compensation and reward systems.	• Programs have strong support from top management. • Programs are developed through the inclusion of employees who will be measured. • Programs include measures that employees and managers need to do their jobs. • Managers demonstrate the impact of measures through linkage to the

a. SOURCE: Peters (1987, 585–593).
b. SOURCE: Davidow and Uttal (1989, 202–204).

ONE FINAL CAUTION ON MEASUREMENT

In addition to selecting the correct parameters to measure, it also is important to establish a system for collecting the correct data. A classic story from World War II illustrates this point.

Suffering tremendous losses of their four-engine Lancaster bombers, the Royal Air Force set up a program to measure their vulnerability to enemy antiaircraft fire. By examining patterns of where the planes were being hit, engineers would be able to design effective countermeasures. Spotters observed the fleets returning to their bases in England and recorded the location of damage on large-scale drawings of the planes.

With great interest, they observed a random pattern of damage over the entire fuselage. Furthermore, the density of gunfire on the wings was significantly lower. The absence of damage to the wings suggested that adding armor plating to the fuselage would be an effective solution. It would be unnecessary to protect the wings, since they did not seem to be vulnerable to gunfire.

Fortunately, before adding the burden of heavy armor to the fuselage, the error in their data collection method was recognized. What was needed instead was to measure the damage to the planes that were shot down, not the ones that were returning safely.

SUMMARY

These guidelines can be combined with the concepts in this chapter to yield the following recommendations for measuring performance at each level:

- *Process:* Process measures are needed to control performance and to improve the efficiency of processes. In processes that are well understood, process measures can be used as predictors of expected outputs.

- *Output:* Output measures quantify the effectiveness of a process to deliver products or services in comparison to specifications. These measure can also be used to represent by-products delivered to shareholders, employees, and the community. The focus of an organization's attention can be adjusted in relation to how much visibility, reward, and attention is devoted to output measures in each dimension. Key output measures and should be posted on the organization's "scoreboard." Output measures should be tested against outcomes to ensure they remain consistent with customers' ever-changing expectations.

- *Outcome:* Outcome measures determine the ultimate success or failure of an organization. Everyone should understand how their process and output measures relate to outcomes, and selected outcomes should be displayed conspicuously. Since outcomes are beyond the control of individual employees, it may be unfair to base individual compensation and reward on these measures. Instead, these measures might be more appropriately tied to whole teams or organizations. Customer satisfaction often represents the key outcome measure.

Lessons learned from the success of leading organizations and the failure of laggards yield the following advice: organizations cannot expect to systematically improve process performance if they do not establish key measures of performance. Guidelines for selecting and using key measures include the following:

- Measure the attributes of products and services (outputs) that are most critical for satisfying customers, and post these as key measures on your "scoreboard."

- Measure performance levels now and how they trend over time. If the correct measures have been selected, they should serve well over the lifetime of the product or service.

- Be specific. Define measures that quantify effectiveness for each product line, business group, or functional team. Recognize that different products and business groups may need different measures.

- Keep it simple. No single organization or individual can focus on more than a dozen or so key measures.

- Measure customer satisfaction directly to validate the key measures.

- Focus on end results (outputs or outcomes) and not on milestones. Supplement key measures with process measures during specific improvement campaigns, but don't lose sight of the ultimate objectives that are represented by the key measures.

- Balance where attention is focused by including an appropriate number of key measures in the dimensions of interest to shareholders, employees, and the community.

- Single out a *critical* performance measure if and when needed. Priorities change, and at any one point in time one measure may be of paramount importance. Concentrate on the measure that is attached to the highest priority need, and if appropriate give it a special name like *critical performance measure*. Don't, however, lose sight of the remaining key measures.

- Tie individual and team compensation systems directly to key measures.

DISCUSSION QUESTIONS

1. Define the dimension (customer, shareholder, employee, or community) and type (process, output, or outcome) for each of the following performance measures:

    a. Employee injuries

    b. United Way contributions

    c. Quarterly operating expenses

    d. Quarterly sales volume (operating income)

    e. Stock price

2. How is performance measured in your organization?

    a. When you report results to your boss, how much time do you spend on measures relating to the process (efficiency), outputs (process effectiveness), and outcomes (product/service effectiveness or customer satisfaction)?

    b. On which dimension do you focus your attention: on organizational/shareholder needs, customers, employees, community impact?

    c. When you discuss key business results with those reporting directly to you, how much time and interest do you allocate to each dimension?

3. How are you collecting performance data?

    a. Are you analyzing your successfully delivered outputs alone without examining and understanding the defective ones?

    b. Are you analyzing desired output characteristics and satisfaction from happy customers? What about the unhappy customers who are not returning, or the ones who have always purchased goods and services from your competitors?

4. Do you understand the relationship among measurements as outputs are processed along the customer-supplier chain?

    a. List the key output measures for your most important product or service.

    b. What are appropriate outcome measures for that product or service?

5. List the key performance measures that should be driving your organization and displayed on your "scoreboard."

ACKNOWLEDGMENT

This chapter is adapted from pages 127–141 in A. R. Tenner, and I. J. DeToro, *Total Quality Management: Three Steps to Continuous Improvement*. Copyright © 1992, Addison-Wesley Publishing Company, Inc. Reprinted by permission of the publisher.

REFERENCES

Carlzon, J. 1987. *Moments of Truth*. New York: Ballinger.

Davidow, W. H., and B. Uttal. 1989. *Total Customer Service*. New York: Harper & Row.

Deming, W. E. 1986. *Out of the Crisis*. Cambridge, MA: MIT Press.

Fishlock, D. 1988. "When Research Is Seen to Make a Profit." *Financial Times* (London) (Aug. 17), p. 12, sec. 19.

Peters, T. 1987. *Thriving on Chaos*. New York: Knopf.

MEASURES

→ *BETTER*
→ *FASTER*
→ *CHEAPER*

8 | Measure Efficiency

Chapter 7 provided a measurement framework to help in the redesign of processes by defining what to measure and where to look for key performance measures. Chapter 8 builds on that chapter by describing *efficiency* measures. Recall from Chapter 7 that efficiency is measured in the process itself and not by examining the outputs or by interviewing customers.

What is efficiency? In the simplest of terms, it is the elimination of waste—waste of money, waste of people, and waste of time. The dictionary definition of efficiency offers a good starting point from which to clarify key points (*Webster's Ninth*, 1989, 397):

> **efficiency 1**: *the quality or degree of being efficient* **2a**: *efficient operation* **2b**: *(1) effective operation as measured by a comparison of production with cost (as in energy, time, and money)* **(2)** *the ratio of useful energy delivered by a dynamic system to energy supplied to it.*

1. *Efficiency is subordinate to effectiveness*. Efficiency is about *doing things right*. This can be contrasted to effectiveness, which is about *doing the right things*. The choice should be clear. When allocating resources for improving how to do the wrong things or how to do the right thing, the ratio should be 0:100. Although success demands being more efficient than competitors, it is useless to invest in the improvement of processes that produce outdated or unwanted goods and services. *Improving the efficiency of doing the wrong things merely slows the rate at which you go out of business.*

2. *Efficiency is relative and not absolute*. Efficiency measures compare actual performance to the best possible. Classical efficiency measures include ones such as the actual amount of energy consumed by a process divided by the theoretical minimum, or the average cost compared to the lowest possible, or the actual time to deliver goods relative to the fastest. Recall from Chapter 7 that effectiveness is also a relative term. The effectiveness of a process is calculated by comparing what is delivered to what is expected by the customers.

3. *Efficiency is multifaceted.* There are numerous ways of defining measures of efficiency or waste. For the purpose of explanation, this chapter divides efficiency measures into three categories: cost, variation, and cycle time.

- *Cost* measures try to minimize the resources consumed in the process.
- *Variation* measures try to eliminate the waste associated with adding fat and contingency into plans and designs that serve to cushion uncertainty.
- *Cycle time* measures try to reduce the total elapsed time required to transform inputs into outputs.

COST

Minimizing the consumption of resources is the cornerstone of efficiency improvement. Strategic advantages are gained in the design of manufacturing processes and facilities to capitalize on the laws of physics and chemistry. Most of these considerations are highly technical, specific to individual industries, and beyond the scope of this book. However, one facet, the cost of quality, pervades all organizations and warrants further discussion.

DEFINING THE COST OF QUALITY

"Quality is free," or so claimed Phil Crosby (1979) in his best-selling book by the same name. Other quality evangelists went beyond Crosby to expound on how quality is not only free but how it even pays dividends. The mystery behind these apparent paradoxes can be unraveled by examining the three components that add to the total cost of prevention, detection, and failure (see Table 8.1). The business goal of

TABLE 8.1	Quality Costs: The Good, the Bad, and the Ugly
TYPE	**EXAMPLE COSTS**
Prevention (good)	Planning, training, design, and analysis
Detection (bad)	Appraisal, inspection, auditing, verifying, and checking
Failure (ugly):	
Internal failure	Rework and repair prior to delivery to customers
External failure	Repair, replacements, refunds, recalls, and warranties after delivery to customers
Exceeding requirements	Features provided that are not valued by the customer
Lost opportunity	Revenue lost when customers purchase from competitors

SOURCE: Adapted from Xerox Corporation (1983).

minimizing costs is achieved by finding the point at which the sum of the three components is minimized. Each component should be included in a comprehensive set of efficiency measures.

The extent to which defects should be eliminated is governed by the relative magnitude of each component. When the consequences of failure are relatively low in comparison to the costs associated with prevention and detection, then a modest level of failures (defects) will yield minimum costs. On the other hand, when the consequences of failure are large, more effort will be justified for prevention and detection.

Controlling the number of carry-on articles per passenger and lowering the wheels prior to landing are two examples from commercial aviation at opposite ends of the spectrum of consequences. Prevention and detection efforts for the former are relatively modest and are consistent with the low consequences attached to failure. On the other hand, lowering the landing gear includes significant prevention and detection—training, written procedures, and warning lights—to match the enormous consequences of failure.

Various rules of thumb have been offered for estimating total quality costs. The *rule of ten* suggests that one act of prevention is worth ten acts of detection, which in turn is multiplied by ten for each failure. Similarly, the *rule of hundreds* could be applied: it replaces the $1 \times 10 \times 100$ relationship with $1 \times 100 \times 10,000$. While interesting for estimating the ballpark value of prevention and detection, these rules of thumb are no substitute for calculating actual costs.

Figure 8.1 shows the results of an example set of calculations. The costs of failure increase in direct proportion to the defect rate for the example product, but prevention and detection costs increase exponentially as efforts increase to eliminate additional failures. Total costs are minimized in example A when 70 percent of the products are free of defects. By contrast, costs are minimized in example B when the product is 100 percent defect free. Dr. Joseph M. Juran explains: "[Example] 'A' represents conditions which prevailed widely during much of the twentieth century. 'Appraisal plus prevention' consisted much of appraisal and little of prevention" (Juran and Gryna, 1988, 4.19). More recently, as priorities have shifted toward prevention and new technology has been introduced, the cost curves have shifted toward the ideal of the "ability to achieve perfection at finite costs" (4.19).

MINIMIZING THE COST OF QUALITY

The shape of the curves and the shifts observed when performance is improving are more important than the absolute values. Four guidelines are offered for redesigning processes:

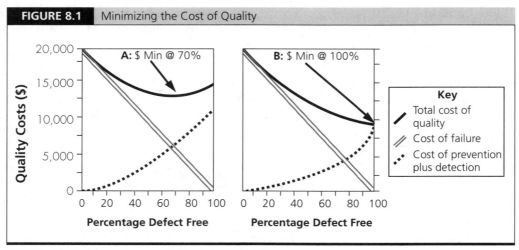

| FIGURE 8.1 | Minimizing the Cost of Quality |

SOURCE: Adapted from Juran and Gryna (1988, 4.19).

- Increase prevention until the marginal cost for the next increment exceeds the marginal cost of detection.

- Increase prevention and detection until the sum of their marginal costs exceeds the cost of the next failure.

- Improve performance further by increasing the effectiveness and efficiency of prevention and detection processes. Refer to Figure 8.1 to visualize how these improvements will shift the minimum point of the curve representing total costs to the right. Minimum costs with the improved process will be lower and will be realized by delivering fewer defective products.

- Reduce the consequences of failures.

Finally, recognize that it is unlikely that you will go beyond the optimum point with excessive prevention and detection efforts. Unlike the clearly visible costs associated with prevention and detection, many elements associated with failures are invisible. The costs to recall and repair defects are visible and measurable, but many remaining costs are hidden, such as those associated with losing customers and with unhappy customers who complain to friends and relatives. Basing the cost of defects on the visiblecomponents understates their impact

- Repairs
- Replacements
- Refunds
- Recalls
- Warranties

and is part of the deadly disease cited by W. Edwards Deming (1986, 121)—that is, "running the company on the visible figures alone and ignoring the unknown or unknowable figures."

VARIATION

While many organizations advanced to just-in-time (JIT) supply lines in the early 1990s, others were stuck in the real world of JIC (just-in-case). You can improve efficiency by eliminating waste associated with adding spare capacity and contingency into plans and designs that serve to cushion uncertainty—variation. This section helps to understand the impact of variation through the use of two measures—process capability index and six-sigma.

- Use the *process capability index* to precisely compare the performance of the process to the expectations of the customers and quantify the level of assurance that defects will not occur.

- Use *six-sigma* analysis as a simple alternative to the process capability index. Motorola built a companywide initiative to satisfy customers around this statistical term, which in essence defines a condition under which defects are exceptionally unlikely.

Note that the measurement of variation is included in this chapter instead of in the chapter on performance measures merely for purposes of explanation. Process capability indices and six-sigma analyses are typically used to quantify outputs (effectiveness) and not efficiency per se.

PROCESS CAPABILITY INDEX

How can the likelihood of failures be estimated in order to determine the cost of quality? Defining the capability of the process and predicting failures through statistical methods is one of the soundest approaches. Additionally, organizations generally produce numerous outputs—either various products and services or significant quantities of the same product or service. How then can the single measurement or set of measurements described in Chapter 7 characterize this vast array of outputs?

The process capability index helps to answer both of these questions by precisely characterizing the performance of the aggregate of the outputs. Calculating capability provides a foundation for estimating the likelihood of defects and offers excellent measures against which the results of improvement efforts can be gauged.

As an example, consider the performance of three processes for delivering quarterly financial reports. In this example (see Figure 8.2), the number of days to complete the reports is the focus of attention, with the performance standard being ten days or less. How might performance be characterized for each process: by their averages, by their maxima, or by qualitative descriptors? None of these terms provides a complete picture by itself. The capability index serves as a better measure.

FIGURE 8.2	Characterizing Performance for Delivering Reports in Less Than Ten Days

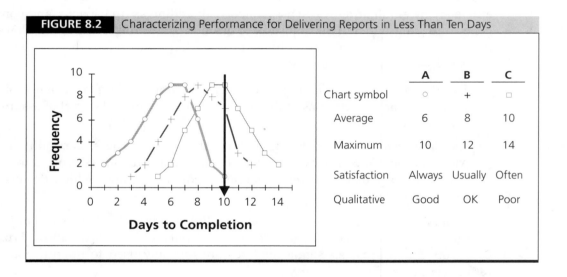

	A	B	C
Chart symbol	○	+	□
Average	6	8	10
Maximum	10	12	14
Satisfaction	Always	Usually	Often
Qualitative	Good	OK	Poor

Defining the Process Capability Index

The process capability index compares the variation expected in performance to the corresponding specifications. It is a way of describing the variability of a process relative to the tolerance between the product's specifications. The process capability index is calculated as the ratio of the tolerance between the specifications divided by the width between the process control limits (see Figure 8.3):

$$C_p = \frac{T}{6\sigma},$$

where

C_p = process capability index,
T = tolerance between upper and lower specification limits, and
σ = standard deviation in performance (sigma).

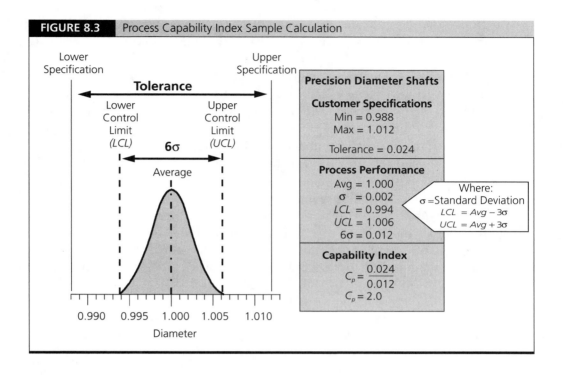

FIGURE 8.3   Process Capability Index Sample Calculation

The capability index is normally calculated for stable processes. That is, capability is determined for processes with variation in performance resulting only from common, random causes. Special, assignable causes have been identified and eliminated. Further, the preceding equation and sample calculation assume that the average (mean) is centered between the upper and lower specifications.

For processes operating nearer to one of the specification limits than to the other (mean-shifted), the equation is revised to measure against the nearer one:

$$C_{pk} = \frac{T_{Min}}{3\sigma},$$

where

C_{pk} = process capability index,

T_{Min} = the minimum of $(USL - X)$ or $(X - LSL)$,

X = mean,

USL = upper specification limit, and

LSL = lower specification limit.

Notice that C_p indicates the spread of the process, whereas C_{pk} indicates both the spread and the setting. When the mean is centered between the specification limits (*LSL* and *USL*), C_p and C_{pk} are identical.

Detailed calculation procedures are beyond the scope of this book, and are described clearly in *Six Sigma Producibility Analysis and Process Characterization* (Harry and Lawson, 1992, 5-11–5-14) or in John Oakland's *Statistical Process Control* (1986, 86–90). Readers interested in further information on stable processes and clarification between common and special causes of variations should refer to W. Edwards Deming's classic book, *Out of the Crisis* (1986, 309–370).

The process capability index is more easily understood for products than for services. Application of capability indices grew rapidly among manufacturers in the 1980s, but use of this tool generally eluded the service sector until the 1990s. The following example shows how the capability index can be used to measure the performance of an insurer's process for paying claims—a service-sector example.

Example: Accelerating Health Insurance Payments

Roger Phillips, employee benefits manager, is responsible for his company's health-care contract with Big-Solid Insurance. In 1993 he attended quality awareness training with his company's management team. Among a number of concepts and techniques learned, three found direct and immediate application to Phillips' work with Big-Solid.

- *A belief in consistent conformance to the customer's requirements and a philosophy to accept no defects.* His company's contract with Big-Solid stated that all valid claims will be paid within two weeks of receipt. He had heard a number of complaints about slow payments, reviewed the records, and recognized that each and every late payment was unacceptable to the affected employee. This situation needed to be improved.

- *Reliance on measurement.* Phillips did not need to work on the basis of vague opinions: he could work from a position of strength with facts and data. In the course that Phillips attended, he learned to record the monthly data received from Big-Solid on what was referred to as a nonconformance chart. His data are shown on Figure 8.4. Big-Solid had been late in paying valid insurance claims seventy-four times in 1993 (6 percent of all claims filed), with incidents nearly every month.

- *A process to eliminate nonconformances through prevention.* The cause for each and every late payment needed to be determined and corrected so that the situation would not recur.

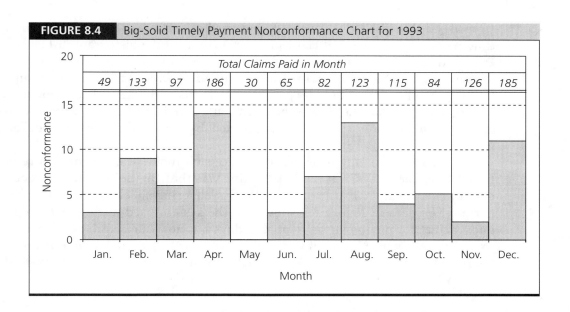

FIGURE 8.4   Big-Solid Timely Payment Nonconformance Chart for 1993

Armed with his new knowledge, data, and the courage of his convictions, Phillips attended the annual contract review meeting with Big-Solid in January 1994. Phillips explained his concepts of quality, reminded Big-Solid of their contractual agreements, and showed that approximately 6 percent of the past year's 1,275 claims were paid late. As a result of this meeting, Big-Solid agreed that in 1994 it would investigate the cause of every late payment and prepare a quarterly report on action required to prevent recurrence.

It was estimated that one additional person would be needed on Big-Solid's staff to coordinate this extra effort. Since this was not covered within the scope of the contract, premiums would have to be adjusted upward. Recognizing the potential payback in improved claims processing, Phillips gladly agreed. The meeting attendees also agreed that some of the corrective actions may increase costs and would need to be reviewed for their effect on premiums prior to implementation.

What Went Wrong with This Analysis?

Phillips' valiant attempts were doomed to failure. True, he was right in not accepting late payments on behalf of his company's employees. True, he was working with data rather than opinions. True, he was looking to improve the process so that causes for late payments would be eliminated permanently. Unfortunately, the reality of the situation was not revealed through his nonconformance chart.

Instead, he should have taken a different view of performance, one that shows the time required to process *all* claims for 1993 (refer to the histogram in Figure 8.5). During this period, claim-processing time averaged about 9.5 days, with a standard deviation of 2.9 days. Adding three standard deviations to the average suggests that nearly all claims should be payable in less than 18.2 days. The problem faced in this case was that the insurer had committed to deliver checks within fourteen days, a specification that is not supported by the actual performance of the process.

Various reasons might be attributed to each incident of payment stretching beyond fourteen days, but the bottom line was that Big-Solid's claim-processing system just was not capable of consistently delivering checks within the specified period. The data in Figure 8.5 show that the system used during 1993 might be appropriate for paying within eighteen days but not fourteen days. Phillips' plan to address the cause for each nonconformance as a specific incident is an example of tampering. Instead, the claim-paying system needed to be examined in its entirety.

What Is a Better Way to Analyze Late Payments?

A far more instructive way to analyze the problem of late payments is to examine the process as a whole and not as isolated incidents. Rather than looking at each nonconformance, Phillips should have first looked at the underlying capability of the process.

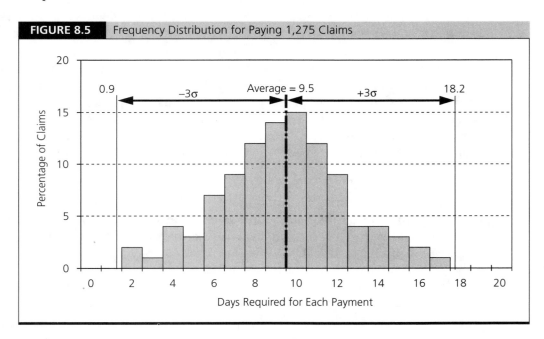

FIGURE 8.5   Frequency Distribution for Paying 1,275 Claims

In the case of paying medical insurance claims, the specification sets the maximum time for payment to be fourteen days. Since no minimum time is specified, the capability index (C_{pk}) compares the observed variation in actual delivery time to the tolerance between the average and the fourteen-day contractual maximum. The calculation of the process capability index is shown in Table 8.2. The capability of this process is about 0.5 and compares poorly to minimum acceptable values for process capability often quoted as 1.0, 1.33, or even 1.5.

Improving Capability

Four options are available to improve the capability of this process:

- Increase customer specification,
- Reduce process average,
- Reduce expected variation, and
- Combinations of the three above options.

Consider the first option—increase customer specification. Performance met the fourteen-day standard for all but about 6 percent of the claims (74 failures out of 1,275 total claims). The maximum expected delivery time is calculated to be 18.2 days. This is the upper control limit for the process and is calculated as the average delivery time plus 3σ (sigma). If the specification was increased to be identical to the eighteen-day upper control limit, capability would equal 1.0. This same process might be expected to fail meeting this relaxed standard about 0.3 percent of the time (997 successes for each 1,000 claims). It is interesting to note that for 1993, all payments were made in fewer than eighteen days.

Although it is usually impossible to "manage the customer's expectations," there are situations when the first option (changing the specification) is appropriate. As the number of days specified in the contract is increased (higher capability index for the same process performance), the likelihood of late payments is reduced.

TABLE 8.2	Calculating Capability Index for Insurance Payment Example

OUTPUT DATA (DAYS)

Customer specification:
  USL (upper spec limit): 14

Calculated process performance:
    X (average): 9.5
  σ (standard deviation): 2.9

CALCULATED CAPABILITY INDEX

$$T_{Min} = (USL - X) = (14 - 9.5) = 4.5 \text{ days}$$
$$3\sigma = (3 \times 2.9) = 8.7 \text{ days}$$
$$C_{pk} = \frac{T_{Min}}{3\sigma} = \frac{4.5}{8.7} = 0.5$$

The second and third options are usually preferred over the first option because they actually yield process improvements. Instead of raising the specification from fourteen days to the eighteen-day maximum delivery time expected for the process, the second and third options would achieve a capability of 1.0 by improving the process such that maximum delivery would be expected to be less than fourteen days. With the second option this would be achieved by reducing the average by four days. The third option would accomplish this objective by reducing the expected variation above the average by the same four days. In actual practice, most improvements would capture the improvements depicted by both the second and third options, since reduced variation would likely accompany reductions in average delivery times.

Figure 8.6 and Table 8.3 compare the process in use during 1993 (base case) with the first three options. Note that the second option would be impossible to achieve. If the variation in the process remained unchanged as suggested in this option, some checks would need to be delivered before the claim was even submitted in order to reduce the average payment time to the required five days. Clearly, the key to success for improving this process is to reduce its variation.

The final option combines gains available through each of the previous options. This option would increase the available tolerance (manage the customers' expectations for later payments) and improve the process (reduce the time actually required for paying valid claims). Motorola drives the performance of its entire organization through this approach, which they refer to as *six-sigma*.

Six-Sigma

An inaugural winner of the United States Malcolm Baldrige National Quality Award, Motorola began its pursuit of six-sigma quality standards in everything they did—both manufacturing and nonmanufacturing operations. They coined the phrase from the Greek character sigma (σ) that statisticians use to represent units of standard deviation. Statistical tables define how much area is under various types of distribution curves at any distance from the mean as functions of sigma.

TABLE 8.3	Options Yielding Process Capability Index = 1.0			
	BASE CASE	**A**	**B**	**C**
	$C_{pk} = 0.5$	INCREASE SPECIFICATION	REDUCE PROCESS AVERAGE	REDUCE PROCESS VARIATION
Process average	9.5	9.5	**5.3**	9.5
Standard deviation	2.9	2.9	2.9	**1.5**
Upper control limit	18.2	18.2	14.0	14.0
Specification	14.0	**18.2**	14.0	14.0

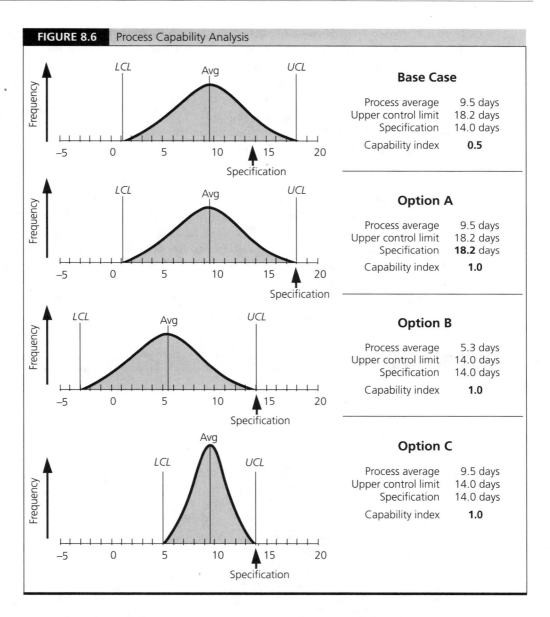

FIGURE 8.6 Process Capability Analysis

Base Case

Process average	9.5 days
Upper control limit	18.2 days
Specification	14.0 days
Capability index	**0.5**

Option A

Process average	9.5 days
Upper control limit	18.2 days
Specification	**18.2** days
Capability index	**1.0**

Option B

Process average	5.3 days
Upper control limit	14.0 days
Specification	14.0 days
Capability index	**1.0**

Option C

Process average	9.5 days
Upper control limit	14.0 days
Specification	14.0 days
Capability index	**1.0**

Motorola adopted the most common curve, the normal distribution, as a model to define the probability of observing defects. It based its terminology on the performance of a process with its average shifted 1.5σ from the center between the specification limits. Its six-sigma goal translates into merely 3.4 defects per million opportunities (3.4 ppm), which is equivalent to 99.9997 percent perfect. Motorola's elegant approach enables assigning a quantitative value to process performance without demanding a strict statistical analysis.

Progress toward the six-sigma goal can be measured by assigning an equivalent performance level (number of sigmas) based on the measured defect rate and a curve such as Figure 8.7. For example, suppose a process is producing 62 defects per 10,000 opportunities (6,200 ppm defects). This is equivalent to 99.4 percent perfect. Figure 8.7 shows that this process is performing at a level equivalent to 4σ.

The six-sigma type of analysis is a simplified version of the previously described process capability index. Rather than requiring the statistical calculation of process variation, the six-sigma type of performance level can simply be looked up in a table or on a graph. Furthermore, the six-sigma type of analysis can be applied to products and services that lack physical or chemical tolerances.

Word processing text, for example, defies classification with a capability index but can be assigned a performance level in the Motorola scheme by examining the number of defects per opportunity. The text in this chapter contains over 40,000 characters. If it had ten errors, which equates to 2.5 defects per 10,000 opportunities (250 ppm), our publication process would be assigned a performance level of 5.0σ. Similarly, two errors in a text of this size would be indicative of a process with a rating of 5.4σ. Error-free performance with 40,000 opportunities would require an error rate below 25 ppm and would be expected from processes rated higher than 5.5σ.

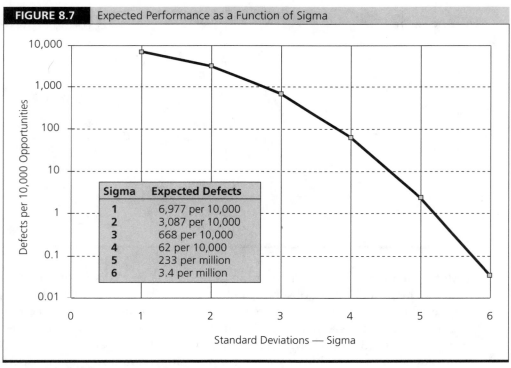

FIGURE 8.7 Expected Performance as a Function of Sigma

Sigma	Expected Defects
1	6,977 per 10,000
2	3,087 per 10,000
3	668 per 10,000
4	62 per 10,000
5	233 per million
6	3.4 per million

SOURCE: Adapted from Harry and Lawson (1992, 5-6–5-7).

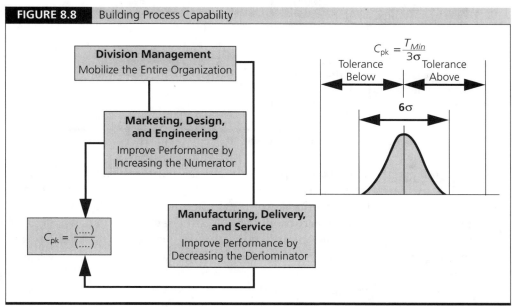

FIGURE 8.8   Building Process Capability

SOURCE: Smith (1990).

Motorola drives its entire organization toward six-sigma performance through a two-pronged attack. First, it seeks to develop more robust designs for its products, a strategy that increases the tolerance for variation and errors. Second, it works toward improving manufacturing capabilities, a strategy that reduces variation and errors. This two-pronged attack is analogous to the last option from the previous insurance payment example and is shown graphically in Figure 8.8. Progress of process improvement efforts toward the six-sigma goal serves as a corporatewide scoreboard. Additional information on six-sigma analysis can be found in Appendix B.

CYCLE TIME

A COMPELLING CASE FOR ACCELERATING PROCESSES

In their book *Competing Against Time*, authors Stalk and Hout present a compelling case for focusing on responsiveness as *the* key means for attaining a competitive advantage. They state that time to complete tasks in Western organizations is dramatically longer than it is for their Japanese counterparts and places the Western firms at a competitive disadvantage. Table 8.4 compares the time differences between Japanese and Western automobile industries in 1982.

TABLE 8.4	World-Class Automobile Comparisons: Representative Cycle Times		
ACTIVITY	WESTERN	JAPANESE	RATIO WESTERN: JAPANESE
Sales order to distribution	16–26 days	5–6 days	7.0
Vehicle manufacture	14–30 days	2–4 days	4.0
New vehicle design and introduction	4–6 years	2 1/2–3 years	1.8
Median age of product offering	5 years	3 years	1.6

SOURCE: Adapted from Stalk and Hout (1990, 29).

Shorter elapsed time to complete product development enables Japanese firms to bring fresher models to the marketplace that capture more recent changes in consumer tastes and incorporate newer technical innovations (Stalk and Hout, 1990, 35). Being first to market in most industries is a money-making advantage in itself. This message was not lost on U.S. auto producers as they saw their dominance in the U.S. market erode during the 1970s and 1980s. To their credit, the big-three U.S. auto companies made impressive gains in reducing the time associated with vehicle assemble and new model development. A 1994 study of the U.S. auto industry by Harbour & Associates (Table 8.5) found that the time required to assemble a vehicle in the big-three's plants has improved to the point of becoming competitive with Japanese firms' performance in their U.S. assembly plants.

The bottom line is profits, and here again, U.S. auto firms have made significant improvement in their financial performance. Chrysler emerged in 1993 as the industry leader in profits per car by streamlining both new product development and manufacturing times in its North American operations (Healy, 1994, 6B). Earnings per vehicle are compared among North American automobile manufacturers in Table 8.6.

The advantages of compressing time apply to other industries as well. FedEx (a registered trademark of the Federal Express Corporation, Memphis, Tennessee) created a new industry by guaranteeing overnight mail delivery. Jiffy Lube (a registered trademark of the Pennzoil Corporation, Oil City, Pennsylvania) created a new auto service business by changing oil and lubricating an auto chassis in twenty minutes.

TABLE 8.5	North America Auto Producers: Workdays per Assembled Vehicle	
	1989	1992
General Motors	4.88	3.94
Chrysler	4.58	3.52
Ford	3.25	2.99
Toyota, Kentucky	NA	2.44
Nissan Motor, Tennessee	NA	2.29

SOURCE: Adapted from Lavin (1994, C22).

TABLE 8.6	Profit per Car in North America, 1993
COMPANY	**PROFIT (LOSS) PER VEHICLE**
Chrysler	$828
Toyota	$358
Ford	$323
Honda	$145
General Motors	($189)

SOURCE: Adapted from Healy (1994, 6B).

H&R Block differentiated itself as tax preparers by offering its clients an instant tax refund. Stalk and Hout (1990, 29) identify four benefits of compressing time in addition to the money-making advantage of being first to market:

- *Increased productivity:* As time in the process decreases, output per unit of time increases, thereby improving productivity.

- *Price premiums:* Customers perceive products and services provided in less time as more valuable. FedEx charges a substantial premium over the U.S. Postal Service's Priority Mail, yet Federal Express has created a multibillion-dollar business by providing such service.

- *Reduced risk:* By producing products and services faster, firms can rely on shorter forecasts, which are likely to be more accurate than longer-range forecasts.

- *Increased market share:* Consumers tend to have more confidence in responsive suppliers and tend to reward them with their business.

Through their investigation of reducing time as a means of securing a competitive advantage, Stalk and Hout (1990, 76–80) offer four rules of responsiveness:

- *.05 to 5 rule:* Surprisingly, studies by the Boston Consulting Group indicate that value is created in only .05 to 5 percent of the total time employed in a process.

- *3/3 rule:* The time lost in most processes is equally attributed to three sources:
  - Waiting for the completion of a unit of work, either for the product itself or for a required component that is not yet available.
  - Waiting for physical or intellectual rework to be completed, and
  - Waiting for a management decision to send work to the next step.

- *1/4-2-20 rule:* If time is compressed in a process by one-quarter, labor productivity doubles, and costs are reduced by 20 percent.

- *3 × 2 rule:* When time is compressed in an organization's processes to be at least 50 percent faster than competition, growth at three times the industry average is likely, and profits of two times the industry average are possible.

MEASURING AND COMPRESSING CYCLE TIME

Time differs from other types of resources in that it cannot be saved, stored, or inventoried for later use. Time is a vital, nonrenewable resource but can be misused or wasted. Understanding how time affects the efficiency of processes avoids such waste and converts time into a competitive advantage.

The total elapsed time in processes is labeled as *cycle time*, and cycle time is defined as "the actual time taken to transform inputs into outputs" (Harrington, 1991, 114). For example, the bread-making process is a sequence of steps in which a baker physically transforms flour and other ingredients into bread. The cycle time to produce a loaf of bread is equal to the sum of the elapsed time for the ingredients to be mixed, kneaded into dough, allowed to rise, and then baked.

Bread-making cycle time totals several hours for weekend bakers, even though they may be directly involved for only a fraction of that time. The baker is employed in the mixing and kneading processes but not in the rising or baking processes. However, each of these steps contributes to the total cycle time. The bread-making example illustrates the following points:

- Cycle time is composed of two components: processing time and nonprocessing time. Processing time includes activities that transform inputs into outputs (refer to Chapter 5). Nonprocessing time includes steps such as waiting and storing, and these steps are generally classified as non-value-added.

- Cycle time is examined from the perspective of the output—the product or service—and not from the perspective of other resources, such as bakers or ovens. The efficient use of these other resources is included in the cost measures discussed at the beginning of this chapter.

Three Categories of Cycle Time

Further, improvement efforts for reducing cycle times are facilitated when the processing component is divided into three categories: real value-added, business value-added, and non-value-added. The length of time consumed by a process in each category represents cycle-time measures.

- *Real value-added (RVA)* includes essential processes that transform inputs into outputs that are necessary to meet customer's requirements and have perceived value to the customer. Examples include

Product development	Fabrication	Packaging
Materials procurement	Assembly	Delivery
Design	Finishing	After-sales service

- *Business value-added (BVA)* includes processes that are installed by management and deemed necessary to support, control, and monitor internal business functions but have little or no perceived value to the customer. Examples include

Scheduling	Career planning	Recruiting
Invoicing	Filing	Auditing
Marketing	Selling	Record keeping

- *Non-value-added (NVA)* includes nonessential processes that contribute to neither customer satisfaction nor improved business operations. Non-value-added activities increase cycle time and add costs rather than value. In addition to nonessential processes, the component of *nonprocessing time* fits within this category. Examples of non-value-added time include

Redundant inspections	Rework	Waiting
Filling in forms	Excessive transit	Storage

Once the categories of time have been assigned and measured for each step in a process, an overall (T_n) efficiency can be calculated. One method for measuring cycle-time efficiency is as a ratio:

$$T_n = \frac{RVA}{T}$$

where

T_n = cycle-time efficiency,
RVA = real value-added time,
T = total cycle time, or
T = $RVA + BVA + NVA$

Eliminating all activities except for those that add real value increases the cycle-time efficiency to unity (1.0, which is equivalent to 100 percent). Further improvements in cycle time are gained through streamlining the remaining essential tasks. The following guidelines can help you to address each category:

- *Eliminate* all non-value-added activities,
- *Minimize* business value-added activities, and
- *Streamline* the real value-added activities.

Criteria for Categorizing Cycle Time

How can real value-added activities be distinguished from business or non-value-added activities? One way to answer this question is to develop criteria for categorizing each activity. Another way is to ask the *external* customer whether this task is necessary.

Why ask customers? These are the best people to answer the question because these people ultimately pay for all processing and nonprocessing steps. Is the customer willing to pay for this step? If the answer is yes, then the activity can be categorized as adding value.

TABLE 8.7	Value-Added Assessment
CHALLENGE	**RESPONSE**
REAL VALUE-ADDED	
❑ Is this step needed to meet a customer's demand?	Can this step be done faster or cheaper? Streamline value-added activities by
❑ Does this step add value to the final product or service that is delivered to the customer?	• Automating, • Improving, or • Performing them in parallel with other steps.
❑ Does this step contribute directly to the customer's satisfaction?	
❑ Is the customer willing to pay for this activity?	
BUSINESS VALUE-ADDED	
❑ Is this step performed to control or manage the business?	Challenge this step with the thought of eliminating or performing it temporarily until the process is redesigned.
❑ Is this step a review, an inspection, or approval?	Eliminate the step by ensuring the performance of previous activities.
❑ Is this step performed because of a trade practice?	Challenge the step with the thought of eliminating it if it is not completely justified.
NON-VALUE-ADDED	
❑ Is this step one of storage, waiting, or queuing time?	Identify and eliminate the root cause of the delays.
❑ Does this step include unnecessary transportation or movement of raw materials or products?	Rearrange or relocate processing activities or sequencing.
❑ Is this step performed to overcome an organizational problem?	Correct the organizational problem, and then eliminate the step.
❑ Is this step necessary to correct errors caused earlier?	Eliminate the step by improving previous activities that are generating errors.

Table 8.7 offers a partial list of the challenges to which each step in the process can be subjected. Affirmative answers to each challenge serve to categorize the step. Table 8.7 also lists possible responses to compress cycle time.

SUMMARY

The improvement of efficiency is accomplished through the elimination of waste—waste of money, waste of people, and waste of time. The elimination of waste depends on the identification and measurement of its contributors, and this chapter divided them into three groups: cost, variation, and time. Efficiency improvements can range from simple defensive moves to remain competitive to offensive attacks that capture a strategic advantage. This brief summary highlights key measures for each group.

Costs are minimized by reducing the resources that are consumed in the process. Most of these are specific to individual industries, but the cost of quality pervades all organizations. The total cost of quality can be equated to the sum of its three components: prevention, plus detection, plus failure. Each component should be included in a comprehensive set of efficiency measures.

Improve efficiency by eliminating waste associated with adding spare capacity and contingency into plans and designs that serve to cushion uncertainty—variation. Either of two measures can be used to characterize variation: the process capability index, or Motorola's six-sigma analysis.

Unlike other resources, time cannot be saved or stored for future use. Cycle time is a measure of the total elapsed time to transform inputs into outputs that are delivered to customers. Three categories of cycle time are real value-added, business value-added, and non-value-added. One method for defining cycle-time efficiency is to calculate the ratio of real value-added time to total cycle time.

DISCUSSION QUESTIONS

1. Select a key product or service from your organization, and calculate the current cost of quality.

   a. Estimate the costs associated with prevention, detection, and failure.

   b. Determine the current marginal costs of prevention, detection, and failure.

   c. Should efforts associated with prevention or detection be increased?

2. What is the capability index for the process that produces the output selected for question 1?

3. Based on the probability of delivering defects for the output selected for question 1, what is the performance level according to the six-sigma type of analysis?

4. Compare the advantages and disadvantages of the capability index and six-sigma type of analysis for characterizing variation.

5. Analyze the cycle time of the process selected for question 2.

   a. List every step in the process, and estimate the total elapsed time for each one.

   b. Categorize the purpose of each step as real value-added (RVA), business value-added (BVA), or non-value-added (NVA).

   c. Calculate the total cycle time (T) by adding all steps. Also calculate the real value-added time (RVA) by adding each step placed in this category.

   d. Calculate cycle-time efficiency by dividing RVA by total T.

ACKNOWLEDGMENT

The section titled "Example: Accelerating Health Insurance Payments" is adapted from pages 149–156 of A. R. Tenner and I. J. DeToro, *Total Quality Management: Three Steps to Continuous Improvement*. Copyright © 1992, Addison-Wesley Publishing Company, Inc. Reprinted by permission of the publisher.

REFERENCES

Crosby, Philip B. 1979. *Quality Is Free: The Art of Making Quality Certain*. New York: Mentor Books, New American Library.

Deming, W. Edwards. 1986. *Out of the Crisis*. Cambridge, MA: MIT Press.

Harrington, H. J. 1991. *Business Process Improvement: The Breakthrough Strategy for Total Quality, Productivity, and Competitiveness*. New York: McGraw-Hill.

Harry, M. J., and J. R. Lawson. 1992. *Six Sigma Producibility Analysis and Process Characterization*. Reading, MA: Addison-Wesley.

Healy, J. R. 1994. "Chrysler per-Car Profit Leaves Rivals in Dust." *USA Today*, June 24, 6B.

Juran, J. M., and F. M. Gryna. 1988. *Juran's Quality Control Handbook*, 4th ed. New York: McGraw-Hill.

Lavin, D. 1994. "GM Would Have to Cut 20,000 Workers to Match Ford Efficiency, Report Says." *Wall Street Journal*, June 24, C22.

Oakland, John S. 1986. *Statistical Process Control*. New York: Wiley.

Smith, W. 1990. "Address to the Exxon Corporation." Total Quality Assurance Conference, Houston, TX, April.

Stalk, G., Jr., and T. M. Hout. 1990. *Competing Against Time: How Time-based Competition Is Reshaping Global Markets*. New York: Free Press.

Webster's Ninth New Collegiate Dictionary. 1989. Springfield, MA: Meriam-Webster.

Xerox Corporation. 1993. *Leadership Through Quality*. Rochester, NY: Xerox Corporation.

9 | Understand the Customer

CUSTOMER REQUIREMENTS MATRIX
(CRM)

Chapter 7 provided a measurement framework that helps you redesign processes by defining what to measure and where to look for key performance measures. Chapter 8 described specific sets of measures for quantifying *efficiency*. Chapter 9 completes the trilogy on measurement by explaining how to connect the customer into measurement systems by quantifying the *effectiveness* of processes and their outputs.

Recall from Chapter 7 that two types of measures are needed to quantify effectiveness. The first type is the measurement of *process* effectiveness—the ability of a process to perform as specified. The second is the measurement of *output* effectiveness—the ability of products and services (outputs) to satisfy customers' needs.

Measures of *process effectiveness* quantify the likelihood of satisfying customers *before* products are delivered. The predictive nature of these measures is enhanced by ensuring that customers' requirements are completely and accurately translated into specifications against which process performance is measured. This chapter offers a choice of three templates to help you build a comprehensive understanding of customers' requirements.

By contrast, measures of *output effectiveness* are retrospective and can be obtained only *after* products or services are delivered. These types of measures, however, are of vital importance because they are the only way to *verify* the accuracy and legitimacy of process effectiveness—the assumptions made regarding customers' requirements and their translation into specifications.

Output effectiveness can be determined either by measuring the performance of your products and services as they are passed down the customer-supplier chain or by measuring customers' satisfaction. The former method was explained in Chapter 7, and models for maximizing the accuracy of the latter are provided in this chapter.

STEPS TO UNDERSTANDING CUSTOMERS' EXPECTATIONS

The quantification of effectiveness relies on understanding customers' requirements. What do customers require? In a word, they require *value*. Customers are satisfied when they feel they have received value: "a fair return or equivalent in goods, services, or money for something exchanged" (*Webster's Ninth*, 1989, 1303).

Unfortunately, predicting a customer's assessment of value is like trying to hit a moving target. Consumers frequently define value in relative terms rather than in absolute terms. They tend to base satisfaction on their comparison of the actual product that was delivered—or the service experienced—to what their expectations were before purchasing it. A product or service is judged to be unsatisfactory when expectations are not met, satisfactory when they are met, and more than satisfactory when they are exceeded. The key to understanding customers' requirements, therefore, is to understand their expectations.

Successful organizations are able to diagnose the full set of customers' expectations and satisfy them completely, every time. World-class organizations have an uncanny ability to understand current requirements and anticipate future ones.

PERFORMANCE MEASUREMENT PARADIGM

A four-step paradigm is offered in Table 9.1 to clarify the measurement of effectiveness. The first two steps in the paradigm require determining customers' requirements and then translating them into specifications. The third step represents the measurement of process effectiveness, and the fourth step represents the measurement of customers' satisfaction.

IDENTIFYING THE CUSTOMER

The term *customer* was introduced with the process model in Chapter 5 as the individual to whom products or services are delivered. The customer of a particular work process can be thought of as the person to whom the output is passed. This simple picture, however, is insufficient for understanding customers' expectations because the world is filled with many different types of customers.

First, there are *internal* as well as *external* customers. The former are employees within the company who work along the customer-supplier chain to produce goods or services for the ultimate customer. This ultimate customer is external to the company and is the only source of revenue. Two schools of thought emerged in the 1980s on the relative importance between these two sets of customers:

TABLE 9.1	Performance Measurement Paradigm

Axiom: Every product and service can be described by a set of performance attributes.

STEP 1. Your job begins by understanding your customers' requirements and identifying the set of attributes applicable to your product or service.

STEP 2. You next must translate these attributes into product or service specifications.

STEP 3. You then must measure your outputs against each specification to quantify the level of performance that your process is capable of delivering.

STEP 4. Finally, you must understand how satisfied customers are with existing performance levels and how much relative importance they attach to changing the level of each.

Three points regarding the first two steps warrant further explanation:

Identify the output: The process of understanding customers is applied to each output (product or service) and begins by selecting the specific output that is subject to analysis.

Identify the customer: Products and services are delivered to people, regardless of whether they are internal to the organization or external. These customers may be grouped or segmented. Organizational names or marketing terms may be assigned to various groups of customers, but that still doesn't change the fact that customers are individual human beings. The second step of the analysis is the identification and segmentation of customers.

Learn the customer's requirements: The needs and expectations of each segment must be determined and then translated into operational definitions that can be measured. These performance measures can be quantitative—such as gasoline octane—or qualitative—such as a service-station attendant's courtesy.

- One school teaches that the needs of the recipient immediately downstream of the process—whether internal or external—should be the focal point for building satisfaction. Each recipient along the customer-supplier chain will work in turn to add value for the ultimate external customer. This approach relies on each internal customer to be the best judge as to what performance levels are needed.

- The other school suggests that a system that focuses on each internal customer along the customer-supplier chain can result in suboptimizing results for the ultimate external customer. This second school teaches that the external customer is the correct focal point. This approach relies on the process owner (see Chapter 6) to integrate needs and performance along the entire customer-supplier chain.

Second there are *buyers* as well as *users*. The picture of learning and understanding customers' requirements is further complicated in many situations because the purchaser is not the user. Suppliers need to satisfy needs of both groups, which are frequently contradictory. Buyers usually focus on price, but users focus on performance:

- As an internal example, desk-top computers in large companies are specified and purchased by information systems specialists but used by novices as well as by experts.
- An external example of the buyer-user distinction is that police cars are purchased by municipal agencies but driven by police.

Finally, within any of these sets, there are customers with numerous different preferences and priorities. Rather than homogenizing the array of differences, each group of customers must be identified. The needs of each segment can then be addressed separately.

LEARNING THE CUSTOMERS' REQUIREMENTS

Once the customers are identified in the targeted market niche for a particular product or service, their expectations can be determined by answering three questions:

- What product/service attributes do customers want?
- What performance level is needed to satisfy their expectations?
- What is the relative importance of each attribute?

Finding answers to the first question begins by postulating a set of features and characteristics that customers might want. This list of hypothetical criteria should next be tested by directly asking customers. Three templates are offered for postulating hypothetical lists of performance criteria. These templates can be used when working in a predictive mode to clarify requirements and specifications or when working in a reactive mode to measure a customer's satisfaction.

WHAT PERFORMANCE ATTRIBUTES DO CUSTOMERS EXPECT?

Customers expect to receive value in the products and services they purchase or use. But how can value be translated into performance measures? Scores of models have been developed to help clarify how customers define quality or value, and this chapter describes three. The first is designed for use with products, and the second is designed for services. The third template is the most comprehensive and is universally applicable. Readers can select any of these templates for preparing preliminary lists of the product and service attributes that their own customers want.

BUILDING BLOCKS FOR TEMPLATES

Value can be viewed most simply as getting things that are faster, better, and cheaper than are available elsewhere. Figure 9.1 shows these basic expectations as three dimensions against which tradeoffs can be made. The first dimension, *time*,

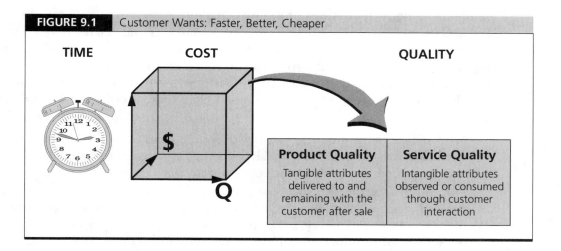

FIGURE 9.1 Customer Wants: Faster, Better, Cheaper

Product Quality	Service Quality
Tangible attributes delivered to and remaining with the customer after sale	Intangible attributes observed or consumed through customer interaction

represents how quickly, easily, or conveniently a product or service can be obtained. The second dimension, *cost*, equates to how expensive the item is. The third dimension, *quality*, is the most difficult one to characterize.

Subdividing quality into two major sets of attributes helps in clarifying this complex dimension: *product* quality includes the tangible attributes that are retained by the customer, and *service* quality includes the characteristics observed or experienced by the customer during the transaction. Most outputs contain both product and service attributes.

An output is usually classified as a product if most of its value-added attributes are tangible and as a service if its value-added attributes are primarily intangible. The attributes used to describe products are frequently different than those used for services. Understanding this distinction helps in establishing the most meaningful set for your own outputs.

Consider the basic hamburger as an example. Ground beef is purchased in the store as a product. The primary value is represented by the beef, and incremental value has been added through services such as transporting, grinding, packaging, and storing. By contrast, a hamburger eaten in a restaurant is dominated by service value: the cost of the beef is usually less than one-third of the price.

- Product attributes represent *what* is delivered and can be measured *after* the output has been delivered. Template 1, Eight Dimensions of Product Quality, defines the attributes of outputs that are characterized as products.

- Customers are often involved directly in the service process. Therefore, some portion of the value in service consists of *how* the output is delivered. Service quality is judged by the customer *during* the service. Template 2, Ten Determinants of Service Quality, defines the attributes of outputs that are characterized as services.

Template 1: Eight Dimensions of Product Quality

David Garvin (1987, 101–109) defined eight dimensions that can be used at a strategic level to analyze product quality. Some of the dimensions are mutually reinforcing, whereas others are not: improvement in one may be at the expense of others. Understanding the tradeoffs desired by customers among these dimensions can help build a competitive advantage. Garvin's eight dimensions can be summarized as follows:

- *Performance* is the product's primary operating characteristic. For example, performance of an automobile includes traits such as acceleration, handling, cruising speed, and comfort; performance of an airline includes on-time arrival.

- *Features* are secondary aspects of performance. These are the "bells and whistles" that supplement the basic functions. Examples include free drinks on planes and sunroofs on cars. The line separating primary performance characteristics from secondary features is often difficult to draw. Further, customers define value in terms of flexibility and their ability to select among available features, as well as on the quality of those features.

- *Reliability* is the probability of successfully performing a specified function for a specified period of time under specified conditions. Reliability of durable goods is often measured as the mean time to first failure or mean time between failures. These measures, however, require a product to be in use for a specified period of time and are not relevant in the case of products or services that are consumed instantly.

- *Conformance* is the degree to which a product's design and operating characteristics meet established standards. Although this is sometimes defined as "conformance to requirements," a sounder analysis will be obtained by examining each characteristic's divergence from its target value. This more robust measure of conformance is built on the teachings of a prize-winning Japanese statistician, Genichi Taguchi. (Refer to the section titled "Process Capability Index" in Chapter 8.)

- *Durability* is a measure of product life. Durability can be defined as the amount of use obtained from a product before it deteriorates to the point that replacement is preferred over repair. Durability is closely linked to both reliability and serviceability. Consumers weigh the expected costs of future repairs against the investment in and operating expenses of a newer, more reliable model.

- *Serviceability* is the speed, courtesy, competence, and ease of repair. The cost of repairs includes more than the simple out-of-pocket costs. Serviceability covers this full dimension by recognizing the loss and inconvenience due to downtime of equipment, the nature of dealings with service personnel, and the frequency with which repairs fail to correct the outstanding problems.

- *Aesthetics* are how a product looks, feels, sounds, tastes, or smells. Aesthetics are largely a matter of personal judgment and a reflection of individual preference; it is a highly subjective dimension.

- *Perceived quality* is reputation. Consumers do not always have complete information about a product's or service's attributes. Indirect measures or perceived quality may be their only basis for comparing brands.

Template 2: Ten Determinants of Service Quality

Research done by Len Berry, Valerie Zeithaml, and Parsu Parasuraman (1985) in the early 1980s provides a strong foundation for understanding the attributes of service quality. Through interviews with business executives and customer focus groups, Berry and his colleagues identified ten determinants of service quality. Their categories, which provide a useful complement to the eight dimensions offered by Garvin, are as follows:

- *Reliability* is consistency of performance and dependability, performing the right service right the first time, honoring promises, accuracy.
- *Responsiveness* is the willingness or readiness of employees to provide service, timeliness.
- *Competence* is possession of the skills and knowledge required to perform the service.
- *Accessibility* is approachability and ease of access, waiting time, hours of operation.
- *Courtesy* is politeness, respect, consideration, and friendliness of contact personnel.
- *Communication* is keeping customers informed in language they can understand, listening to customers, adjusting language to different needs of different customers, explaining the service itself and how much it will cost, explaining how problems will be handled.
- *Credibility* is trustworthiness, believability, honesty, company reputation, personal characteristics of personnel.
- *Security* is freedom from danger or doubt, physical safety, financial security, confidentiality.
- *Understanding the customer* is making the effort to understand the customer's needs, learning the customer's specific requirements, providing individualized attention, recognizing the regular customer.
- *Tangibles* are physical evidence of the service, physical facilities, the appearance of personnel, tools or equipment used to provide service, physical representation of the service (such as a plastic credit card or a bank statement), other customers in the service facility.

Template 3: A Compendium of Quality Attributes

We have synthesized a single comprehensive set of quality attributes from Templates 1 and 2. Shown in Table 9.2, this compendium integrates Garvin's eight dimensions and Berry's ten determinants into the macro-set of faster-better-cheaper. Rather than

TABLE 9.2	Compendium of Quality Attritubes	
	DELIVERABLES	**INTERACTIONS**
FASTER	Availability	Responsiveness
	Convenience	Accessibility
BETTER	Performance	Reliability
	Features	Security
	Reliability	Competence
	Conformance	Courtesy
	Durability	Credibility
	Serviceability	Empathy
	Aesthetics	Communication
	Perceived quality	
CHEAPER	Price	Price

APPLICATION OF THE COMPENDIUM

Quality is characterized through two sets of elements:

- *Deliverables* describe *what* attributes are provided.

- *Interactions* describe the characteristics of staff and equipment that affect *how* customers experience the service process while it is performed.

Both elements apply to all products and services, and the list of attributes can be used to confirm that all major attributes have been considered.

distinguishing between elements of product and service quality, this set reclassifies quality into two components: deliverables and interactions. The *deliverables* define *what* attributes are provided to customers. The *interactions* characterize *how* behaviors and styles affect customers while they are experiencing the service process.

The delineation between deliverables and interactions offers an explicit framework within which to identify and measure process and product effectiveness. Furthermore, interactions are not limited to face-to-face contact. As shown in Figure 9.2, your staff also interacts through the telephone as well as through electronic and print media. The service experience is further affected by physical facilities, and customers can interact with many services without any human interface. The quality characteristics expected by customers must be assured in all modes.

Use Table 9.2 as a worksheet in your dialogue with customers to test the attributes of your own outputs. Which characteristics differentiate you from your competitors? Which ones represent your strengths and your weaknesses? Which ones are most important to the customers in your targeted market niche?

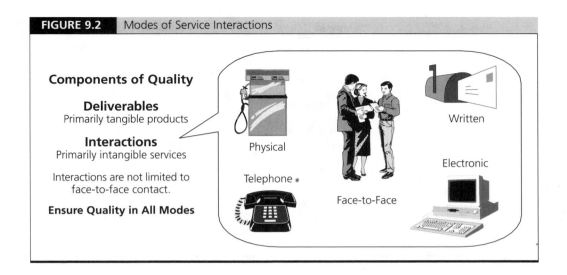

FIGURE 9.2 | Modes of Service Interactions

TRANSLATING ATTRIBUTES INTO SPECIFICATIONS

After defining and verifying the list of characteristics that are important to customers, the next step is to translate each characteristic into measurable terms. This step is sometimes referred to as creating *operational definitions*. These measurable terms are next translated into product and service specifications, and then data are obtained to define the level of performance actually delivered (process effectiveness). The sequence of steps is the same whether the feature is an element of a product or a service—a deliverable or an interaction.

Some people have argued that product quality (deliverables) can be measured but service quality (interactions) cannot. Although the two sets of characteristics might be different and one might be easier to measure, data can be obtained and analyzed for both sets. Service attributes often are measured in subjective, qualitative terms based on observations and comparisons. Product attributes usually are measured in absolute, quantitative terms based on physical or chemical properties. Exceptions to these generalizations are numerous, but a general comparison is presented in Table 9.3.

Two examples of exceptions to these general tendencies might be instructive. The physical design of a car is certainly a product attribute, but how can style be measured? It is measured in the same way as service quality—by subjective comparison to other cars. What about customer comfort while eating in a restaurant? This is certainly a service characteristic, yet the features of chairs are measured in the same objective way as product quality.

TABLE 9.3	Comparing Typical Quality Measurements	
	PRODUCTS (DELIVERABLES)	**SERVICES (INTERACTIONS)**
ATTRIBUTES	Objective Tangible	Subjective Intangible
MEASURES	Absolute terms such as physical or chemical properties	Comparative terms relative to expectations
EXAMPLES	Size Weight Volume Delivery time Material Count Color	Attitude Courtesy Cooperation Attention Reputation Dependability Friendliness

WHAT PERFORMANCE LEVEL IS NEEDED TO SATISFY EXPECTATIONS?

The measurement of a customer's satisfaction is fraught with problems. It is intrusive and places an uninvited burden on your customer to respond. Practitioners frequently try to overcome this problem by making the task as simple as possible or by offering incentives—either in cash or merchandise. The measurement of customer satisfaction is also plagued with errors—including the moodiness of a respondent due to external circumstances, design flaws in the survey instrument or sampling procedure, and limited knowledge on the part of the customer. Two concepts are presented to help minimize some of these inherent difficulties: (1) a model relating customer satisfaction to expectations and (2) delineation of three distinct expectation levels.

A MODEL FOR PREDICTING CUSTOMER SATISFACTION

Understanding a customer's dissatisfaction helps to direct improvement efforts but is not as powerful as being able to predict satisfaction in advance. How can a customer's satisfaction be predicted and ensured? This task is particularly difficult because customers' needs and expectations are constantly escalating as their requirements are met and they learn of new possibilities from competitors (Tenner and DeToro, 1992, 56). In the simplest of terms, satisfaction can be ensured by promising less and delivering more. Consider your own experience and mark your level of satisfaction for each of the situations shown in Table 9.4.

	LEVEL OF SATISFACTION		
SITUATION	**HIGH**	**NEUTRAL**	**LOW**
1. You buy a high-priced luxury automobile. It is delivered in perfect condition, performs like a dream, wins the admiration (and envy) of your friends and neighbors, and never suffers a mechanical problem.	❑	❑	❑
2. You watch an Academy Award-winning movie after reading rave reviews. The movie is good, but you leave the theater feeling disappointed.	❑	❑	❑
3. You are in an unfamiliar neighborhood. You are tired and hungry. Everything is closed but one low-priced greasy-looking dive. You go in for a bite to eat out of desperation and are amazed at the quality of the food and service.	❑	❑	❑
4. You have been buying a particular brand of teeshirt for years and chronically complain about how it shrinks. You decide to buy a larger size and find that it fits perfectly after a few hot-water washings.	❑	❑	❑

TABLE 9.4 Determining Levels of Satisfaction

By generalizing the above situations and customers' natural responses you can predict satisfaction through the following equation:

$$\text{Satisfaction} = \frac{\text{Actual}}{\text{Expectation}}$$

Two of the three terms in this equation are relatively straightforward. *Satisfaction* is the outcome measurement described in Chapter 7. *Actual* represents the performance of the output (product or service) that was delivered. But what about the third term—*expectation*? Customers' expectations are established through the integration of five factors:

- *Specific needs:* The performance required to achieve a fundamental need.
- *Word of mouth from others*: Positive or negative comments of family and friends who have previous experience with similar products or services.
- *Mass-media images:* Portrayals of suppliers or competitors in advertising, feature, or news stories in print or broadcast journals.
- *Explicit or implicit statements of performance:* Written or verbal contracts that specify performance of the product or service that is promised or delivered to the customer.
- *Prior experience:* Previous positive or negative experiences of the customer with similar products or services.

IMPLICIT, EXPLICIT, AND LATENT REQUIREMENTS

The performance of products and services expected by customers can be viewed as a progressive hierarchy of three levels: implicit, explicit, and latent (see Figure 9.3). This differentiation provides a model for understanding the level of performance needed to satisfy customers' expectations.

Customers' implicit expectations form the base or lowest level. These characteristics (or levels of performance) are always assumed to be present, and if they are missing, customers will always be dissatisfied. When buying a car, customers assume certain basic attributes will be included without any discussion with the dealer. Examples of customers' base expectations about cars include the following implicit requirements:

- *Cornering stability:* The vehicle will not be prone to roll over when subjected to sudden evasive maneuvers.

- *Collision protection:* The vehicle is not likely to burst into flames as the result of a rear-end collision.

- *Motor vehicle regulations:* The vehicle is built in compliance with applicable local or national regulations and will pass any mandated inspections.

The next level is represented by the specifications and requirements that are visible to customers and are actively involved in their selection process. At the explicit level tradeoffs are made and terms negotiated. Continuing with the car example, this level of performance covers the features that are advertised and those that are discussed with dealers. They include such characteristics as fuel economy, horsepower, acceleration, color, number of seats, body style, interior decor, price, delivery, and warranty protection.

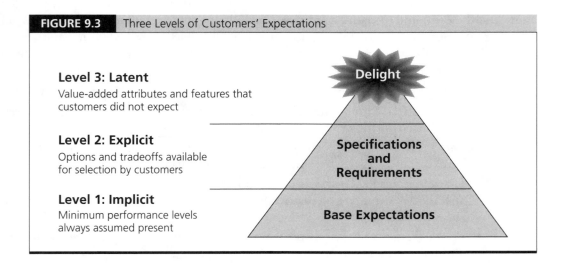

FIGURE 9.3   Three Levels of Customers' Expectations

Level 3: Latent
Value-added attributes and features that customers did not expect

Level 2: Explicit
Options and tradeoffs available for selection by customers

Level 1: Implicit
Minimum performance levels always assumed present

Delight

Specifications and Requirements

Base Expectations

The highest level of performance is represented by the value-added features that the customer did not even know about but is delighted to receive. Performance at this latent level can be described as delivering all of the implicit and explicit requirements as well as latent ones. Latent requirements are real but are not visible or obvious to the customer. From your own experience, think about a product or service that absolutely thrilled you. What were the features or characteristics that caused you to feel this way? Were they attributes that you did not even know enough to ask for?

Some people define quality as simply "conformance to requirements," but this is an incomplete definition that does not account for occasions when your competition is able to ascertain and provide features that exceed expectations and delight customers. As an example, consider Thomas Edison's invention of the light bulb at a time when customers did not even have electricity in their homes. How could he be bound by the requirements of a population that did not even know what questions to ask—direct current or alternating, incandescent or fluorescent, high- or low-voltage, 60 or 100 watts, long-life or standard, soft-white or clear? In comparison to the specifications of gas lamps, the electric light satisfied latent requirements for bright, safe, reliable, and inexpensive lighting. It represented a level of delight.

Note, however, that performing at the level of delight is not simply a matter of delivering more than specified. For example, a company that blends lubricants in a batch process orders 20,000 gallons of a particular component. The supplier, thinking that more is better, delivers a full railcar containing 22,000 gallons. But this does not delight the customer, since the batch must then be reformulated for the greater-than-expected amount of this component. As another example, this same lubricant blender orders feedstock for delivery in four weeks. Faster delivery—in, say, one week—might not delight the customer if the customer is then billed for three weeks of demurrage (rent for the idle railcar).

Table 9.5 offers another example to help clarify the three-level performance model. This table compares two characteristics of automotive performance through the three-level hierarchy.

TABLE 9.5	Example Performance Characteristics at Three Levels	
LEVEL	**CORNERING**	**ACCELERATION**
PROVIDES DELIGHT	Lateral acceleration exceeds 1.0.	0–60 MPH in less than 4.0 seconds
MEETS SPECIFICATIONS	Lateral acceleration is in the range of 0.65–0.85.	0–60 MPH in 7.0–10.0 seconds
VIOLATES BASE EXPECTATIONS	The vehicle rolls over on evasive maneuvers.	The vehicle cannot be driven at 60 MPH.

Customer satisfaction ratings respond differently to changes in performance at each of these three levels. As explained by Bernard Zions (Figure 9.4), meeting base expectations can be thought of as a defensive strategy. The implicit characteristics at this lowest level must always be present to earn merely a neutral rating from customers; their absence leads to disaster. By comparison, delivery against agreed-on explicit specifications yields a proportionate gain in customer satisfaction. Assuming that both the lower levels have been achieved, providing the unanticipated value-added features at the highest level yields delighted customers.

APPLICATION OF THE EXPECTATION MODELS

Recognizing the performance level of any particular attribute offers three advantages. First, it clarifies which attributes should be discussed with current or prospective customers when validating a hypothetical list of requirements. Second, it helps to predict how the level of customer satisfaction might respond to a change in performance. Third, it indicates possible future trends in expectations. This knowledge can be applied as follows:

- Focus discussions with customers around the characteristics that represent the conspicuous specifications and requirements (level 2). Customers take the base expectations (level 1) for granted and assume that knowledgeable suppliers know this. Similarly, customers cannot be expected to appreciate level 3 features until they are experienced.

- Meeting level 1 expectations is a defensive requirement that at best will help you avoid creating dissatisfied customers. The information systems division (ISD) within one large company conducted an extensive survey of its customers

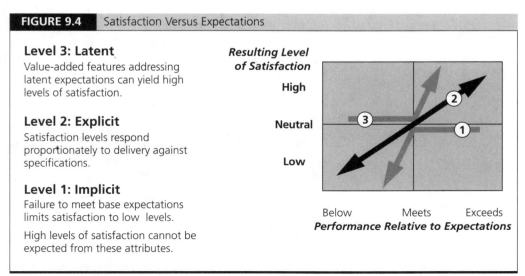

FIGURE 9.4   Satisfaction Versus Expectations

Level 3: Latent
Value-added features addressing latent expectations can yield high levels of satisfaction.

Level 2: Explicit
Satisfaction levels respond proportionately to delivery against specifications.

Level 1: Implicit
Failure to meet base expectations limits satisfaction to low levels.

High levels of satisfaction cannot be expected from these attributes.

Resulting Level of Satisfaction

High

Neutral

Low

Below   Meets   Exceeds
Performance Relative to Expectations

SOURCE: Adapted from Zions (1990).

to learn how important various ISD services were and how satisfied customers were with each. ISD had thought it was doing an excellent job in offering security and data protection and could not understand why customers regarded this service as unimportant and only average in satisfaction level. Had ISD recognized that security is a base expectation, it would have known that "average" was the best that could be expected.

- High levels of customer satisfaction can be expected by consistently delivering the implicit base expectations (level 1) and every explicit specification (level 2), as well as including the value-added features (level 3) that delight customers.

- Over time customers' expectations will escalate, and performance levels will migrate down through the hierarchy. For example, at one time, U.S. motorists did not understand or appreciate the benefits of radial tires. Those who found them on their foreign cars were delighted with how long radial-ply tires lasted in comparison to the bias-ply tires they had always known (level 3). Later, radials became a desirable option (level 2), and by the 1980s radial tires became embedded in consumers' base expectations (level 1). The escalation of motorists' expectations moved radial tires from a latent requirement to an explicit specification and then to an implicit expectation.

RESPONDING TO COMPLAINTS: THE HIDDEN LEVEL

There is one more level of performance, a hidden one that is discovered only after unhappy customers bring problems back to their suppliers. A study by the Technical Assistance Research Program shows that a positive response to complaints can create advantage out of adversity (see Figure 9.5). Rather than seeing disappointed customers defecting to your competitors, your ability to "recover" by handling complaints effectively can actually build customer loyalty (Goodman, 1989).

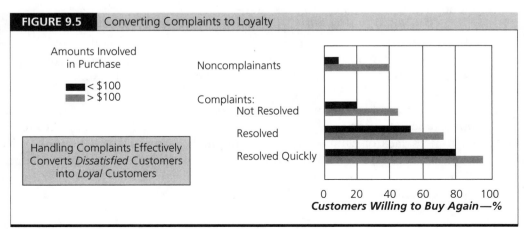

FIGURE 9.5 Converting Complaints to Loyalty

SOURCE: Adapted from Goodman (1989).

One course of action available to a dissatisfied customer is to accept the problem begrudgingly and not complain to the supplier. Unfortunately, this customer is likely to complain to friends and influence them to avoid buying from this supplier.

The other course of action for a dissatisfied customer is to seek compensation from the supplier (such as replacement, refund, repair). By providing convenient avenues for complaining, dissatisfaction will be reduced. Depending on how the problem is handled, three outcomes are possible:

- If the supplier's corrective action does not meet the customer's expectations, the original feeling of dissatisfaction will be exacerbated.

- If the supplier's corrective action meets the customer's expectations, the original feeling of dissatisfaction will likely be neutralized.

- If the supplier's prompt, effective, complete, and courteous action exceeds the customer's expectations, the original feeling of dissatisfaction can potentially be converted into delight.

WHAT IS THE RELATIVE IMPORTANCE OF EACH ATTRIBUTE?

The literature is filled with studies and advice trying to define which are the most important quality characteristics. In our experience, no universal prescription has been developed. The relative importance of each attribute varies in relation to the specific expectations of the customer at any particular time.

Your own purchase of groceries helps to illustrate the variability in the relative importance of performance attributes. Under one set of circumstances, the quality of the food might be paramount to you, and at another time, the ambiance of the supermarket could be of major importance. At another time, convenience might be the critical factor, as in the case of running out of soda for a party you are giving late at night on a holiday weekend. Finally, there may be situations when price alone dictates your shopping decisions.

Rather than attempting to prioritize customers' needs on a global basis, the relative importance of performance characteristics should be determined with customers for each product and service and then updated frequently. The relative rating of importance can be used to guide the allocation of resources for process or product/service improvement efforts.

Unfortunately, building an understanding of how customers rank the relative importance of quality characteristics is not a simple task and can be confounded by customers' lack of perspective. For example, how important is safety in selecting a flight on a commercial airline? Although safety might be the single most important characteristic, the majority of passengers take safety for granted. Many feel that "accidents always happen to the other guy."

Suppliers who understand the three levels of performance that were explained earlier in this chapter can avoid contaminating their findings by recognizing that characteristics like flight safety are among customers' implicit expectations. As long as these base-level expectations are satisfied, they will not command the attention or interest of customers. An airline with a pattern of safety incidents will be shunned by passengers, since it has violated their implicit expectations.

Another degree of complexity occurs because customers will seemingly change their priorities overnight. Whereas the types of features and characteristics expected by customers might remain stable for long periods of time, their relative importance and level of expectation will *appear* to change with headline news, weather, competitors' advertising, and technology advances. The word *appear* is emphasized to draw attention to the need to differentiate between fads and fundamental beliefs or between topical headlines and underlying values.

When customers are asked about the importance of a characteristic, their replies might be confused with their level of satisfaction. For example, many customers will underrate the importance of telephone system reliability because of complacency resulting from their satisfaction with current performance. On the other hand, if this same characteristic were tested with customers who are experiencing telephone service interruptions, a significantly higher level of importance will be attached to reliability.

SUMMARY

The development of measures to define the effectiveness of any product, service, or process relies on understanding the customer's underlying expectations. The measurement of process effectiveness offers a predictive tool for gauging customers' satisfaction. The direct measurement of customers' satisfation, however, is required to validate and tune performance measurement systems.

Consumers tend to base satisfaction on their comparison of the actual level of performance that they experience with a product or service to what their expectations were before purchasing it. The process of satisfying customers therefore begins by fully understanding their expectations. This process requires learning about the features and characteristics customers want, the performance level they expect, the relative importance they attach to each attribute, and their satisfaction with performance at the current level.

Faster, better, and cheaper are basic attributes that describe how customers define value. These three terms provide a springboard for building other, more detailed templates that can be used when defining the comprehensive set of performance attributes expected by customers.

The level of performance expected by customers for any individual attribute can be measured, although some data will be obtained through subjective comparisons instead of objective measures against absolute standards. The three-level hierarchy helps in the analysis of performance measures: the base level's implicit expectations must never be violated; the intermediate level's explicit specifications can be discussed and negotiated; and the highest level's latent requirements might not be evident to customers but when provided will lead to their delight. Furthermore, customers' expectations escalate: features that currently delight customers may eventually become embedded in their base expectations.

Building an understanding of customers' satisfaction and the relative importance customers attach to each performance attribute is a complex and difficult task that is fraught with opportunities for errors. For example, a customer survey might tend to underrate the importance of a vital performance characteristic because customers are satisfied with its current delivery and distracted by other irritants. Knowledgeable suppliers are able to discern customers' true underlying values.

DISCUSSION QUESTIONS

1. Select a specific output and identify its performance attributes.

   a. Would you categorize this output as a product or as a service?

   b. Does your list of attributes include speed, cost, and quality?

   c. Comment on the advantages and disadvantages of using Template 1 (Eight Dimensions of Product Quality), Template 2 (Ten Determinants of Service Quality), or Template 3 (Compendium of Quality Attributes) for defining output attributes.

2. Define the specifications that should be attached to each attribute identified in question 1.

   a. What is the current performance level provided for each specification?

   b. Categorize each attribute or performance level as to whether it satisfies implicit, explicit, or latent requirements.

3. Describe the process that you can use to validate the list prepared in question 1 with customers.

   a. Will your process delineate the relative importance of each attribute?

   b. Will your process show the relative level of satisfaction that customers have with current performance for each attribute?

   c. Will you be able to learn which attributes are important to customers but were missed in your answer to question 1?

ACKNOWLEDGMENT

This chapter is adapted from pages 60–75 of A. R. Tenner and I. J. DeToro, *Total Quality Management: Three Steps to Continuous Improvement*. Copyright © 1992, Addison-Wesley Publishing Company, Inc. Reprinted by permission of the publisher.

REFERENCES

Berry, L. L., V. A. Zeithaml, and P. Parasuraman. 1985. "Quality Counts in Service Too." *Business Horizons* 28, no. 3: 44–52.

Farley, J. M., D. F. Carson, and D. H. Pearl. 1990. "Service Quality in a Multinational Environment." In *ASQC Quality Congress Transactions* (96–101). San Francisco: ASQC.

Garvin, D. A. 1987. "Competing on the Eight Dimensions of Quality." *Harvard Business Review* (November-December): 101–109.

Garvin, D. A. 1988. *Managing Quality*. New York: Free Press.

Goodman, J. 1989. "The Nature of Customer Satisfaction." *Quality Progress* 22, no. 2: 37–40.

King, C. A. 1987. "A Framework for a Service Quality Assurance System." *Quality Progress* 20, no. 9: 27–32.

Peters, T. 1987. *Thriving on Chaos*. New York: Knopf.

Peters, T., and R. H. Waterman. 1982. *In Search of Excellence*. New York: Harper & Row.

Rosander, A. C. 1989. *The Quest for Quality in Services*. Milwaukee: Quality Press.

Tenner, A. R. and DeToro, I. J. 1992. *Total Quality Management: Three Steps to Continuous Improvement*. Reading, MA: Addison-Wesley.

Webster's Ninth New Collegiate Dictionary. Springfield, MA: Meriam-Webster.

Zions, B. 1990. Conversations with the authors.

10 Document Processes

Before beginning to improve a process, we need to understand how we currently complete its various tasks and activities. A general understanding of the process is insufficient to support comprehensive improvement. A *thorough* understanding is needed, and the required depth of understanding is gained by documenting the process. Some organizations document their processes as "standard operating procedures," while others merely rely on the experience of their employees. Although these practices may have been sufficient in the past, our experience reveals that building a thorough understanding of processes typically requires preparing a graphical representation—a flowchart.

This chapter explains approaches that can help a team acquire process knowledge and capture this information in a flowchart. The flowchart is one of the seven basic quality tools: it transcends language and nationality and is universally understood and appreciated. The chapter begins by providing a technique for flowcharting high-level core processes and then follows with an approach to create more detailed flowcharts of subprocesses. The chapter also offers guidance and examples for applying the five keys to drawing effective charts:

1. *Define purpose.* Begin by identifying the information you need. Processes exist at many levels, and different types of charts are better suited to describe different aspects of certain ones. We have not discovered the single all-purpose "best" chart. A flowchart design should be selected because it is best able to reflect the work performed.

2. *Identify boundaries.* Identify the scope of the process under investigation—what is to be included and what is excluded.

3. *Enlist resources.* Involve the right people in drawing flowcharts—the people who work in the process, know how it functions, and know where the problems and opportunities exist.

4. *Control details.* Good judgment is essential for striking a delicate balance on the level of detail included in the chart. Too much detail clutters the chart and makes

it difficult to follow. Too little detail renders the chart superficial and useless. Revisit the stated purpose of the chart to determine the appropriate level of detail.

5. *Revise for accuracy.* Review the chart with people who are familiar with the process, and revise the chart until it reflects reality—what *really* happens in the process and not what is *supposed* to happen.

Having the appropriate materials on hand will make flowchart preparation go smoothly. At a minimum, you'll need the following:

- Existing documentation: process flowcharts and procedures or policies,
- An erasable white board or large flipchart,
- Pads of Post-It™ notes, and
- Colored markers.

HOW TO CHART A CORE PROCESS

A map of a core process is not a detailed blueprint of work steps but more like a high-level, graphic representation of the sequence of work as it flows through and across the organization. It reveals the departments involved and enables the people to

- See the sequence of events,
- Draw boundaries around the process,
- Identify key players and functional groups within the bounded process,
- Identify hand-offs between subprocesses, and
- Identify supplier and customer interfaces.

An analogy for charting a core process is to think of this chart as the map of a country that you intend to visit. This national map orients us to the boundaries of the country, its major geographic features, and the relative location of its cities. Similarly, a core-process flowchart should position the boundaries of the overall process and the relationship of subprocesses with regard to when and where work is performed.

At this high level it is not necessary to depict decision points, approvals, control points, or specific tasks or to worry about using precisely correct symbology. These details will be captured in the subprocess maps at the next level of detail. Staying with the mapping analogy, detailed diagramming of subprocesses will show the highways and by-ways and enable drilling down to find points of interest within the cities. Two sample flowcharts commonly used for documenting core processes are illustrated in Figure 10.1.

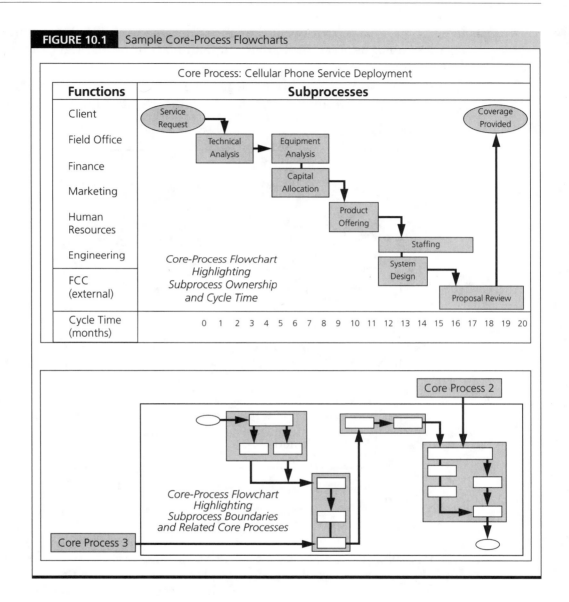

FIGURE 10.1   Sample Core-Process Flowcharts

STEP-BY-STEP GUIDE TO DOCUMENT CORE PROCESSES

1. Set up a work area for charting the process on a white board or on several sheets of flipchart paper taped to a wall.
2. Determine the process name and process owner and write them at the top of the chart.
3. Briefly describe the process mission—what it's supposed to do and why it exists—to test and clarify the scope.

4. Identify the final output (what the process produces). Write this output on a Post-It™ note, draw an oval around it, and place it on the right side of the work area.

5. Identify the starting point (what triggers the process). Write it on a Post-It™ note, draw an oval around it, and place it on the left side of the work area.

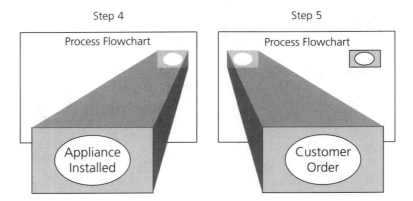

6. List all major functional groups involved in the process in sequence down the left side of the chart area (alternatively, list them horizontally across the top from left to right).

7. Use a Post-It™ note as a box for each subprocess within the core process and place it on the chart. As an option, include the name of subprocess owner to provide clarification for team members who are creating the chart.

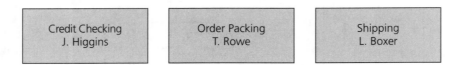

8. When all subprocesses are identified, rearrange the boxes from left to right. If any subprocesses occur simultaneously, place them one above the other on the same time line. Move the boxes around the chart until the team is satisfied that it accurately describes the process.

9. Draw connecting lines in pencil between the subprocess boxes using right angles. Use arrowheads to show the direction of flow.

10. Finalize the flowchart by rearranging, combining, or adding missing steps, and ink in lines connecting each step. Be careful to show the appropriate level of

detail—the "big picture." The purpose now is to show the relationship of work as it flows across major areas. Don't be bogged down in too many details.

11. Test the accuracy of the map by posting it in a convenient, well-visited location. Invite associates who work in the core process to comment on the degree to which the map reflects reality. Their suggestions can be captured by asking them to attach a Post-It™ at any point in question.

HELPFUL HINTS FOR CHARTING CORE PROCESSES

- Strive to fit the chart on a single sheet of letter-size paper.
- Capture the chart on a PC using flowcharting or drawing software. This electronic approach facilitates using the flowchart as a working document and revising it throughout the life of the process or improvement project.
- Identify each internal output (what each subprocess produces), and write it on the flowchart.
- Use shading or draw lines around subprocesses to indicate their boundaries and clarify ownership.
- Identify subprocesses with a decimal numbering system. For example:

9.0 Core process

    9.1 Functional process A

        9.1.1 Subprocess X

        9.1.2 Subprocess Y

        9.1.3 Subprocess Z

    9.2 Functional process B

    9.3 Functional process C

HOW TO CREATE A SUBPROCESS FLOWCHART

COMMON TYPES OF FLOWCHARTS

The design of a chart depicting workflow in a subprocess should fit its intended purpose; no single type of chart is necessarily best. Frequently used chart types are listed below. The examples provided in Figures 10.2 through 10.4 portray how different types of charts can be used to display different aspects of the same process. Note that the name shown for each type of chart is merely a common one. Many organizations have developed their own jargon to identify these same types of charts.

- *Process map:* Create a step-by-step schematic picture of a process by connecting standard symbols with arrows to reveal the sequential flow of work (see Figure 10.2). Two variations of a conventional flowchart can be used to show functional responsibility or cycle time for each task:
  - *Functional:* This type of process map is constructed to clarify the specific organization that is responsible for each step along the process and to show hand-offs across functional boundaries. It is prepared by listing each of the participating organizations (or individual employees) along the left side of the page and showing their respective activities in corresponding rows along the page. Alternatively, the organizations are listed across the top, and their respective roles are shown in columns (see Figure 10.3).
  - *Time line:* The time line is constructed to show cycle time along the process. It is prepared by placing a time scale down the left side of the page (or along the bottom) and showing respective activities in their corresponding time slots. This special-purpose chart is most commonly used when working to reduce cycle time. Application, however, is limited to relatively simple processes, since branches and alternative paths tend to clutter the chart. The complication of multiple branches is shown in Figure 10.3, where the branches for approved and unapproved orders are shown. This chart, however, does not include the delays resulting from the required goods not being in stock. Consider how adding this branch would complicate the chart.

FIGURE 10.2	Sample Subprocess Flowchart

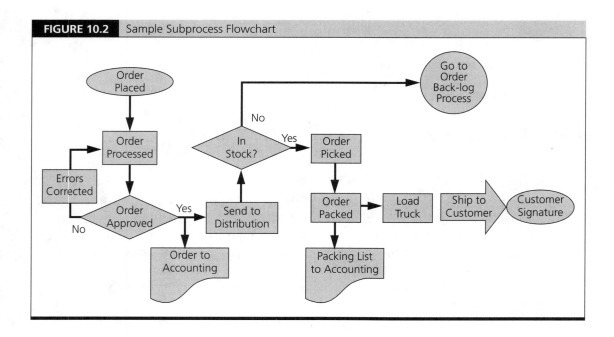

FIGURE 10.3   Sample Functional and Time-Line Flowcharts

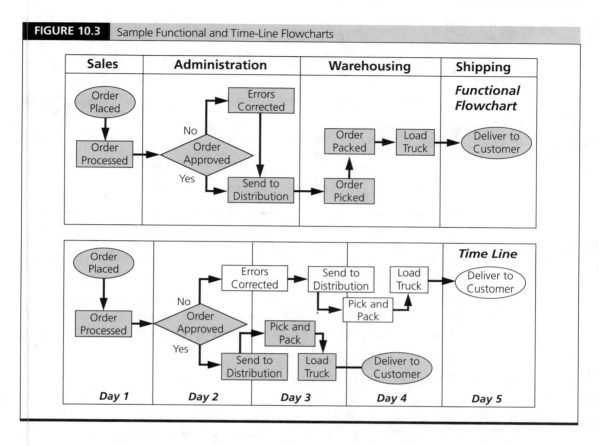

- *Top-down:* Useful in planning activities, the top-down chart shows the major elements along the top of the chart and lists details below each element. This type of chart provides the best of both worlds: the big picture can be seen easily by looking across the top portion of the chart, and details can be found in the lower portion (see Figure 10.4) (Scholtes, 1988, 2–19).

- *Workflow:* Show the physical movement of people, materials, tools, equipment, or information by tracing their paths on a sketch of the floor plan or map of the workplace. This type of chart helps teams to visualize inefficiencies and is used to understand where to redesign work space and streamline process flow. Like the time line, application of this special-purpose chart is limited to relatively simple processes (Scholtes, 1988, 2–22).

- *Block diagram:* Simply show the major components of the process by placing activities in boxes without worrying about details. Block diagrams can be designed to show organizational boundaries, time lines, or both. Block diagrams

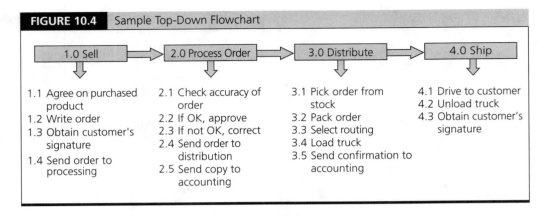

FIGURE 10.4 Sample Top-Down Flowchart

| 1.0 Sell | 2.0 Process Order | 3.0 Distribute | 4.0 Ship |

1.1 Agree on purchased product
1.2 Write order
1.3 Obtain customer's signature
1.4 Send order to processing

2.1 Check accuracy of order
2.2 If OK, approve
2.3 If not OK, correct
2.4 Send order to distribution
2.5 Send copy to accounting

3.1 Pick order from stock
3.2 Pack order
3.3 Select routing
3.4 Load truck
3.5 Send confirmation to accounting

4.1 Drive to customer
4.2 Unload truck
4.3 Obtain customer's signature

are commonly used to depict core processes (see Figure 10.1). Since they lack details, block diagrams should be supplemented with additional charts that clarify each major component.

The technique for creating subprocess flowcharts is similar to the one explained earlier for creating a core process flowchart but has more detail. The remainder of this chapter describes the additional steps required for flowcharting subprocesses.

CONDUCT PROCESS WALK-THROUGH

Walking through the process and observing it firsthand helps to document what actually occurs instead of what is expected to occur. James Harrington (1991, 15) explains, "Team members may not truly understand the procedures that are being used; individuals may have departed from the approved process because they have found better ways to do the work; they may not have adequate time to follow the approved process, or perhaps someone told them to do it differently." Walking through the process overcomes these limitations. When interviewing job performers, consider asking some of the questions listed in Table 10.1 to learn details about the process and remember three critical steps:

1. Decide what you need to know.

2. Observe and interview job performers. Ask them to describe precisely how they perform their jobs.

3. Take careful notes.

TABLE 10.1	Sample Questions for Process Walk-Through

- What work do you perform, and how do you do it?
- What is the sequence of events, and how much time does each one take?
- What tools do you use?
- What measurements are used?
- What does this step cost?
- What decisions are made during production?
- What approvals are required?

- What skills are necessary to do your work?
- Have you been trained? Was it a formal program?
- Who supplies the inputs, and how much is in stock?
- To whom do you deliver your work?
- Do you follow documented procedures?
- How are exceptions handled?
- Are there incentives or rewards for performing well?

HELPFUL HINTS FOR CHARTING SUBPROCESSES

- Display the type of activity with standard symbols. Be sure to show decision points, approvals, recycle loops, as well as the physical movement of materials, documentation, and information. A listing of frequently used symbols is provided in Figure 10.5.

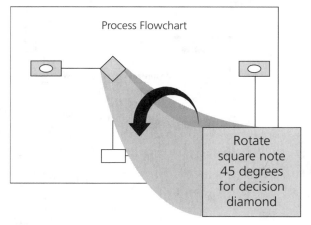

- Identify all suppliers who provide inputs and draw arrows connecting them to the subprocess that they support.

- Unlike the core-process flowchart, which should fit on a single sheet of paper, the details required to describe subprocesses may require multiple sheets. Use the connecting symbol (circle) to show how sheets are joined together.

- Drill down into each task (box) in the subprocess flowchart to discover details of various tasks and activities (see Figure 10.6).

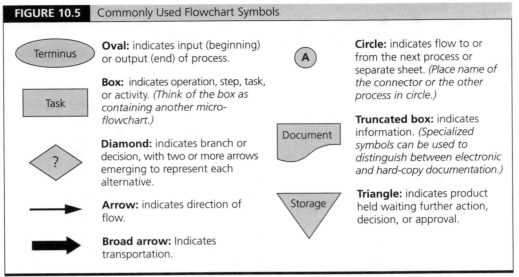

FIGURE 10.5 Commonly Used Flowchart Symbols

Oval: indicates input (beginning) or output (end) of process.

Box: indicates operation, step, task, or activity. *(Think of the box as containing another micro-flowchart.)*

Diamond: indicates branch or decision, with two or more arrows emerging to represent each alternative.

Arrow: indicates direction of flow.

Broad arrow: Indicates transportation.

Circle: indicates flow to or from the next process or separate sheet. *(Place name of the connector or the other process in circle.)*

Truncated box: indicates information. *(Specialized symbols can be used to distinguish between electronic and hard-copy documentation.)*

Triangle: indicates product held waiting further action, decision, or approval.

SOURCE: Adapted from Leitnaker, Sanders, and Hild (1995, 502).

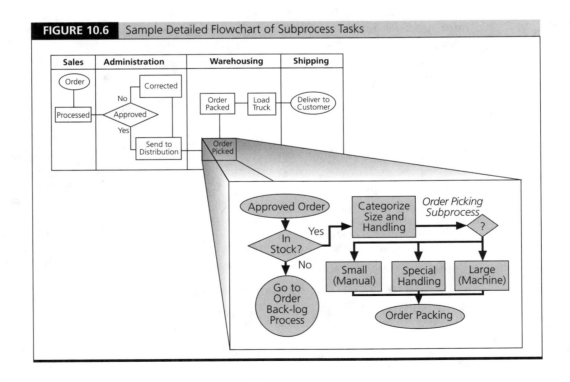

FIGURE 10.6 Sample Detailed Flowchart of Subprocess Tasks

SUMMARY

Documentation is the best method to ensure that a complete understanding of a process is obtained before redesign begins. All too often, everyone assumes they understand the various procedures that produce an output, but unfortunately, everyone's understanding is different. This chapter explains the simple techniques used to chart the flow of each core process and all related subprocesses, and thereby bring everyone on the team to a common understanding of what needs to be redesigned.

DISCUSSION QUESTIONS

1. Select one core process in your organization and construct a flowchart that depicts its major components.
2. Select one subprocess from the core process used in question 1.
   a. Describe how you would choose the best type of flowchart to document this process.
   b. Draw a flowchart of the selected subprocess.

REFERENCES

Harrington, James H. 1991. *Business Process Improvement*. New York: McGraw-Hill.

Scholtes, P. R. 1988. *The Team Handbook*. Madison, WI: Joiner Associates.

11 | Assess the Process

This chapter concludes our discussion of process analysis and sets the stage for redesigning and systematically improving processes. It provides a three-step approach for analyzing performance data in order to establish priorities and set direction for improvement projects.

Before continuing, however, let's step back and examine whether all the cultural requirements have been satisfied (refer to Table 1.1 in Chapter 1 for details). Positive answers to *all* of the following questions show a readiness to proceed; a negative answer to any question suggests a need to strengthen the foundation before continuing to build:

- *Process management:* Does the organization focus on processes and customers or on bosses? If the focus is on processes and customers, is this demonstrated in the existing organization structure or in a willingness to consider changes to it? If not, refer back to Chapter 2.

- *Leadership:* Is a compelling vision articulated and accepted? Is the mission clear? Are goals and objectives clear and meaningful? If not, refer back to Chapter 3.

- *Organizational assessment:* Is the organization's health conducive to process improvement? If not, refer back to Chapter 4.

Building on the foundation of a supportive culture, analysis of performance data will point toward improvement targets. This analysis can proceed on a process-by-process basis or across any number of processes. Regardless of the scope of the analysis, it is assumed that the array of processes employed by the organization, their relationship to each other, and their relative importance are understood through flowcharts and other forms of documentation (refer to Table 1.2 in Chapter 1 and to Chapters 5, 6, and 10).

The objectives at this point are to determine *where* and *how* to direct improvement efforts for the maximum benefit of the company. Process improvement is an investment, with its return realized over the remaining useful life of the improved process. It would be imprudent to invest significant resources in a process that was destined to be abandoned in the near term.

Investment in improvement efforts is prioritized on the basis of importance, opportunity, and feasibility. Gap analysis enables defining importance and opportunity and is covered here. Feasibility (covered in Chapter 12) accounts for the difficulty of closing gaps as well as the level of risks and resources required.

Gaps represent the differences between how well a process currently performs and how well it should perform. The sets of measures described in Chapters 7, 8, and 9 allow quantifying gaps across all critical dimensions of performance. Gap analysis is presented in three steps. The objective of the first two steps is to rank the relative size and importance of gaps in order to determine which ones to close first—*where* to work. The third step is used to set direction and determine what type of improvement is needed—*how* to work.

The first two steps of gap analysis show where efforts should be focused by defining the size and relative importance of improvement opportunities. The first step can be thought of as coarse tuning, and the second as fine tuning. Following the approach recommended in the first step provides information that will be needed in the third step for setting direction.

STEP 1: QUALITATIVE ASSESSMENT

The general condition of an organization's processes can be defined using a pair of five-point scales—one to rate effectiveness and the other to rate efficiency. It is critically important to rate each dimension independently in order to set direction correctly in the third step of the analysis. Combining the assessment of effectiveness and efficiency is likened to comparing apples and oranges: don't do it.

The axes along Figure 11.1 provide five qualitative descriptions for assigning values to effectiveness and efficiency. Rate effectiveness by analyzing data that quantify how well products and services perform, including their acceptance by customers as measured by satisfaction (refer to Chapters 7 and 9). Rate efficiency by analyzing data on costs, variation, and cycle time (refer to Chapter 8).

Plot the results on a chart like Figure 11.1 to determine a process's overall condition—unhealthy, fair, satisfactory, healthy, superior, or world-class. For example, a point would be mapped in the satisfactory band for a product that meets *most* customer requirements and is produced by a process that is characterized as being *fairly* effective. The relative health of an organization's outputs and processes can be easily visualized by plotting each one on this type of chart.

The size of improvement opportunities can be characterized by counting how many bands separate process ratings from the ideal—world-class. Processes in the poorest condition tend to offer the greatest opportunities. For example, a process rated as fair will likely offer more opportunity for improvement than one rated as superior.

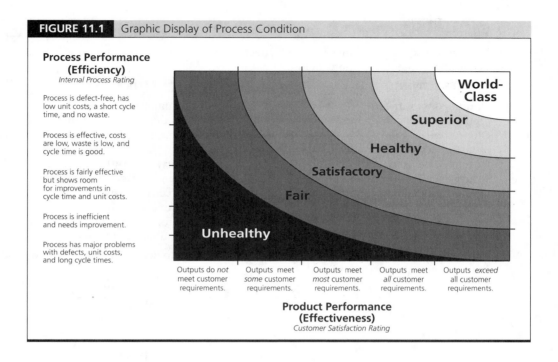

FIGURE 11.1   Graphic Display of Process Condition

Figure content:

Process Performance (Efficiency)
Internal Process Rating

Process is defect-free, has low unit costs, a short cycle time, and no waste.

Process is effective, costs are low, waste is low, and cycle time is good.

Process is fairly effective but shows room for improvements in cycle time and unit costs.

Process is inefficient and needs improvement.

Process has major problems with defects, unit costs, and long cycle times.

Zones (from inner to outer): Unhealthy, Fair, Satisfactory, Healthy, Superior, World-Class

Outputs do *not* meet customer requirements. | Outputs meet *some* customer requirements. | Outputs meet *most* customer requirements. | Outputs meet *all* customer requirements. | Outputs *exceed* all customer requirements.

Product Performance (Effectiveness)
Customer Satisfaction Rating

STEP 2: QUANTITATIVE ASSESSMENT

Some organizations will be satisfied with a qualitative analysis (Step 1) for defining the relative size of improvement opportunities, but other organizations will demand more information. Step 2 is optional and is intended for those organizations that need a closer look. Two alternative techniques are offered.

The first technique is an arithmetic analog of the qualitative approach employed in Step 1. Use the top portion of Table 11.1 to rate the effectiveness and efficiency of your processes and the bottom portion to score their overall health. Remember, the point of this exercise is merely to build consensus on the current condition of processes and relative size of performance gaps. Don't overwork the numbers trying to derive an overly precise assessment.

Process performance can be analyzed more precisely by examining each specific attribute of effectiveness and efficiency. Table 11.2 shows how the performance of four financial service processes might be compared. In this simplified example, efficiency and effectiveness are each comprised of two components—cost and cycle time for efficiency and accuracy and completeness for effectiveness. Alternatively, the performance criteria listed in Table 11.2 could have been represented quantitatively instead of qualitatively. For example, accuracy and completeness could have been defined through a capability index or six-sigma type of analysis (see Chapter 8). Similarly, the efficiency components of cost and cycle time might have been defined as ratios relative to minimum theoretical values.

TABLE 11.1	Five-point Scale to Rate Process Condition

Instructions: Assign ratings (1–5) for effectiveness and independently for efficiency according to the descriptions below.

EFFECTIVENESS	RATING	EFFICIENCY
Outputs do *not* meet customers' requirements.	1	Process has major problems with defects, unit costs, and long cycle times.
Outputs meet *some* customers' requirements.	2	Process is inefficient and needs improvement.
Outputs meet *most* customers' requirements.	3	Process is fairly effective but can use improvement in cycle time and unit costs.
Outputs meet *all* customers' requirements.	4	Process is effective, costs are low, waste is low, and cycle time is good.
Outputs *exceed* customers' requirements.	5	Process is defect-free and has low unit costs, short cycle times and no waste.

Instructions: Add ratings for effectiveness plus efficiency to determine score. Assign condition based on score shown below.

SCORE	CONDITION
<5	Unhealthy
5	Fair
6–7	Satisfactory
8	Healthy
9	Superior
10	World-class

Tabulating performance for a large array of processes is often impractical on a spreadsheet like Table 11.2. Unless the analysis is confined to a set of relatively similar processes, the list of effectiveness attributes will become unreasonably long, with many being inapplicable to numerous processes. This limitation can be overcome by listing each process (or a small subset) on a separate worksheet. The bottom-line performance figures from each worksheet can then be plotted on a chart like Figure 11.1.

RANK RELATIVE IMPORTANCE

Rather than calculating overall performance with arithmetic averages, weighting factors can be assigned to performance attributes proportionate to their relative importance. Another scheme might use the minimum value (capability index or six-sigma rating) of any attribute, instead of the average of all attributes. Choices here need to reflect the values, priorities, and business realities of the organization and its customers.

Assess the value for closing effectiveness and efficiency gaps independently. For each one, look at the value of the effort as the ratio of its importance relative to the size of the gap.

TABLE 11.2	Sample Process Performance Analysis Spreadsheet

Instructions: List processes across the top, and performance attributes down the side of the spreadsheet. Score performance of each process for each attribute:

(4) = Outstanding, (3) = Excellent, (2) = Average, (1) = Fair, (0) = Poor.

	FINANCIAL REPORTING	BUDGET PLANNING	BILL PAYING	INVOICE PREPARING
EFFICIENCY				
1. Cost				
2. Cycle Time				
EFFECTIVENESS				
1. Accuracy				
2. Completeness				
Total score				
Average score				

- For effectiveness, assign an importance weighting for each gap according to relative priorities assigned by customers. Then calculate the value of the improvement effort by dividing the importance by the size of the opportunity (rating assigned by use of Table 11.1 or 11.2). Rank order the priorities by descending scores (see the example in Table 11.3).

- By contrast, assign values to closing efficiency gaps by a direct comparison of costs or cycle times. These values then can be compared to the resources required for improvement efforts to establish priorities and justify action.

- Alternatively, if costs or revenues can be attributed to closing effectiveness gaps, this common currency can be used to compare these values to those of the efficiency gaps. In our experience, the required quantitative data rarely exist.

HIT THE MOVING TARGET

Another level of sophistication can be gained by "looking into the crystal ball." In all likelihood, you analyzed gaps by comparing current performance to current targets or specifications. Unfortunately, time passes between launching improvement efforts and implementing them.

Gaps will tend to widen because the expectations of customers and the capabilities of competitors both increase over the course of time. Real success might depend on being able to hit a moving target. Ideally, your competitors' capabilities are known, including what they might become in the future. Consider reexamining the size of your gaps by comparing current performance to future expectations.

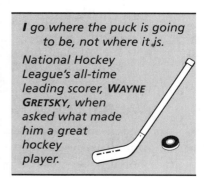

I go where the puck is going to be, not where it is.

National Hockey League's all-time leading scorer, **WAYNE GRETSKY**, when asked what made him a great hockey player.

TABLE 11.3	Example Ranking of Effectiveness Opportunities			
REQUIREMENTS	**IMPORTANCE (A)**	**Opportunity (B)**	**Value (A ÷ B)**	**Priority**
On-time delivery	5	1	5.0	1
Reliability	4	3	1.3	2
Accuracy	3	3	1.0	3
Durability	1	2	0.5	4

CLARIFY SCOPE OF IMPROVEMENT

You might also want to step back and examine the scope of processes covered in your assessment. What types of processes have been included—all processes, core processes, subprocess within one core process, or a random selection? If the analysis covers a random selection of processes, it is recommended that you go back and complete related groups.

Assessing all subprocesses within a selected core process ensures that no important area will be overlooked. If performance data are accurate and weighting factors are appropriate, this comprehensive analysis will enable you to prioritize improvement plans with a high degree of confidence. Similarly, subjecting all core processes to this assessment will help you direct and balance strategic improvements.

Needless to say, the assessment of processes is not a one-time event. Periodic updates will enable reprioritizing and redirecting improvement efforts to yield maximum benefits.

AVOID SUBOPTIMIZING

After analyzing the performance of all subprocesses within a selected core process, it may be appropriate to reassess plans. The improvement targets that were identified through gap analysis may require further scrutiny to avoid suboptimizing.

As an example, consider the situation where most of the subprocesses are rated fair or satisfactory when their performance is plotted on a chart such as Figure 11.1 (or score in the range of 5 through 7 using Table 11.1). This situation would likely lead to planning improvement projects for each subprocess. This might not be the best choice, and a superior path might be to redesign the overall core process.

CAVEAT: If the performance of many subprocesses within the same core process is weak, then an attractive alternative might be to redesign the overall core process rather than to address each subprocess in isolation.

VALIDATE CHOICES

Just as looking at each individual process in isolation could lead to suboptimization, trusting the aggregate performance score for any individual process can occasionally be misleading. Users of the quantitative analysis were offered two options—to assign equal importance to each attribute or to establish a weighting system to recognize relative importance. The choice of weighting factors is insignificant if performance of all attributes is about the same.

On the other hand, consider the situation where the performance of one or two attributes is far weaker than the others. If equal weight is assigned to each attribute, but these weaker ones are more important, the analysis will understate their priority. Similarly, if a weighting is assigned to each attribute and these are overweighted, the analysis will overstate their priority.

> CAVEAT: *If performance of a few attributes is very different from the others, consider reexamining the weighting factors assigned to each attribute to ensure that the overall aggregate score is reasonable.*

STEP 3: SETTING DIRECTION

ORDER OF PRIORITIES

Having identified which gaps to close first, the next step is to determine what type of improvement is needed. The value of improvement efforts will be maximized by recognizing the inherent priority of three basic objectives and respecting their order (refer back to Chapters 7, 8, and 9 for definitions and details of performance measures):

1 *Outcomes:* Improve the design of products or services to increase their value to customers.

2 *Outputs:* Improve the capability of the process to deliver outputs as designed.

3 *Processes:* Reduce resource consumption, variation, and/or cycle time.

Outcomes

The first priority is to produce and deliver the right products and services. It is useless to invest in the improvement of processes that produce outdated or unwanted goods and services. Therefore the first priority must be to ensure the acceptance of your goods and services in the marketplace.

Determining how well your outputs are accepted by customers was explained in Chapter 7 as an outcome measure—with customer satisfaction commonly used as a surrogate (Chapter 9). If these data show that you are trying to sell the wrong products to the wrong people at the wrong time, efforts must concentrate on improving these outputs and not on their production processes. Solutions will likely be in the form of new product designs or new marketing strategies. Improving the efficiency of your production processes would yield negligible value here. A process's condition being mapped toward the left side of Figure 11.1 is indicative of a process that delivers poorly rated products and services.

> CAVEAT: *If shortcomings in the marketplace are attributable to the process's inability to deliver specified outputs, then improvment should be sought through the process.*

Outputs

The second priority is to ensure that processes are capable of delivering products or services consistent with the specifications of their designs. Process effectiveness is measured by examining the output and comparing what was actually produced with the specifications (see Chapter 7). Process capability indices and six-sigma type analyses (Chapter 8) are two techniques for quantifying process effectiveness. Process effectiveness is improved by tuning or redesigning the process.

The term *process effectiveness* is usually represented by aggregating the process's ability to meet each individual specification. Aggregation is useful at this stage for an overall assessment to establish priorities and choose improvement paths. Once into the improvement effort, however, work must address each performance attribute and not the aggregate. As with poorly rated products and services, the condition of ineffective processes will be mapped toward the left side of Figure 11.1.

> *CAVEAT: Ensure that the performance attributes that are desired by customers (Chapter 9) are accurately translated into specifications.*

Processes

The third priority is to improve efficiency—to stop wasting money, people, and time. Efficiency is measured in the process and compares the actual consumption of resources to minimum possible levels.

Efficiency is multifaceted (see Chapter 8). It includes the cost of the resources consumed in the process. Efficiency also encompasses variation—the waste associated with adding fat and contingencies into plans and designs to cushion uncertainty. Reduced cycle time is the third facet of efficiency. As with effectiveness, prioritizing and direction setting may be based on an aggregate of the efficiency measures, but improvement efforts will need to attack each individual facet. A process's condition that is mapped in the lower portion of Figure 11.1 indicates an inefficient process.

Analogy for Ordering Priorities

The relative importance of the three improvement objectives for processes finds an analogy in the piloting of aircraft. Improving efficiency, effectiveness, and product/service effectiveness and customer satisfaction are analogous to setting speed, direction, and altitude. Speed is useless if the plane is heading in the wrong direction. Neither speed nor direction can compensate for the most serious of all aviation problems—lack of altitude.

The location of the landing site has minimal influence on takeoff. At this point in the flight, the layout of runways, wind direction, and avoiding other aircraft are of paramount importance. The pilot's first priority is to gain altitude. Little else matters at the beginning of the flight beyond safely climbing.

Once airborne, the pilot can set a course. Adjusting (improving) altitude will continue, but heading toward the destination gains added importance. Finally, the pilot can trim the plane at an efficient cruising speed. Adjusting (improving) altitude and heading will continue through the remainder of the flight.

The three types of improvement are not strictly sequential. As with piloting an airplane, the improvement of outputs, effectiveness, and efficiency should be viewed as a continuum of overlapping tasks. In most cases, product and process improvements will proceed concurrently.

DIFFERENTIATE PRODUCT FROM PROCESS IMPROVEMENT

Having completed an analysis of performance gaps, it is time to decide on the course of action and determine the type of improvement needed. Do the goods or services delivered to the marketplace have sufficient acceptance to justify investing in the improvement of their production processes? Does analysis of customer satisfaction data offer sufficient encouragement on the viability of these goods or services? If not, efforts should focus on *product* improvement—a subject that is beyond the scope of this book.

On the other hand, if the market appears to be viable, then priorities should focus on launching *process* improvement efforts. Projects might focus on improving process effectiveness, efficiency, or both. As with adjusting the altitude of an aircraft, improvement of the underlying goods or services should continue in conjunction with the improvement of their production processes. Step-by-step guidance for improving processes begins in Chapter 12.

SUMMARY

The choice of improvement strategies is predicated on knowing the degree to which the process is efficient in the use of internal resources and effective in generating favorable outcomes. Without adequate assessment, subsequent investment in improvement projects could be a misuse of organizational resources.

DISCUSSION QUESTIONS

1. Select a group of processes from the process inventory of your organization (Chapter 5), and compare their relative health by plotting them on a chart like Figure 11.1.

2. Based on your answer to question 1:

    a. Do any outputs or processes demand immediate improvement?

    b. What type of improvement is needed for those with the largest gaps—product or process?

REFERENCES

Leitnaker, M. G., Sanders, R. D., and Hild, Cheryl. 1995. *The Power of Statistical Thinking: Improving Industrial Processes*. Reading, MA: Addison-Wesley.

PART III | PROCESS IMPROVEMENT

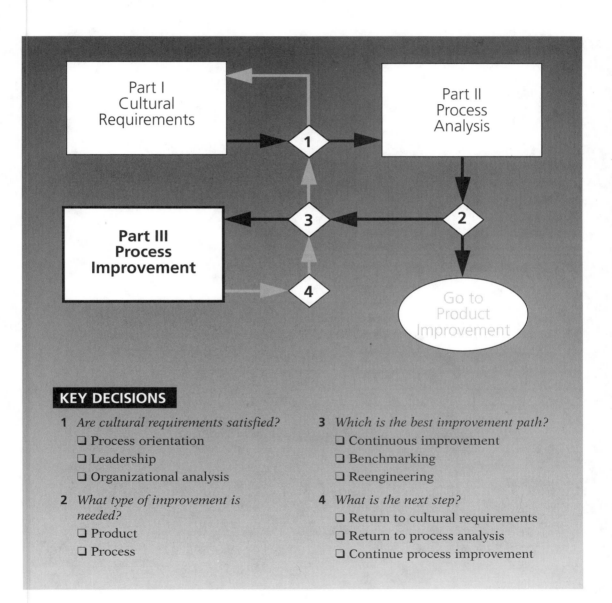

KEY DECISIONS

1 *Are cultural requirements satisfied?*
   - ❑ Process orientation
   - ❑ Leadership
   - ❑ Organizational analysis

2 *What type of improvement is needed?*
   - ❑ Product
   - ❑ Process

3 *Which is the best improvement path?*
   - ❑ Continuous improvement
   - ❑ Benchmarking
   - ❑ Reengineering

4 *What is the next step?*
   - ❑ Return to cultural requirements
   - ❑ Return to process analysis
   - ❑ Continue process improvement

12 | Planning the Improvement

Part III offers a step-by-step guide for process improvement in three blocks (Figure 12.1). The first block (Chapter 12) describes the elements commonly needed at the outset for planning improvement efforts. The second block (Chapters 13, 14, and 15) covers three alternative paths for improving processes: continuous improvement, benchmarking,

> *If you do it right, it should take forever.*
> **MARSHALL FISHER (1995, 20),** when asked by companies how long the improvement effort will take.

and reengineering. The third block (Chapter 16) explains the actions required at the conclusion of each of these paths to install the improved process.

Three elements common to the planning of process improvement projects are covered in this chapter: the identification of the project, the selection of improvement alternatives, and the launching of improvement teams (which includes criteria for designing teams, selecting team members, and ensuring their success).

IDENTIFY THE IMPROVEMENT SUBJECT

If everything went according to plan, the analysis of performance gaps (Chapter 11) would have identified improvement opportunities and defined their relative importance. But what if the opportunities are still not clear? Or if you have identified opportunities, how can you ensure that you have selected the most important ones? These questions can be answered by understanding three common triggers of improvement efforts and by working to clarify your project through three short exercises.

RECOGNIZE IMPROVEMENT TRIGGERS

Any of three triggers can cause an organization to launch improvement efforts. Recognizing the type of trigger your organization is experiencing can help you to clarify the selection of improvement opportunities:

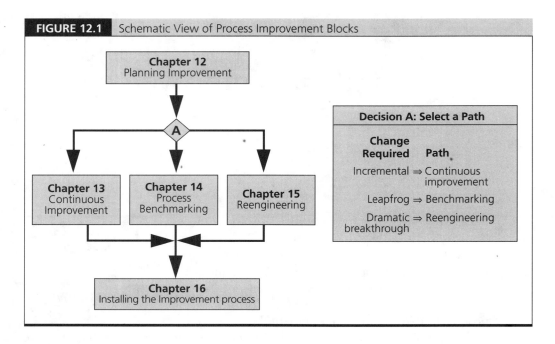

FIGURE 12.1 Schematic View of Process Improvement Blocks

- *Acute crisis:* A huge cost overrun or a major customer threatening to cancel a contract can trigger an improvement project by itself. No further effort is required to identify what the organization should target to improve when it is hit by a crisis or when it sees clear signals such as customer complaints, loss of market share, or sudden declines in reorders. Another clear signal that triggers improvement is learning about an innovative technology, practice, or process employed by a competitor. Similarly the organization may seek to seize an opportunity created by new technology or by the discovery of a new market.

- *Chronic problem:* Learning how customers' expectations are constantly increasing or how competitors are strengthening may well cause an organization to commission an improvement project. As with the crisis-type trigger, the topic for improvement is clear.

- *Internal driver:* The selection of a project will be more difficult when the organization is not hammered by an acute problem or when it doesn't face the chronic disadvantage of struggling against competitors with apparent advantages. The situation of not being certain what to address is often encountered when launching a total quality management process, since *everything* is a candidate for improvement. In this case the question of "what to improve first" requires careful screening to ensure that appropriate areas are selected. Effective gap analysis is an essential first step, and additional work often is required to clarify the project.

CLARIFY THE IMPROVEMENT PROJECT

The most commonly encountered problems in selecting improvement projects result from selecting a topic that is too large, one that is trivial, or one that has no measurable impact on securing a competitive advantage. Three exercises can be used to confirm a topic already selected, to narrow or broaden its scope, or to find a topic that is clearly important to the organization's success.

Exercise 1: Map the Process

Draw a picture that maps the elements and boundaries of the current process. Various forms of such flowcharts are explained in Chapter 10.

A map of the training process within a service department is shown in Figure 12.2 as an example. It covers the steps from the origin of identifying a training need

FIGURE 12.2   Sample Process Map for a Technical Training Group

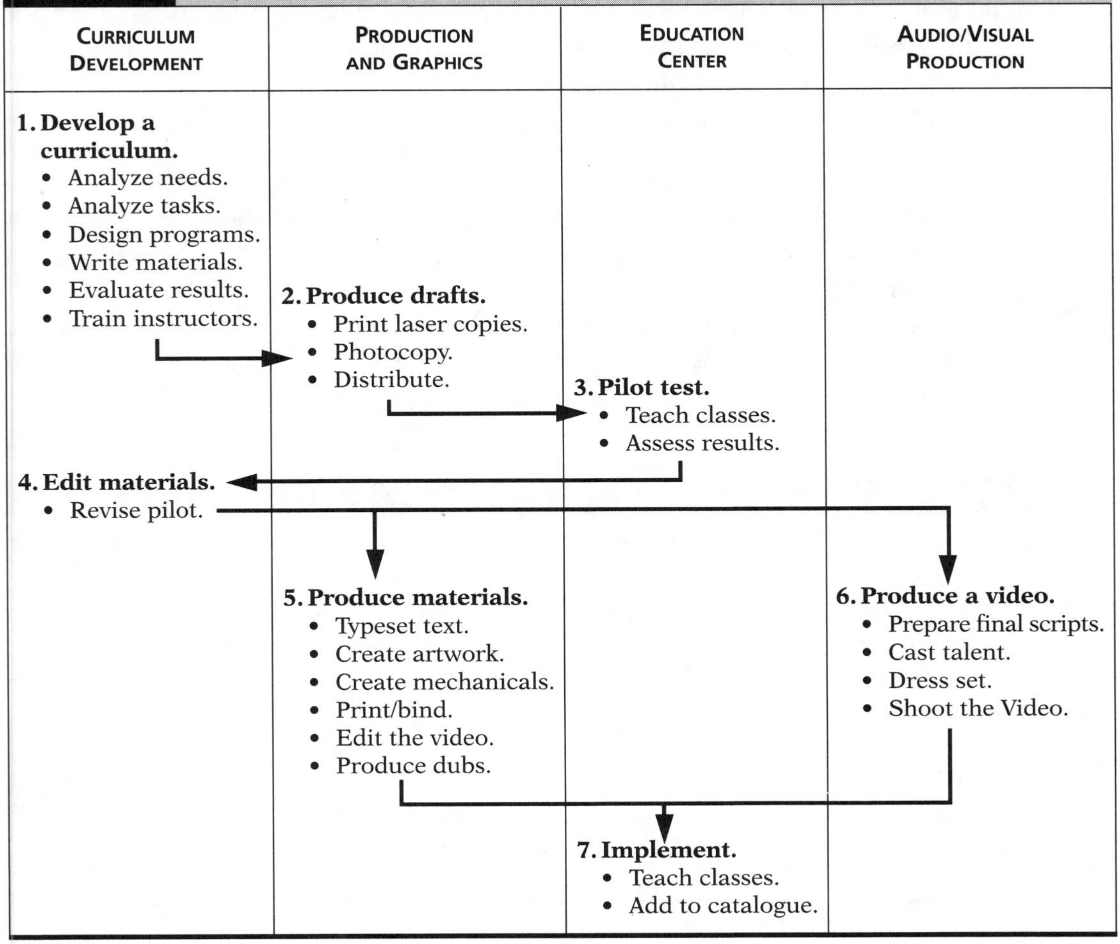

CURRICULUM DEVELOPMENT	PRODUCTION AND GRAPHICS	EDUCATION CENTER	AUDIO/VISUAL PRODUCTION
1. Develop a curriculum. • Analyze needs. • Analyze tasks. • Design programs. • Write materials. • Evaluate results. • Train instructors.	**2. Produce drafts.** • Print laser copies. • Photocopy. • Distribute.	**3. Pilot test.** • Teach classes. • Assess results.	
4. Edit materials. • Revise pilot.	**5. Produce materials.** • Typeset text. • Create artwork. • Create mechanicals. • Print/bind. • Edit the video. • Produce dubs.	**7. Implement.** • Teach classes. • Add to catalogue.	**6. Produce a video.** • Prepare final scripts. • Cast talent. • Dress set. • Shoot the Video.

to the end product—delivery of training to the service technicians. The process map can help define or clarify the boundaries and thereby assists in the selection of the improvement project.

Process documentation is a prerequisite to systematic improvement, and any attempt to shortcut this exercise will undermine the entire effort. Don't underestimate the effort required for documenting processes. Our experience reveals that a team devoting one-third of its time to the improvement project may require up to two or three weeks to complete their flowcharts. This documentation provides a common understanding of the process and can be used for ongoing analyses. The results of process flowcharting are often gratifying. We frequently are amazed to see individuals who work together enter this exercise with completely different pictures of the workflow and emerge with a common view.

Exercise 2: Review Direction-Setting Statements
Where do you start when the organization issues a policy requiring that everyone must improve everything? The answer is to go back to the basic direction-setting statements—mission, goals, and objectives.

When a functional organization is working to improve its processes, its mission, goals, and objectives will serve to set the improvement project's direction (refer to Chapter 3 for additional information). A sample description of the Technical Training Group's mission, goals, and objectives is shown in Table 12.1. The relative importance of candidate improvement projects can be tested against these statements.

These first two exercises may be sufficient to enable a team to select a topic or specific set of processes to improve. If, however, the topic defined through these previous exercises appears to be correct but still too large, a third exercise

TABLE 12.1 Technical Training Group: Mission, Goals, and Objectives	
DIRECTION-SETTING STATEMENT	**TIMING**
MISSION	
• Provide training to all technical personnel and continually improve their skills and productivity, so that they achieve their job targets and satisfy all end-user service requirements.	Ongoing
GOAL	
• Achieve the industry's best technical training.	2–5 years
OBJECTIVES	
• Improve mean time-to-repair test scores from 1.4 to 1.2 hours. • Reduce program development time and costs by 10%. • Increase interest level in class by 20%.	0–2 years

can help to narrow its scope. Our example continues with the Technical Training Group's goals and objectives. If they cannot improve all of their processes, which should they select?

Exercise 3: Rank Output Priorities

Rank the relative importance and improvement potential of the outputs (products or services delivered to customers) produced by each of the subprocesses.

Outputs are not all equal in their contribution toward attainment of the organization's goals and objectives. By ranking the relative importance of each output, the team can clarify the scope of its project. For example, if cycle-time reduction is the team's primary objective, then any outputs with long cycle times would be ranked as *1*. If cost reduction is the primary objective, then any high-cost output would be ranked as *1*. Rankings of *2* and *3* would be assigned to outputs with less impact on the stated objectives.

Each output also can be judged as to its improvement potential. Outputs and associated processes that are assessed to have little opportunity for improvement are ranked *L* for low. Those outputs with medium- or high-improvement potential would be marked *M* or *H*, respectively. (Refer to the gap analysis procedure explained in Chapter 11.)

This exercise leads a team to find the few 1-H outputs that offer the greatest combination of importance and opportunity. The processes that produce these outputs would be assigned the highest priority to be improved. A sample exercise applied to the Technical Training Group is illustrated in Table 12.2. It suggests that highest priority should be assigned to improving the curriculum development process. A second candidate might be the process for conducting classes in the education center.

The Technical Training Group might address both areas as a joint project or select one. If resources are available for only one process, preference should be given to the upstream process, since its improvement may offer benefits to all downstream processes as well.

The completion of these exercises clarifies which process should be improved to gain the greatest impact on performance. The candidate process should be further tested for reasonableness by asking such questions as, "Is this the area that customers complain about the most? Does this area contribute to major cost overruns? Is there something that needs to be fixed immediately so that we can avoid being affected in the marketplace?"

TABLE 12.2	Technical Training Department Outputs Ranked		
FUNCTION	**OUTPUTS**	**PRIORITY**	**IMPROVEMENT POTENTIAL**
Curriculum development	Needs analyzed	1	H
	Tasks analyzed	1	M
	Programs designed	1	H
	Materials written	1	H
	Results evaluated	1	M
	Instructors trained	1	H
Production	Type specified	2	M
	Material typeset	2	H
	Materials proofread	2	L
	Transparencies prepared	2	L
	Materials printed	2	M
Graphics	Artwork prepared	2	M
	Page layout designed	2	M
	Materials printed	2	M
Education center	Classroom set up	3	H
	Pilots conducted	1	M
	Classes conducted	1	H
	Students evaluated	2	L
	Bills paid	2	L
	Travel booked	2	L
	Facilities cleaned	2	M
	Student expenses monitored	3	H
	Memos typed	3	M
	Food served	2	H

SELECT IMPROVEMENT ALTERNATIVES

The selection of improvement alternatives follows a sequence of four steps. First, you need to set your target—the size of the gap to be closed and speed required for closing it. Second, you need to define the improvement path that represents the best approach to reach the target. Third, you need to determine the feasibility of reaching your target by the selected path. Finally, you may need to recycle back through these steps if the risks and costs determined in step 3 exceed the value expected to be returned by reaching your target.

SET A TARGET

Most organizations have business drivers that enable them to set improvement targets. Other organizations will find that the quantification and analysis of performance gaps will likely lead to defining targets. Competitive benchmarking offers yet another approach. No additional guidance is offered on target setting.

Clarifying note: Readers should recognize the distinction between *competitive* benchmarking and *process* benchmarking. The former looks at performance of competitors in order to set targets. By contrast, process benchmarking continues the search to include finding the *means* by which competitors and others have achieved their superior performance. Process benchmarking not only helps to set targets; it also provides guidance on what to emulate in order to achieve those targets (see Chapter 14).

SELECT AN IMPROVEMENT PATH

Select an improvement path for each process at any given time based on the size of performance gaps, the potential opportunity for improvement, and the relative difficulty expected for the improvement effort. Consider the following questions when choosing the improvement path:

- How much improvement is required?
- How outdated is the process?
- Which subprocesses are obsolete?
- How does our performance compare to that of our competitors?
- How rapidly are customers' requirements changing?
- How much will it cost to fix?
- What are the risks?
- How difficult will it be?
- How long will it take?
- How long do we have?
- Do we have to start from scratch?
- Do we have the resources and time?
- Will we need outside help and if so, what kind?

Answers to these questions in combination with information provided in Table 12.3 can help in deciding which of the following paths to select:

- *Continuous improvement* on an ongoing basis for incremental gains: the magnitude of these gains should not be expected to improve performance above the process condition band determined in Chapter 11 without repeated reapplication (go to Chapter 13);
- *Benchmarking* periodically for larger gains that should be sufficient to propel the process condition up one level (go to Chapter 14);
- *Reengineering* selectively to achieve dramatic breakthroughs that offer the potential of rocketing the process condition up more than one level (go to Chapter 15).

TABLE 12.3	Comparison of Typical Expectations for Improvement Paths				
PATH	**REWARD**	**RISK**	**COST**	**DURATION**	**DIFFICULTY**
Reengineering	Up to 1,000%	Very high	Very high	Long	High
Benchmarking	20–50%	Low	Moderate	Long	Moderate
Continuous improvement	3–10%	Low	Low	Short	Easy

DETERMINE FEASIBILITY

With the path defined, you are now ready to ensure that the efforts required to reach your target are justified. How likely is success? What are the risks? What resources—time and effort—will be required? In determining resources, consider each of the following:

- Will the work be performed by your own staff, or will incremental staff be needed? What will be the costs for personnel over the timeframe projected?

- What will be the costs for supporting resources—technical specialists, tools, equipment, samples, travel, and training?

- Is the improvement effort justified if total costs are double the predicted level? Triple?

Even if you are unfamiliar with the improvement process, you should be able to estimate its costs. You don't need to work this in isolation, since others have undoubtedly attempted similar tasks before. Ask others to help define the scope of what is needed. Estimate the resources required consistent with guidelines of your organization.

LAUNCH IMPROVEMENT TEAMS

"Corporate America is having a hot love affair with teams. And why not? When teams work, there's nothing like them for turbo-charging productivity" (Dumaine, 1994, 86). Management consultants, too, love teams and have found a huge niche within which to launch thriving careers. Teamwork and team building have become popular terms in business circles, but look at their evolution. Before the industrial revolution, a *team* was usually seen as horses, mules, or oxen drawing carts or plows. During the past century, a *work team* might more aptly have been described as a gang or crew (Tenner and DeToro, 1992, 183–184).

> **Teams** *are the Ferraris of work design. They're high performance but high maintenance and expensive.*
> **EDWARD LAWLER**
> *(Fisher, 1995, 20)*

Only relatively recently have teams been recognized in industry and discussed in the context of collaboration, cooperation, and sporting events. But even now the terms are frequently misused. In traditional, hierarchical, autocratic organizations, *teamwork* has often meant compliance, and a *team player* is often a euphemism for a conformist who suppresses his or her own goals for the sake of the organization (Keidel, 1988, 11).

Some managers mistakenly stereotype teams in a certain mold and glamorize them with analogies to professional sports or circus aerial acts. These managers assume that a group cannot be called a high-performing team if it doesn't fit some idealized model of total autonomy and equality. This idealized picture, however, needs a dose of reality. All teams are not alike, all teams are not autonomous, and equality among members is more frequently the exception than the norm. Furthermore, using teams is not always the right answer. Robert Keidel (1988, 11) explains:

> *TEAMS ARE OVERUSED. Many companies will create teams where they're not really needed. The key is to analyze the work before you form a team. Does the task really require that people interact with each other? Can work be done faster by a single person? . . . You don't use teams with insurance salesmen or long-haul truckers.*

The remainder of this chapter is intended to help team sponsors effectively launch improvement teams—whether they are teams of one, natural work groups, or special-purpose management teams. This help is provided in three ways: guidance on how the type of tasks that teams will face influences how the team is designed, criteria for defining who needs to be included on the team's roster, and a pair of keys to ensure success.

THREE DIMENSIONS OF TEAM DESIGN

How can a team's sponsor know the degree of autonomy, control, independence, and collaboration that best suits a process improvement team that he or she is about to launch? The answer can be found in understanding three dimensions of team design and selecting the "sweet spot" in the design on the basis of the types of tasks that the team will perform. Teams can be designed to operate anywhere across the spectrum of three independent dimensions: tenure, dependence, and control (see Table 12.4).

Different types of tasks demand different types of teams (Harbour, 1990, 1–7). Consider the differences in dependence and control required to perform the following tasks: driving spikes into miles of railroad tracks, deciding on the guilt or innocence of an alleged criminal, winning a football game, or improving the design of a data processing system. Following are four types of tasks commonly encountered by process improvement teams and the design best suited to each type:

TABLE 12.4	Three Dimensions for Defining Teams	
Tenure:	Longest ↕ Shortest	**Natural work team:** operates, maintains, and improves own process on an ongoing basis
		Special purpose team: is responsible for specific task(s) and disbands on completion
Dependence:	Most ↕ Least	**Collaborative:** is highly interactive and interdependent
		Independent: includes individual contributors, "teams of one," and task groups
Control:	Closest ↕ Furthest	**Autonomous:** is internally directed and self-managed
		Authoritarian: is controlled and directed from outside, above, or by a designated individual

- *Additive tasks:* Constructing miles of railroad track is an example of an *additive* task, and the accomplishment of the team equals the summation of individuals' contributions. In this type of task, the team will accomplish more than any individual; however, the contribution of each member is frequently below that of the same individual performing on his or her own. The maximum potential capability of teams performing additive tasks is proportionate to the size of the team, but the actual work accomplished will be less. The key to leading this type of team is to minimize this gap (Harbour, 1990, 1–7). Teams performing additive tasks will likely require little collaboration among members and should benefit from direct control of a designated leader.

- *Disjunctive tasks:* A jury deciding on guilt or innocence represents a team performing a *disjunctive* task. Solving problems and making decisions are common disjunctive tasks. In this type of task, the performance of the team will approximate that of the most knowledgeable member. Teams cannot perform beyond their available resources, and optimal performance will be realized through identification and support of the most knowledgeable member (Harbour, 1990, 1–7). Popular corporate team-building exercises such as Desert Survival and Lunar Landing games provide practice for teams performing disjunctive tasks. The best levels of collaboration and autonomy for teams performing disjunctive tasks will depend on the styles and inclinations of their members.

- *Conjunctive tasks:* By contrast, playing a football game is a *conjunctive* task. Here, each member must perform his or her task, and the team's capability may be limited by the ability of the weakest member, not the strongest

(Harbour, 1990, 1–7). Teams performing conjunctive tasks will likely operate best with a high level of collaboration among members and direct control from a designated leader.

- *Optimizing tasks:* A team working to improve the design of a data processing system is performing an *optimizing* task. Here, the goal is to produce some specific, most preferred outcome. Collaboration and cooperation among members result in the team's performance potentially exceeding the summation of the abilities of all the individuals. Furthermore, this team will likely address subtasks that are additive, disjunctive, or conjunctive. The mode of operation of the team should adjust for each subtask. Teams performing optimizing tasks will likely operate best with high levels of collaboration and autonomy.

CRITERIA FOR SELECTING TEAM MEMBERS

Four rules of thumb help team sponsors to determine the composition of their improvement teams.

RULE 1: Minimize the number of members on any improvement team. Why minimize the number of participants? The answer is simple—to minimize costs. Costs for running teams increase disproportionately with their size. In addition to the direct costs of each incremental member, complexity increases—slowing progress and complicating the scheduling of meetings.

Some might challenge this rule as shortsighted and missing the benefits attributed to collaboration. This is not the case, as long as the remaining three rules are satisfied. Ask yourself whether each of the next three rules are satisfied when looking to assign members to a team, and reduce the team's membership to the smallest number for which you can still answer yes three times.

RULE 2: Populate the team with members in positions of authority. Does the team have the authority to make the changes they determine necessary? If not, look to include people who have the authority to act, either through inclusion as full-fledged members or through their legitimate sponsorship.

RULE 3: Populate the team with stakeholders. Does the team include or represent the individuals and groups that will be impacted by the outcome? These people are frequently called the stakeholders, and their participation on process improvement teams helps to ensure buy-in during implementation.

RULE 4: Populate the team with individuals who have the skills and knowledge needed for the intended mission. Does the team have the required skills, knowledge, and perspective to fulfill its charter? This includes both the *content* of what needs to be accomplished and the *process* by which the team will operate. If required competency is not included, look to add appropriate members or engage them as consultants to the team.

These four rules help to dispel two myths about selecting improvement team members that were unleashed on the corporate world over the past decade. One myth dictated the inclusion of customers on improvement teams, and the other myth required the inclusion of individuals who offered diversity. While not disagreeing that some types of teams require both types of players, you can determine your team's composition by examining the roles of customers and diversity in their proper perspective.

A Role for Customers

Including customers on improvement teams was one of the myths built into many ill-fated quality improvement programs. Customers are clearly stakeholders when the products or services sold to them are being improved, since their buy-in is the objective of the improvement effort (Rule 3). Similarly, customers have firsthand knowledge of their requirements (Rule 4), which is another reason to represent them on teams charged with improving products or services.

On the other hand, customers generally don't have a stake or expertise—nor should they be expected to show interest—when improvements focus on improving efficiency.

A Role for Diversity

A second myth is the selection of members who offer diversity in thinking, background, and styles. This is needed under some situations but not all. Sometimes the key selection criterion is simply expertise (Rule 4). Adding diversity may be a way to find expertise, but this is trusting to luck. If expertise is needed, it is more productive to define the capabilities that are needed and then seek them directly.

Include Customers?	
Type of Improvement	
Product/Service	Yes
Process Effectiveness	Maybe
Efficiency	No
Include Diversity?	
Type of Task	
Additive	No
Disjunctive	Maybe
Conjunctive	Maybe
Optimizing	Yes

The need for diversity becomes clearer when looking at the type of tasks that the team will be performing. Additive tasks typically call for a multitude of similar members—big, strong men for driving spikes into miles of railroad tracks, for example. By contrast, a team needing to find new ways of doing things will likely benefit from members who can bring different perspectives into their discussions. These latter teams will obviously benefit from the deliberate inclusion of members with diverse backgrounds.

TWO KEYS TO BUILDING SUCCESSFUL TEAMS

Launching teams is a natural process in some organizations but is artificial and stilted in others. Two keys to success are offered to help tune the process.

Clear Direction

Team members need to know what is expected of them. The information needed to clarify the direction and scope of a team's effort can be documented in a project description—or team charter. (Team charters differ from the mission statements in that charters exist only for the duration of their projects. Mission statements are long-lived and rarely change.) Three essential elements in this document are (1) a general description of the problem or opportunity to be addressed, (2) the expected outcome, and (3) the boundaries—including the delineation of resources and authority. Special-purpose teams formed to resolve specific issues will benefit from clear and comprehensive charters.

> NOTE: *Teams that are natural work groups should find these three elements embedded in their direction-setting documents (see Chapter 3)—mission statement (description); vision, goals and objectives (expected outcomes); and core values, policies, strategies, and plans (boundaries).*

The team's charter must mate with the organization's stated mission, vision, goals, and objectives. Examining alignment between the team's charter and the organization's direction-setting statements may

- Redefine the charter,
- Identify required revisions to the organization's goals and objectives (but this examination is *not* likely to impact the mission or vision),
- Influence the approach to the improvement effort,
- Help to define key performance measures for the project, and
- Help lend credibility to the project when the team seeks support, resources, and approval of its recommendations.

The charter relates directly to the event or situation that triggered the project. It should position the team with a clear goal and well-defined objectives. Although not necessarily included within the charter, all members should know their roles and responsibilities on the team.

The project team can use this description to ensure that its project receives support, approval, and resources from the sponsor. If sponsorship is unclear, vague, or indecisive, improvement should not be undertaken until the support is more concrete. It hardly makes sense to embark on a seemingly important improvement effort without support from a sponsor.

Teams should expect to revise their charters as they clarify what they expect to accomplish and as more information is gathered during the course of improvement activities. These updates can be used to keep the sponsors informed, or for justifying mid-course corrections. A sample project description is provided in Appendix C.

Motivation

Organizations launch teams to improve products, services, and/or processes—all for the betterment of the organization. But what are the benefits for the members? "Our employees are our most valuable resource." If this claim is to ring true, then clear evidence of how the team's performance will benefit participants is needed. Benefits can include improved quality of work life, development of skills, new job opportunities, and increased authority. Benefits also include timely rewards and recognition.

These benefits, however, are pale in comparison to a "stake in the action." There is no greater driver for team building than a life-or-death stake that each member has in the outcome. Evaluate the stake that members have in the outcome. Is it high (will it impact on members' jobs, pride, or compensation?) or is it low (will it impact merely on others and on members' consciences)? How does your compensation system tie to the team's performance? Can you do anything to increase members' stakes in the outcome if it is low?

Team-building exercises are not always required. These exercises are most needed when individual stakes are low, unclear, or conflicting. Team-building exercises should be a last resort; preferred choices are to increase members' stakes, clarify the impact, and align individual self-interests.

SPECIAL CONSIDERATIONS FOR CORE-PROCESS IMPROVEMENT TEAMS

Forming teams to address relatively complex objectives—like the improvement of core processes—deserves additional clarification. Chapter 6 described how to identify those large key processes that are critical to an organization's success. We assume, at this point, that senior management has identified these vital few core processes and is now launching an improvement effort of selected ones.

The Roles of Champions and Owners

Improvement of a core process begins by identifying and appointing individuals to several key roles. According to Paul Allaire, Xerox's CEO, "Each [core-process improvement] effort has a process champion and a process owner. The process owner is responsible for orchestrating the daily details of redesign and improvement; it's a full-time job for a vice president. Process champions, in contrast, are members of my senior management team, with broad oversight responsibilities" (Garvin, 1995, 85).

The *champion* in concert with the other senior managers who have supported the improvement activity should select the process owner. This individual should

TABLE 12.5	Core Process Owner's Roles and Responsibilities
ROLES	**RESPONSIBILITIES**
Improve performance (effectiveness) to increase customer satisfaction.	• Understand customers and their requirements. • Understand the capabilities of the process. • Understand the capabilities of competitors.
Improve efficiency.	• Reduce costs. • Reduce variation. • Reduce cycle time.
Improve workflow across the organization in the assigned core process.	• Manage cross-functional conflicts and disconnects between functions.
Recommend improvement strategies.	• Assess processes for efficiency and effectiveness and commission improvement teams.
Support improvement activities.	• Select the right resources for each team, including participants in subprocesses and in other functions. • Allocate support, and arrange for training.
Set agendas, approve mandates for change, and hold teams accountable for timetables and results.	• Ensure that the direction is clear and expectations are understood. • Establish effective tracking and monitoring systems.

SOURCE: Adapted from Rummler and Brache (1991, 135–137).

be able to work across the organization, relying on a mix of line authority and personal persuasion. The individual assigned as process owner is frequently a high-potential manager needing additional experience before assuming still greater responsibility. The role is usually full-time but may be part-time depending on the magnitude and urgency of the improvement required. The core process owner's role and responsibilities are listed in Table 12.5.

The Role of Team Members

The process owner can assemble a core-process improvement (CPI) team by selecting senior managers, department heads, or supervisors who are responsible for and have vested interest in this workflow now called a core process. These members must be credible and respected across the organization and be capable of devoting considerable time and personal energy to the project.

The CPI team is an executive improvement team that will work at two levels—to improve the core process itself and to commission subprocess improvement teams within selected functional groups that interact within this core process. A team may also include technical experts or specialists, customers, suppliers, and information technology specialists. A typical CPI's team member's roles and responsibilities are listed in Table 12.6.

TABLE 12.6	Core Process Team Roles and Responsibilities
ROLES	**RESPONSIBILITIES**
Process owner	See Table 12.5.
Functional process coordinator	• Manage improvement projects for all functional subprocess teams. • Approve all subprocess recommendations.
Functional leaders, department heads, and supervisors	• Identify subprocesses improvement opportunities. • Improve all hand-offs between subgroups. • Commission subprocess teams.
Process personnel	• Perform ongoing operations of process. • Provide an operating perspective as members of improvement teams. • Handle improvement initiatives.
Process improvement specialist	• Support efforts to map and document processes. • Support data collection systems and use of analysis tools • Support application of improvement tools and techniques.
Customers	• Provide the customer's perspective to clarify requirements and satisfaction levels.
Suppliers	• Provide information on all inputs. • Identify issues and opportunities.

SOURCE: Adapted from Rummler and Brache (1991, 135–137).

SUMMARY

Planning improvement initiatives includes selecting an improvement path from a number of alternatives, and utilizing the talents and skills of employees. Descriptions of roles and responsibilities, and guidelines on how to best select team members and work with individuals to launch improvement projects are provided.

DISCUSSION QUESTIONS

1. Pick one process in your organization that requires improvement. Quantify the magnitude of improvement needed and the timeframe in which this should be achieved.

2. What path would you take to reach the target for the process selected in question 1—continuous improvement, benchmarking, or reengineering?

3. Estimate the resources required to pursue the path selected in question 2.

4. Examine a team that you are forming or on which you currently serve. What type of task(s) will be performed: additive, disjunctive, conjunctive, and/or optimizing?

5. How best should this team operate in the dimensions of interdependence and decision making?

6. Does membership include appropriate staff? Are the rules of authority, buy-in, and competence satisfied?

   a. If not, what is missing, and who needs to be added to the team?

   b. Is the team larger than it needs to be?

7. Does the team have a clear and comprehensive charter that describes the problem/opportunity, the expected outcome, and the boundaries?

   a. Is the charter understood and supported by all members?

   b. Is the expected outcome realistic, ambitious, but achievable?

   c. Is the scope within the authority of the team or its sponsor?

   d. Do all members know their roles and responsibilities?

8. Do all members have a clear stake in the outcome, and will they benefit if the team is successful? If not, what can be done to cement member's allignment?

REFERENCES

Dumaine, Brian. 1994. "The Trouble with Teams." *Fortune* (September 5), 86.

Fisher, Marshall L. 1995. "Soups and Ski Parkas: Two Ends of the Spectrum." *Wharton Alumni Magazine* (Winter), 20.

Garvin, D. A. 1995. "Leveraging Processes for Strategic Advantage." *Harvard Business Review* (September-October), 85.

Harbour, Jerry. 1990. "Understanding and Improving Small Group Performance." *Performance and Instruction* (January), 1–7.

Keidel, Robert W. 1988. *Corporate Players*. New York: Wiley.

Rummler, G. A., and A. P. Brache. 1991. *Improving Performance: How to Minimize the White Space on the Organizational Chart*. San Francisco: Jossey-Bass.

Tenner, A. R., and I. J. DeToro. 1992. *Total Quality Management: Three Steps to Continuous Improvement*. Reading, MA: Addison-Wesley.

13 | Continuous Improvement

When CEOs are demanding use of the latest tools like benchmarking and reengineering, the idea of continuous improvement retains about as much excitement as watching paint dry. Compounding the problem are managers who have had little success in convincing their organizations to buckle down and methodically address work processes. These managers tend to seize the latest mandate as a refreshing opportunity to drop unsuccessful projects and start over—championing a tool that has just been reported in a popular business magazine or touted in a best-selling book.

In many respects, this reaction is part of our tendency in the United States to look for shortcuts, the silver bullet, or the single perfect solution to a complex issue. While there are valid and appropriate applications for new tools, there is also an appropriate and permanent place for basic ones—like continuous improvement. In our experience, approaches like benchmarking and reengineering rarely succeed in organizations that neglect continuous improvement.

Continuous improvement is a key weapon in an organization's arsenal for moving toward world-class performance. Sustaining incremental improvements of 5 percent per year will compound to 30 percent within five years. When coupled with breakthroughs provided by benchmarking and reengineering, the combination leads to world-class performance.

Our experience shows that an organization should select a single disciplined method, common language, and set of tools for continuous improvement. This standardization enables individuals to jump from one team to the next and across functional boundaries without having to relearn new tactics. This chapter illustrates one such methodology. It builds on the concepts and tools introduced in earlier chapters with step-by-step plans that enable readers to proceed in their own organizations.

Six-Step Improvement Model

The improvement methodology needs to be disciplined, methodical, and robust. No team should struggle to develop a methodology for its specific project because this development work already has been completed. A model is available that has been tested and proven successful by a number of organizations around the world.

This model serves as a road map to move a process from its current state along a path to world-class performance. A road map differs from a prescription. People who are unfamiliar with the route use a road map as a guide for getting from point A to point B. On the other hand, a prescription specifies requirements that must always be followed. The journey is illustrated graphically in Figure 13.1 along with the six-step model.

The model offers a six-step approach that enhances the likelihood for success. These steps are explained in the remainder of this chapter and previewed as follows:

1. *Understand the customer.* Understand the end customer's stated requirements and unstated wants, needs, and expectations. Measure the organization's ability to meet these requirements and identify gaps. Determine competitor's performance and project future levels that may be required to maintain and improve customer satisfaction (see Chapters 7 and 9).

2. *Assess efficiency.* Select internal process measures that reveal how well the process is performing. Gather data and determine how well it meets internal requirements like cost, variability, and cycle time (refer to Chapter 8).

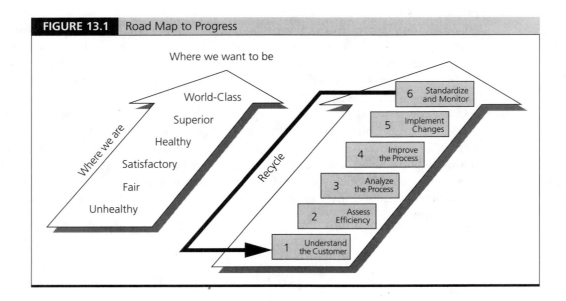

FIGURE 13.1   Road Map to Progress

3. *Analyze the process.* Rate the condition of the process. Is it effective but inefficient, or ineffective but efficient, or worse, both ineffective *and* inefficient? Select the appropriate improvement path—continuous improvement for incremental gains, benchmarking for step changes, or reengineering to achieve dramatic breakthroughs (see Chapters 11 and 12). Continue to step 4 if continuous improvement is the selected path. Alternatively, benchmarking and reengineering are covered in Chapters 14 and 15, respectively.

4. *Improve the process.* Continuous improvement relies on building a fundamental understanding of customers' requirements, process capability, and the root cause for any gaps between them. Hypotheses are developed and tested, and improvement is gained through the cycle of plan-do-study-act. This is a systematic approach as opposed to the classic short-cut of problem detection and subsequent solving—an approach resembling plan-do-plan-do instead of plan-do-study-act.

5. *Implement changes.* Pilot the revised process before adopting it on a full scale. Simulate the new process or test critical facets. Make appropriate adjustments. Develop and document an implementation plan by working with appropriate subprocess teams (see Chapter 16).

6. *Standardize and monitor.* Implement the changes. Continue to track performance, monitor cycle time, cost, and variation. Observe competitive moves, and measure customer satisfaction. Continuously improve the process to sustain your competitive edge (see Chapter 16).

Actions required in Steps 1, 2, and 3 are common to all improvement efforts—continuous improvement, benchmarking, and reengineering—and are covered in previous chapters. Key activities in these steps that pertain to continuous improvement are amplified in this chapter.

STEP 1: UNDERSTAND THE CUSTOMER

Assess the customer's satisfaction with the end product or service produced by this process. Most organizations are surprisingly ill informed on the identity of their external customers, their requirements, and the degree to which these requirements are being met. The team can build the required understanding by completing Step 1 (see Figure 13.2).

1.1 Identify the Final Output

Identify what your process produces—not what individuals do but what is produced and sold to the end customer. Most processes produce numerous outputs, but the team should focus on the final output that the external customer receives.

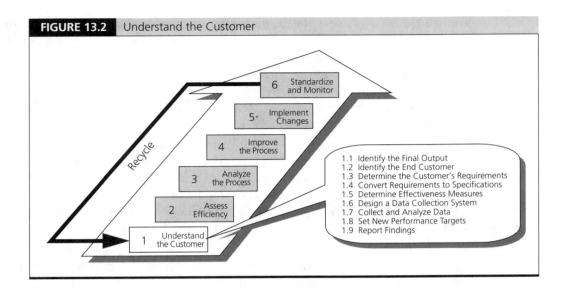

FIGURE 13.2   Understand the Customer

This final output could be the laptop computer sold or the health-care service provided by a hospital. It could be the new long-haul, large-capacity truck or the transportation provided by an airline. The final output is the product or service that the end customer purchases and uses that should be the focus of the team.

1.2 Identify the End Customer
Having identified the final output, the team needs to identify the person(s) or specific group(s) for whom the process produces the final output. This could be the corporate user of the laptop computer, the hospital patient for health-care services, the long-distance truck driver, or the airline passenger.

1.3 Determine the Customer's Requirements
Once the specific customers have been identified for the final output, the team needs to understand their needs, requirements, and expectations. As consumers, we are being asked with increasing frequency how well we enjoyed our hotel stay, our degree of satisfaction with the auto rental, or whether we would recommend a particular restaurant to a friend. These questions are being asked by providers who are looking for feedback on the performance of their processes. Successful organizations understand the complete array of customers' requirements. They also know which ones are being met and which are not.

In cellular communications, for example, the "dispatch" service—or ability to broadcast the same message to a group—differs across customer groups. Commodities brokers, for example, may not want to be interrupted in the trading pit but may want dispatched messages retained and transmitted when they leave the floor and activate their cellular phones. By contrast, police officers need to be ready and continuously accessible because of the critical nature of protecting public safety. Understanding the unique requirements of each of the different end-user groups is necessary for tailoring services and succeeding in the wireless communication market.

A number of techniques are available to collect data for learning customers' requirements. Focus groups, mail surveys, telephone surveys, interviews, analysis of customer complaints, warranty claims, and letters of appreciation are but a few. The team can distill data from these sources to identify the customer's requirements.

Caution: Many improvement projects are derailed from the outset by claims that customers don't know what they want. While this may be true on the surface, this is not a valid reason to ignore customers and go off doing what you want. The challenge is to dig beneath the surface and help customers describe their requirements.

Beginning with a list like the examples in Table 13.1, determine the performance that the end customer wants, needs, and expects. Write a brief description of each requirement, and determine its relative importance to the customer.

TABLE 13.1 Example Product Quality Measures

REQUIREMENT	MEASURES
Customer satisfaction	• Percentage of reorders • Number of customer referrals • Number of complaints • Number of commendations • Market share
Reliability	• Number of service calls • Percentage of equipment downtime
Availability	• Percentage of back orders
Delivery	• Percentage of on-time deliveries • Average delivery time
Conformance (defects)	• Percentage of customer returns • Number of customer complaints
Durability	• Percentage of warranty claims • Average product life
Ease of use	• Number of service calls • Average time to learn use

1.4 Convert Requirements to Specifications

Create operational definitions and translate each requirement into a specification that precisely prescribes what needs to be produced or delivered. If customers demand *hot, fresh* coffee, then the specification might state that coffee must be brewed every fifteen minutes and served at 180 degrees. If customers require *responsive* service on malfunctioning equipment, the specification could state that a specialist will phone within fifteen minutes, and if required, a technician will be on site within ninety minutes and repair the equipment within 180 minutes of the original call. Responsiveness is measured in time, and these limits represent the organization's service specification in this dimension.

1.5 Determine Effectiveness Measures

Measures of effectiveness quantify what is actually delivered to customers in comparison to what they required. Two distinct types of effectiveness measures are used (see Chapter 7). One type compares the product or service to its specifications and quantifies the effectiveness of the *process*. Process effectiveness is measured when the product or service is produced. The second type measures the effectiveness of the *product* or *service*. Product or service effectivness shows how well the output satisfies the user, and these data cannot be collected until after the output is delivered to the customer. Examples of the latter type include the typical customer-satisfaction measures compiled by most organizations, as well as other data such as warranty claims, complaints, and customer retention rates. See examples in Table 13.2.

1.6 Design a Data Collection System

Identify sources from which data can be otained and build a database. Three common sources of data on customer satisfaction (product or service effectiveness) are outlined in Table 13.3, and five methods for surveying customers are compared in Table 13.4.

TABLE 13.2	Example Effectiveness Measures	
REQUIREMENTS	**SPECIFICATIONS**	**MEASURES**
Prompt delivery	30 days from order	• Customer complaints for late deliveries • Number of late deliveries • Average delivery time
Correct quantity	No over- or undershipment	• Customer complaints for incorrect quantities • Number of incorrect shipments
etc.		

TABLE 13.3	Three Sources of Customer Satisfaction Data	
INTERNAL	**THIRD-PARTY**	**CUSTOMERS**
Complaints	Independent surveys	Interviews
Warranty claims	Industry analysts	Focus groups
Field-service reports	Trade magazine surveys	Mail surveys
Credits and refunds issued		Telephone surveys
Lost customer reports		Comment cards
Delivery receipts		

TABLE 13.4	Comparison of Customer Survey Methods		
METHOD	**DESCRIPTION**	**PROS**	**CONS**
Interviews	• Ask individual customers for direct feedback.	• Controllable response rate • In-depth data obtained • Can ask clarifying questions	• Expensive • Requires interviewer skills • Requires extensive time
Focus groups	• Assemble 6 to 12 customers. Probe for feedback, and stimulate interaction among participants.	• Controllable response rate • In-depth data obtained • Can ask clarifying questions • Fosters discovery by participants	• Expensive • Requires interviewer skills • Requires group interaction skills
Mail surveys	• Send survey questions to a random list of customers (consider offering incentive to encourage responses).	• Inexpensive • Can reach a large number of customers	• Low response rate • Possible non-response bias • Cannot clarify responses • Difficult to follow up
Telephone surveys	• Telephone a random list of customers.	• High response rate • Can reach a large number of customers • Automated compilation • Rapid analysis possible	• High call-back rate required to ensure integrity of sample
Comment cards	• Provide written response card at point of purchase	• Inexpensive	• Low response rate • Nonrandom sample • Cannot clarify responses or follow up

TABLE 13.5	Sample Customer Satisfaction Survey Instrument				
REQUIREMENTS	**SURVEY QUESTIONS—CIRCLE THE APPROPRIATE RESPONSE**				
	How would you rate us on each requirement?				
Fit and finish	1 Poor	2 Fair	3 OK	4 Good	5 Excellent
Billing accuracy					
Timely delivery					
Product availability					
Price					
Durability					
Reliability					
Responsiveness					
Ease of use					
Primary usage	What is your primary use for this product?				
	1 Business	2 School	3 Home	4 Travel	5 Other
Competitor rating	How would you rate competitor's product? Model: _____				
	1 Poor	2 Fair	3 OK	4 Good	5 Excellent

CAUTION: Your customers are probably bombarded by surveys. Don't waste their time and your money on poorly designed surveys. Ask only what you cannot determine through less intrusive methods. Minimize efforts required to respond, and test your questions before use. Although the design of survey instruments is beyond the scope of this book, an example is illustrated in Table 13.5. Start by listing customers' requirements, and determine the information required to test how well each requirement is satisfied.

1.7 Collect and Analyze Data

Data collected should be compiled and analyzed to determine the extent to which gaps exist, and what those gaps suggest about process or product/service deficiencies. A sample summary is shown in Table 13.6.

1.8 Set New Performance Targets

Even if an organization is meeting all of its customers' requirements, improvement may be required. Complacency is risky. Performance gaps will likely open as competitors innovate and customers' expectations escalate.

In a fiercely competitive marketplace organizations need to know how they stack up against their best competitor and project the future direction of their industry. If an organization knows its advantages over competition, it can exploit competitors' weaknesses while addressing its own performance gaps.

TABLE 13.6	Sample Process Effectiveness Summary

Process: <u>Order fulfillment</u>   Customer Group: <u>Western Region</u>
Product: <u>Model 96-A</u>   Date: _____

REQUIREMENTS	PRIORITY	SPECIFICATIONS	MEASURES	PERFORMANCE	GAP
Correct quantity shipped	2	• As per purchase order—no short orders	• Percentage of correct shipments	95.3	4.7
Timely delivery	1	• 2 business days from order	• Percentage of on-time deliveries	65	35
			• Average time (days)	1.5	—
			• Maximum time (days)	4.0	2.0
Product availability	1	• Available at order—no back orders	• Percentage of orders filled completely	92.1	7.9
Responsive to inquiries	1	• Return calls within 15 minutes	• Percentage of on-time responses	89	11
			• Average time (minutes)	15	—
			• Maximum time (minutes)	30	15

NOTE: Priorities are determined by customers.

Set new performance targets, and assign a time frame in which these new targets will be reached. Set these targets on the basis of existing gaps and projections of industry trends and customers' future expectations.

1.9 Report Findings

Integrate the findings of Step 1 into a status report, and update the team's charter as needed. Communicate findings to all stakeholders, including the team's sponsor. This status report might recommend making a midcourse correction. Preparing a short presentation will help to educate senior managers on the issues and opportunities involved in improving this process.

STEP 2: ASSESS EFFICIENCY

Step 2 is a logical extension of the activities completed in Step 1 to understand the customer. In Step 2 the team turns its attention inward to learn how efficiently the process is capable of satisfying internal requirements for conserving resources. These internal requirements will likely include the need to reduce costs, reduce variation, and reduce cycle time. Efforts might also be directed toward satisfying the needs and expectations of internal customers. The team can assess efficiency by completing Step 2 (Figure 13.3).

2.1 Determine Efficiency Measures

Select efficiency measures that quantify how well the process satisfies internal requirements. Typical indicators include cycle time, unit cost, defect and scrap rates, rework, productivity, asset utilization, and cost of quality.

> **Don't** be a DRIP: <u>D</u>ata <u>R</u>ich but <u>I</u>nformation <u>P</u>oor.

Computer-controlled production facilities can overwhelm any organization with more data than it can handle. An understanding of gaps in meeting the external customer's requirements (Step 1) may help narrow an otherwise huge list of efficiency measures. For instance, if customers complain about late deliveries, perhaps the improvement team should focus on cycle-time reduction. If customers complain about price, perhaps the internal focus needs to be on unit cost. Rank or prioritize these measures, and select the critical ones from the interesting many. A sample of common efficiency measures is listed in Table 13.7.

Efficiency measures are often relative and expressed as ratios or percentages rather than as absolute numbers. Commonly used units include defects per 1,000 units of output, or non-value-added time as a percentage of total cycle time.

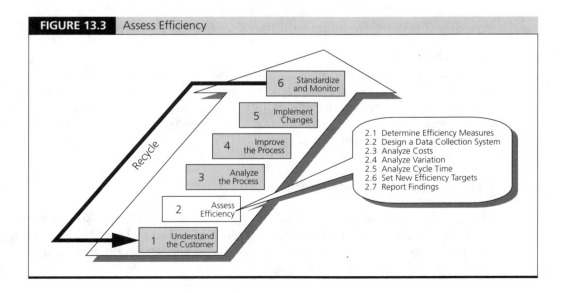

FIGURE 13.3 Assess Efficiency

TABLE 13.7	Common Efficiency Measures

OVERALL

(handwritten annotation: → Fall into one of three categories → Better → Faster → Cheaper)

- Cost
- Output variation
- Cycle time
- Incremental cost added by each work step
- Variation in output conformance to specification
- Time consumed performing each work step

OUTPUT CONFORMANCE

- Defects
- Scrap
- Rework
- Percentage of outputs that are defective or rejected
- Percentage of outputs that are scrapped (not recycled)
- Percentage of outputs that are recycled for repair

PROCESS

- Cost of quality
- Productivity
- Inventory turns
- Asset utilization
- Costs for prevention, detection, and failure of nonconforming outputs
- Quantity produced per employee per unit time
- Frequency of sale and restocking
- Resources used in work processes, including capital, materials, personnel, space, equipment, and materials

INPUTS

- Meet specifications
- On-time deliveries
- Percentage of materials rejected
- Percentage of late deliveries

> *CAUTION: Don't waste your time downgrading sound data on quantities, cost, and time by translating them to arbitrary scales or values—like high, medium, or low. Instead, use the data directly. The only translating required at this stage might be to define relative values between time and costs. Relative scales are more appropriate in Step 3, after integrating your analysis and assigning priorities for action.*

2.2 Design a Data Collection System

With the vast amounts of efficiency data available in most organizations, developing formats for displaying relevant data is usually more important than looking to find additional data. Graphic displays that reveal trends are often perferred solutions.

Determine your sources of efficiency data, and be certain to establish a baseline representing current performance of each key indicator. A sample of a blank worksheet for summarizing efficiency data is shown as Table 13.8.

For processes that are not rich in data, the improvement team may need to launch its own data-gathering program. This is frequently encountered in processes that deliver services—as contrasted to those that produce tangible products. Walking through and observing the process may supply the required data.

Collect data on how the process performs through a technique referred to as a *process walk-through* (see Chapter 10). Using the team charter and list of inefficiencies generated earlier, determine the data you need to gather (see Table 13.9). Observe the process in operation, interview job performers, and take careful notes.

Analysis of efficiency in terms of cost, variation, and cycle time is explained in Steps 2.3, 2.4, and 2.5, respectively. Complete any or all of these steps depending on the team's objectives.

2.3 Analyze Costs

Identify and measure the resources used (costs incurred) for producing and delivering products and services. Consider using *activity-based costing* for attributing costs to each process step. Although a detailed explanation is beyond the scope of this book, an example later in this chapter shows how this method

TABLE 13.8	Sample Efficiency Worksheet

Process: _____

Product: _____   Date: _____

OBJECTIVE	MEASURE	PERFORMANCE	EXPECTATION	GAP	TARGET
Defects	% of rejects				
Scrap	% of total units % of unit costs				
Rework	% of total units Avg. rework cost				
Costs	Avg. unit cost Avg. gross margin				
Cycle time	Avg. days/unit				
Asset utilization	Output units/day Floor space/process				
Productivity	Workhours/unit				
Cost of quality	% of revenues				

TABLE 13.9	Data Collection Through Process Walk-through
SYMPTOM	**NEED TO LEARN**
Low customer satisfaction	• How would *you* rate customer satisfaction? • How frequently do customers complain? • What do they complain about most? Like most? • What percentage of the time are your outputs rejected?
High defect rates	• What percentage of your outputs are defective? • What are the most frequent types of defects? • What appear to be the causes of defects • How much is scrapped or reworked? • How do you measure variation of your outputs?
High cost of quality	• How many inspection points are in the process? • How many approvals do you need to obtain for your work? • How much time is inspecting outputs?
Late deliveries	• What percentage of your outputs is late? • Why are outputs late? • How do *you* think this affects your customers?
Long cycle time	• How long does it take to produce an output? • How much does this time vary? • How much time is wasted?
Poor productivity	• How many people work with you in this subprocess? • How much time do *you* think is spent productively?
Poor asset utilization	• How much floor space is devoted to your subprocess? • What is the total number of outputs produced? • What quantity of raw materials is used? • What other resources are used?
Process problems	• What are your most frequent problems? • Where do they occur? • What might be the cause?

can be used to find high-cost processing steps. Also consider delineating costs associated with assuring quality through use of a checklist like the one shown in Table 13.10.

2.4 Analyze Variation

Analyze the spread of the data (variability) to understand the underlying capabilities of processes and to determine whether limitations and defects are the result of common casues of variation or special causes. Display data graphically to show patterns; alternatively use process capability indices or Motorola's six-sigma values.

TABLE 13.10	Cost of Quality Checklist

PREVENTION (COST OF CONFORMANCE)

Activities designed to prevent poor quality *before* production:
- Design reviews
- Double-checking drawings
- Specification reviews
- Quality audits
- Planning
- Supplier management programs
- Pilot or prototype studies
- Product qualification
- Training
- Process capability studies
- Preventive maintenance

DETECTION (COST OF APPRAISAL)

Activities designed to measure, evaluate, and audit products *during* production:
- Inspection of raw materials
- Inspection of finished products
- Proofreading
- Product audits

FAILURE (COST OF NONCONFORMANCE)

Internal failures:

- Scrap and rework
- Engineering changes
- Corrective action
- Adjustments
- Over- or underproduction
- Redesigns

External failures incurred *after* production:
- Misshipments
- Redeliveries
- Recalls
- Service calls
- Billing adjustments
- Retrofits
- Replacements
- Warranty costs

LOST CUSTOMERS/OPPORTUNITY (COST OF NONCONFORMANCE)

Costs incurred when customers do not reorder or when they buy from competitors:

- Lost customers
- Lost revenues
- Lost goodwill

2.5 Analyze Cycle Time

Calculate the elapsed time in each activity and subprocess. Identify the non-value-added activities, business value-added activities, and real value-added activities, and allocate the associated cycle times among these categories. Identify opportunities to eliminate non-value-added, minimize business value-added, and streamline real value-added activities.

2.6 Set New Efficiency Targets

Identify your industry's best performers, and learn how efficiently they perform as part of your plan for setting targets. Compare current performance to these benchmarks, calculate gaps, and set improvement targets for each efficiency measure. Table 13.11 provides a sample of a partially completed worksheet that displays the results of these analyses.

2.7 Report Findings

As with Step 1, integrate the findings of Step 2 into a status report, and update the team's charter as needed. Communicate findings to all stakeholders, including the team's sponsor.

TABLE 13.11	Partially Completed Efficiency Worksheet

Process: Order fulfillment
Product: Model 96-A   Date: _____

OBJECTIVE	MEASURE	PERFORMANCE	EXPECTATION	GAP	TARGET
Defects	% of rejects	4.0	0.02	3.98	1.0
Scrap	% of total units	1.5	0.5	1.0	
	% of unit costs	3.8	2.3	1.5	
Rework	% of total units	5.7%	4.0%	1.7%	
	Avg. cost of rework	$11	$6	$5	
Costs	Avg. unit cost	$109	$100	$9	
	Avg. gross margin	29	40	11	
Cycle time	Avg. days/unit	3.4	2.3	1.1	
Asset utilization	Output units/day	250	325	75	
	Floor space/process	18 sq. ft.	10 sq. ft.	8 sq. ft.	
Productivity	Workhours/unit	275	220	55	
Cost of quality	% of revenues	8.0	2.5	5.5	

STEP 3: ANALYZE THE PROCESS

The information compiled in the first two steps should provide the team with a comprehensive performance assessment of its targeted process. The team now needs to set a course of action for improvement that provides the greatest benefits. This can be accomplished by completing Step 3 (Figure 13.4).

3.1 Assess Process Condition

The team can determine overall process condition by integrating the team's assessments of effectiveness (Step 1) and efficiency (Step 2) with a pair of five-point scales (see Chapter 11). The composite score will yield a qualitative rating in one of six categories: unhealthy, fair, satisfactory, healthy, superior, or world-class. The size of the improvement opportunity will generally be larger for processes rated in poorer categories.

3.2 Prioritize Improvement Opportunities

Set priorities for improvement projects by considering both the importance and size of performance gaps (see Chapter 11).

3.3 Prioritize Subprocess Opportunities

Core-process improvement (CPI) can progress at either of two levels: at the core-process level or at the subprocess level. For example, if a CPI team is trying to improve responsiveness by reducing cycle time and determines that most of the elapsed time is concentrated in one certain subprocess, that subprocess should be

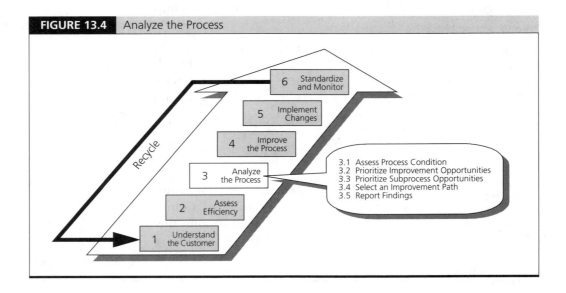

FIGURE 13.4 Analyze the Process

targeted for improvement. The CPI team representative from the function in which the subprocess resides would likely be asked to commission an improvement team. This subteam would develop its own charter and report to the broader CPI team.

The CPI team representative would likely be the leader. Members would include individuals who work in the targeted area. Posing the following questions should help determine who needs to join the subteam:

- Who knows most about the process?
- Who is available to work in the required time?
- What specialists do we need (e.g., scribes, chart makers, technicians, statistical analysts, quality experts)?

Note: The concept of commissioning subteams under a wider core-process improvement team offers a structure for harnessing the talents of all employees in a way that quality circles could not. Working on a subteam addressing issues for the CPI team lends the importance, legitimacy, and support from management that quality circles usually lacked.

3.4 Select an Improvement Path

Select an improvement path for each process at any given time based on the size of performance gaps, the potential opportunity for improvement, and the relative difficulty expected for the improvement effort (see Chapter 12). Choices of paths are

- *Continuous improvement* on an ongoing basis for incremental gains. The magnitude of these gains should not be expected to improve performance above the process condition band determined in substep 3.1 without repeated reapplication (proceed to Step 4).
- *Benchmarking* periodically for larger gains that should be sufficient to propel the process condition up one level (go to Chapter 14).
- *Reengineering* selectively to achieve dramatic breakthroughs that offer the potential of rocketing the process condition up more than one level (go to Chapter 15).

3.5 Report Findings

As with Steps 1 and 2, summarize the analysis completed in Step 3 in a status report, and update the team's charter as needed. Communicate findings to all stakeholders, including the team's sponsor. At this point the team will be recommending a definitive course for action. Therefore, be certain to secure a clear understanding of support and a firm commitment to proceed. If the direction is unclear, or if your sponsor's commitment is not resolute, *stop*!

STEP 4: IMPROVE THE PROCESS

Continuous improvement is also known by the Japanese term *kaizen*. It relies on building a fundamental understanding of customers' requirements, process capability, and the root cause for any gaps between them. Hypotheses are developed and tested, and improvement gained through the cycle of plan-do-study-act. This is a systematic approach as opposed to the classic short-cut of problem detection and subsequent solving—an approach resembling plan-do-plan-do (Tenner and DeToro, 1992, 124).

The sequence of improvement activities will depend on the project's objective. For example, a team working to improve responsiveness could reduce cycle time by eliminating non-value-added activities, minimizing business value-added activities, and reducing the time required to perform real value-added tasks. If improving product or service quality is the objective, then efforts would focus on minimizing variation, errors, and defects. Similarly, if price is a competitive disadvantage, then cost reduction could be pursued using activity-based costing.

Regardless of the improvement objectives, project teams should adhere to four basic principles:

1. *Attack the vital few*. You will find numerous things to improve, but don't be distracted from addressing those few that are the most important.

2. *Diagnose root causes*. Don't merely seek the cause of the limitation, but look for the underlying root cause.

3. *Understand sources of variation*. Recognize two fundamental sources of variation—common causes and special causes—and use the correct approach to eliminate or minimize the identified source.

4. *Plan-do-study-act*. Test and verify that the root cause attributed to the limitation is in fact correct. Design experiments to test your hypothesis.

Example of Cycle-Time Reduction

Chapter 8 presented cycle-time reduction as a weapon for gaining a strategic advantage. Many firms have pursued cycle-time reduction because it is relatively easy for employees to recognize wasted time and because it offers a beneficial side effect—reduced costs. Corporations pursing cycle-time reduction on a large scale include the following:

- Texas Instruments has a *2X Program* to reduce current cycle times to less than two times the theoretical minimum time they should take.

- Xerox has a *A Delta T Program*, which calls on all employees to reduce the delta (difference) between the *a*ctual time and the *t*heoretical time taken to complete work.

- ABB has a *T50 Program*, which is driving for a 50 percent reduction in cycle time in all its processes worldwide.

Cycle-time reduction is as good a place as any to use as a starting point; explanations on reducing variation and costs will follow later in the chapter. The process for filling a customer's orders serves as an example, and key points for reducing cycle time are illustrated in Figure 13.5. This chart was constructed through the following sequence:

1. Prepare a *flowchart* that displays every step in the process. Note that processes with alternative branches from decision points sometimes require completing the analysis for each branch separately. Additionally, note that this figure deliberately strays from conventional flowchart symbols and uses octogons (representative of a stop sign) to highlight non-value-added steps.

2. Estimate the *total elapsed time* for each step. Alternative sets of measurements include typical times, averages, or ranges—normal minimum to normal maximum. Regardless of the specific set adopted, the elapsed time *begins* as soon as the input enters one step and *ends* when the output is received at the next step in the process. The example shown in Figure 13.5 uses typical times for each step.

3. *Categorize* the purpose of each step as real value-added (RVA), business value-added (BVA), or non-valued-added (NVA). Refer back to Chapter 8 for an explanation of each category.

4. *Enter* the time required to complete each step in a column on a worksheet according to its assigned category.

5. *Add* total times for each category, and calculate cycle-time efficiency by dividing RVA by the total cycle time.

The analysis illustrated in Figure 13.5 offers a springboard to the order-fulfillment improvement team charged with reducing the cycle time. What were some of the team's observations? First, total cycle time is nearly seven hours and includes less than two hours (30 percent) of value-added activities. Second, a 50 percent improvement could be achieved by eliminating two non-value-added steps—*correcting errors* in order processing and *sending orders to distribution*. Furthermore, elimination of errors will enable removal of yet another step—*order approval*—a business value-added activity that consumes another 5 percent of total cycle time.

The team's first efforts were directed at removing the order-approval and error-correction steps. Simply eliminating these steps reduces cycle time by one-third but does nothing to ensure that the orders are correct. Therefore, before eliminating these steps, the team needed to understand why order-entry errors occur and how they could be prevented.

Attack the Vital Few
Dr. Joseph M. Juran believes that a fundamental law of nature dictates that 80 percent of the problems are the result of 20 percent of the causes. One key to improvement is to identify those crucial 20 percent and focus attention on them. Juran

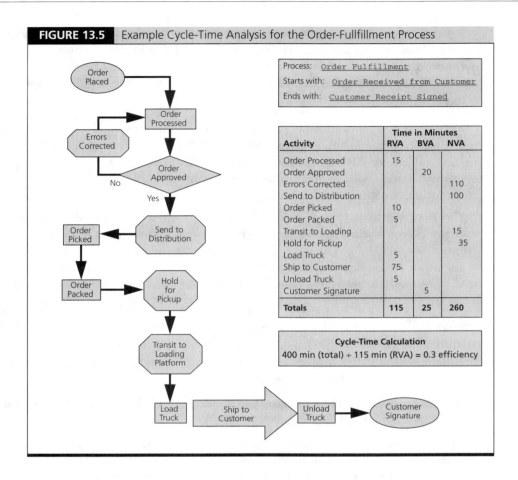

FIGURE 13.5   Example Cycle-Time Analysis for the Order-Fullfillment Process

Process: Order Fulfillment
Starts with: Order Received from Customer
Ends with: Customer Receipt Signed

Activity	Time in Minutes		
	RVA	BVA	NVA
Order Processed	15		
Order Approved		20	
Errors Corrected			110
Send to Distribution			100
Order Picked	10		
Order Packed	5		
Transit to Loading			15
Hold for Pickup			35
Load Truck	5		
Ship to Customer	75		
Unload Truck	5		
Customer Signature		5	
Totals	**115**	**25**	**260**

Cycle-Time Calculation
400 min (total) ÷ 115 min (RVA) = 0.3 efficiency

named this concept, which represents a maldistribution of quality losses, in honor of Vilfredo Pareto, a nineteenth-century Italian economist. Pareto found a large share of wealth was owned by a relatively few people—a maldistribution of wealth. The Pareto analysis is a method for categorizing and recategorizing causes until the vital few are found (Tenner and DeToro, 1992, 118).

To find the most important source of order-entry errors, a team member recorded errors according to their type on a check sheet (Figure 13.6). The results were then plotted on a Pareto-like bar chart that revealed that the entry of price is the most common type, accounting for nearly one-half of the fifty-four errors identified in the 500 orders prepared over a thirty-day period.

Diagnose Root Causes

Kaoru Ishikawa suggests that the first signs of a problem are its symptoms and not its causes. Actions taken on symptoms cannot be permanently effective. It is necessary to

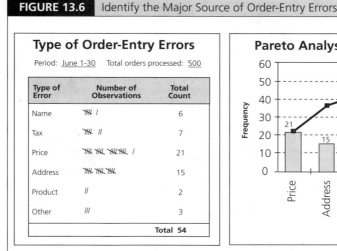
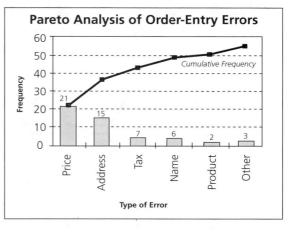

FIGURE 13.6 Identify the Major Source of Order-Entry Errors

understand and act on the underlying root causes. *Cause-and-effect diagrams, fishbone charts*, and *Ishikawa diagrams* are synonyms for a basic tool that can be used to help differentiate among symptoms, causes, and root causes (Tenner and DeToro, 1992, 124).

Having identified incorrect pricing as the most frequent source of order-entry errors, a fishbone chart can be used to identify the underlying causes of the problem (see Figure 13.7). A horizontal straight line (spine) is drawn from a box (head) in which the symptom that is being diagnosed is written. Ribs are drawn from the spine—hence the name fishbone—that identify the major sources that can contribute to the problem of incorrect pricing. Detailed factors are then added to the ribs.

The major sources were classically termed the five M's: *men, machines, materials, methods,* and *measurements*. More recently these terms have been replaced by *people, procedures, equipment, materials,* and *environment*. This last category includes physical contributors like temperature and pressure, as well as cultural and organizational ones.

The order-fulfillment improvement team brainstormed to try to identify all causes and the causes of these causes. As general guidance, a team should ask *why* five times in order to penetrate to the potential root causes. A team should spend several hours at this task, perhaps adding hundreds of causes to their diagram.

Drawing the chart is only a small piece of the job. Next the team needs to narrow the array of causes down to the one (or a few) true root causes. For simple problems, this can sometimes be accomplished by a brief discussion and voting by members. More complex problems, however, will require more work. In some cases

Ishikawa Diagram

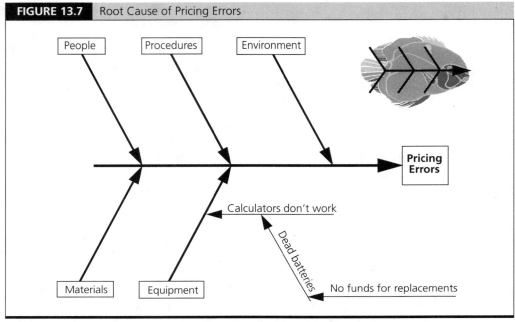

FIGURE 13.7   Root Cause of Pricing Errors

the team will be able to find the root causes after gathering and analyzing additional data. In other cases, finding the root causes might take months and involve formal experimentation. For more information, refer to Leitnaker, Sanders, and Hild's book, *The Power of Statistical Thinking* (1996).

The team discovered that errors in entering prices were caused by inadequate funding. As a consequence, batteries were not purchased for the sales representatives' pocket calculators. Hand-calculated prices were principal contributors to errors. As a solution, the team is considering either revising the funding process or replacing battery-dependent calculators with solar-powered ones.

Understand Sources to Reduce Variation

Everyone makes decisions daily based on his or her interpretation of observed variation. Traffic has been heavier on the bridge on Fridays: should I take the by-pass today? Sales have been higher in each of the last three months: is this a trend indicating that we should increase production capacity? My stock has reached a new high: is it time to sell? Inflation has increased in four of the last six months: should the federal government tighten credit to control it?

We are looking for a signal that something has changed, and we are often looking for this signal among data points that always seem to jump around anyhow. Technically speaking, we are looking to attribute variation in the patterns observed to either of two types of sources. In the preceding examples we were looking to identify or confirm some sort of *special* cause—an incident or series of identifiable events that are outside of (or new to) the system. Alternatively, variation is the result of *common* causes—chronic small changes that are part of the system and occur randomly within predictable bounds.

A process that has only common causes affecting its outcome is called a *stable* process and is said to be in a state of statistical control. A process that is affected by both common and special causes is called an *unstable* process because its variation is unpredictable from one period to the next (Nolan, 1990, 70).

Dr. W. Edward Deming explained that all variation is caused and that the causes can be classified. Common causes are inherent within the system and yield random variation within predictable bounds. Special causes are assignable to specific reasons or events and result in sporadic variation that defies prediction (Tenner and DeToro, 1992, 119).

Making the right decision on controlling variation requires knowing its source, since appropriate actions differ according to the source—or type—of variation. Common causes (stable process) can be eliminated only by addressing the underlying system. On the other hand, special causes (unstable process) are removed by acting on their specific, identifiable source. Being able to distinguish between stable and unstable processes is essential before beginning improvement activities: continually adjusting a stable process actually increases variation and makes the process worse.

But how do we know the source of the variation, so that we can take appropriate action? The answer can be determined from control charts, a tool developed by Walter Shewhart in the 1930s. The control chart (illustrated in Figure 13.8) is typically constructed by plotting data values (e.g., length, width, temperature, size, cost, or frequency of errors) on the vertical axis and time along the horizontal axis. In addition to a line connecting the data points, the control chart includes three horizontal lines. One line represents the average value of the data points, and the other two are the upper (UCL) and lower (LCL) control limits. These three lines are based on a statistical analysis of the process's performance. Refer to Leitnaker, Sanders, and Hild's *The Power of Statistical Thinking* (1996) for a complete explanation on how to construct control charts.

Figure 13.9 displays five examples of chart patterns and possible meanings behind them. Of these five, only the first represents a stable process. Each

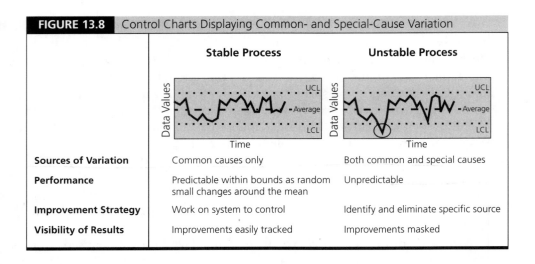

FIGURE 13.8   Control Charts Displaying Common- and Special-Cause Variation

	Stable Process	**Unstable Process**
Sources of Variation	Common causes only	Both common and special causes
Performance	Predictable within bounds as random small changes around the mean	Unpredictable
Improvement Strategy	Work on system to control	Identify and eliminate specific source
Visibility of Results	Improvements easily tracked	Improvements masked

of the remaining four examples exhibit variation attributable to an assignable special cause. Another pattern indicative of special causes is exhibited when data points exceed either control limit, as shown for the unstable process in Figure 13.8.

For unstable processes, corrective action begins by bringing the process into control by removing special causes of variation. This is usually accomplished through problem-solving techniques and root-cause analysis. Some quality programs popularized in the 1980s trained employees to find and remove special causes.

Even if all special causes are removed, the range of variation may still be unacceptable. For example, a corporation's expenditures may be in statistical control, with annual costs exhibiting random variation within a range of ±15 percent. But what if management demands that costs remain within 10 percent of budget? Rather than recognizing that their processes may be incapable of meeting the goal, managers may burden the organization with endless reconciliation of every item or incident exceeding their 10 percent limit. If managers are not aware that common-cause variation must be addressed, they may wait in vain for quality teams to generate improvements that never come. Rather, they must either redesign the process or revise their expectations (refer back to Chapter 8 for an explanation of process capability, capability indices, and six-sigma analysis).

Example of Variation Reduction

In the example of cycle-time reduction in the order-fulfillment process, the team determined that order-approval and error-correction steps should be removed.

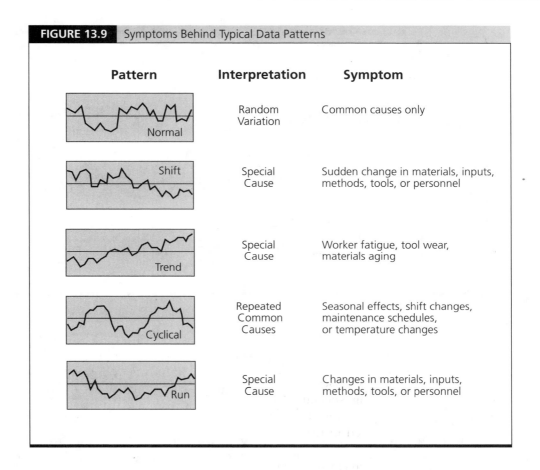

FIGURE 13.9 Symptoms Behind Typical Data Patterns

Pattern	Interpretation	Symptom
Normal	Random Variation	Common causes only
Shift	Special Cause	Sudden change in materials, inputs, methods, tools, or personnel
Trend	Special Cause	Worker fatigue, tool wear, materials aging
Cyclical	Repeated Common Causes	Seasonal effects, shift changes, maintenance schedules, or temperature changes
Run	Special Cause	Changes in materials, inputs, methods, tools, or personnel

Team members next faced the task of error proofing the process to allow these steps to be removed. Recall that they found nearly one-half of the errors could be eliminated by ensuring that the sales representatives had working calculators to enter correct pricing data. But this is only the first stage of improvement. How do they go about eliminating the rest of the errors?

Figure 13.10 displays the number of order-entry errors detected each week. The mean, UCL, and LCL are based on a statistical analysis of the error rate and are redrawn each time the process changes. This chart provides a clear picture of the trends of improvement efforts, and confirms the successful attack on pricing errors at the end of stage 1.

Work continued, and in stage 2 the team found sporadic episodes of high error rates (special causes of variation). Perhaps they were attributed to a particular office, and training was instituted to correct the specific problems. In stage 3, the

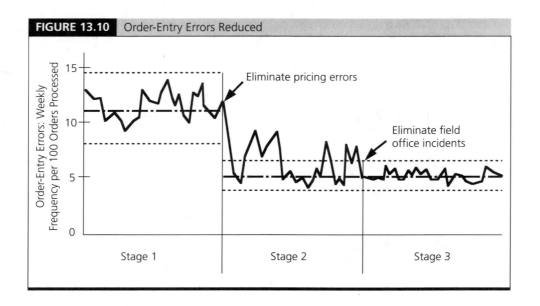

FIGURE 13.10   Order-Entry Errors Reduced

team will again focus on attacking common causes within the system. As in stage 1, the team will construct Pareto charts to find the most important types of errors and then look for root causes using a fishbone chart. Changes will be implemented, and work will continue until errors have been either eliminated or reduced to a low enough level to permit removal of the approval and error-correction steps.

The improvement stages followed by the order-fulfillment improvement team in this example typify the natural sequence for reducing variation. The steps outlined in Table 13.12 are offered as general guidance to any improvement team working to reduce variation.

> *NOTE: Readers interested in six-sigma analysis (refer to Appendix B) will note that this process was initially rated at 2.7. This rating was determined by interpolation in Figure B.1 (the average of 11 errors per 100 orders processed is equal to 1,100 errors per 10,000 opportunities). In stage 2, the performance rating was improved to 3.1 (the average of 5 errors per 100 orders is equal to 500 errors per 10,000 opportunities).*

Example of Cost Reduction

When costs need to be reduced, most managers think it would be a simple task to run a cost analysis to determine where costs are incurred. Although their analysis might be simple, it wouldn't necessarily reveal the type of cost information needed. Don't be surprised if your organization lacks a complete understanding of where costs are incurred to produce your current slate of products or services. The reason behind this information deficiency rests with typical accounting systems that were built to determine the

TABLE 13.12	Sequence of Steps for Reducing Variation		
WHAT	**HOW**	**WHO**	**OPPORTUNITY**
1. **Stabilize the process.**	Eliminate special causes until the process is in control.	Employees working in the process	6%
2. **Redesign the process.**	Reduce common-cause variation.	Managers who own the process	94%
3. **Monitor and continuously improve.**	Track performance, investigate and eliminate special causes, and redesign to minimize common causes.	Everyone	100%

costs of running a department or functional unit but not the cost of outputs produced by that unit. Questions naturally arise when reducing costs and improving margins:

- What is the real cost of our output?
- What are our real margins?
- How can we provide this output for less cost?
- Where are we incurring the most cost?
- Which processes or subprocesses are contributing the most cost?
- Where can we best trim expense?

When the order-fulfillment improvement team eliminates non-value-added activities, minimizes business value-added activities, and streamlines real value-added activities, they will likely have already made significant progress in reducing costs. After all, the removal of non-value-added activities automatically reduces the need for labor, facilities, equipment, and other related expense items. Depending on priorities (refer back to Chapters 11 and 12), at some point in time it is appropriate to address costs directly.

To find where to focus cost-reduction efforts, consider using *activity-based costing*. Traditional accounting places costs in various expense categories and enables calculating the cost of products by dividing the total cost by the number of units produced. But how accurately are costs allocated among different types of outputs, and how well does the traditional method account for the cost of each step or subprocess? Activity-based costing overcomes these limitations by allocating costs to process steps (see Figure 13.11).

Activity-based costing enables a team to analyze costs in the same way that it analyzed cycle time. This technique can be used to gain new insights into improvement opportunities by spotting high-cost activities and establishing yardsticks by which progress can be measured. Although details of activity-based costing are

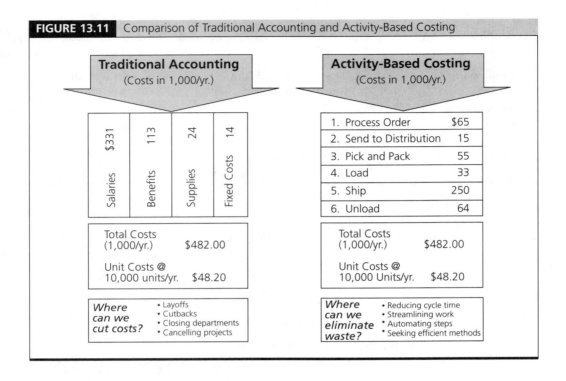

FIGURE 13.11 Comparison of Traditional Accounting and Activity-Based Costing

Traditional Accounting
(Costs in 1,000/yr.)

Salaries	Benefits	Supplies	Fixed Costs
$331	113	24	14

Total Costs
(1,000/yr.) $482.00

Unit Costs @
10,000 units/yr. $48.20

Where can we cut costs?	• Layoffs • Cutbacks • Closing departments • Cancelling projects

Activity-Based Costing
(Costs in 1,000/yr.)

1. Process Order	$65
2. Send to Distribution	15
3. Pick and Pack	55
4. Load	33
5. Ship	250
6. Unload	64

Total Costs
(1,000/yr.) $482.00

Unit Costs @
10,000 Units/yr. $48.20

Where can we eliminate waste?	• Reducing cycle time • Streamlining work • Automating steps • Seeking efficient methods

beyond the scope of this book, the approach can be illustrated through an example. Readers interested in more information should refer to *Activity-Based Costing for Small and Medium-Sized Businesses and an Implementation Guide* by Douglas T. Hicks, John Wiley, New York, 1992.

The order-fulfillment improvement team dissected their cost components and allocated an appropriate portion to each step in their process. Their cost components included such items as

- Materials,
- Personnel (including salary plus benefits),
- Equipment, and
- Facilities (including utilities).

The team then listed the cost for each process step on a worksheet like the one illustrated in Table 13.13. Although this rough-cut analysis did not provide extremely accurate costs, it was sufficient for its purpose. In this example, the highest-cost step *(ship to customer)* also consumes the most cycle time. The team's next stage of improvement activities will focus on this step.

TABLE 13.13	Cost-Reduction Worksheet

Process: Order Fulfillment   Date: _____

| | CYCLE TIME IN MINUTES | | | COST |
ACTIVITY	RVA	BVA	NVA	(THOUSANDS/YR.)
Order processed	15			$65
~~Order approved~~ ~~Errors corrected~~	—	—	—	—
~~Send to distribution~~			100	15
Order picked	10			25
Order packed	5			25
Transit to loading			15	5
Hold for pickup			35	3
Load truck	5			30
Ship to customer	75			250
Unload truck	5			34
Customer signature		5		30
Totals	115	5	150	$482

Plan-Do-Study-Act

Ideas for improvement must address the root causes of the problem, regardless of whether efforts are focused on reducing cycle time, variation, or costs. Develop new and different ways to design and operate the process to eliminate the root causes of its limitations. All of the activities in Steps 1, 2, and 3 were *planning*.

Step 4 is the time to *do* something. Design and conduct experiments to test the hypotheses of underlying root causes. Also, design experiments to test the ideas for eliminating these causes before implementing them as solutions.

Study the results of the tests and experiments. When tests fail to produce the desired results, determine the cause. Was the test invalid? Was the improvement idea ineffective? Were you mistaken about the root causes of the problem? Were measurements inaccurate or taken on the wrong parameters? Was the process completely identified? Were the customer's requirements misunderstood? Recycle back to the appropriate step on the process improvement road map before continuing.

Act to complete the cycle by implementing the proven improvements by advancing to Steps 5 and 6.

STEPS 5 AND 6: IMPLEMENT CHANGES, AND STANDARDIZE AND MONITOR

Actions required in Steps 5 and 6 are common to all improvement efforts—continuous improvement, benchmarking, and reengineering—and are covered in Chapter 16. Key activities pertinent to continuous improvement include the following:

- *Pilot the improved process.* Test the new process in a scaled-down version or test critical facets to identify unanticipated problems. Make appropriate adjustments after evaluating results of the pilot test.

- *Implement plans.* Install the improved process, manage the changeover, and update documentation.

- *Monitor results.* Track performance, monitor cycle time, costs, and variation. Continue to measure customer satisfaction.

- *Reward participants.* Reward and recognize successful team contributions.

- *Identify next steps.* Define where the next increment of improvement will be obtained, and repeat the improvement cycle to sustain your competitive edge.

SUMMARY

Continuous improvement of an existing process is the easiest and most often selected improvement path. Whether processes require the added benefit gained from benchmarking and reengineering is sometimes open to discussion, but no one should assume that their process is so perfect that it could not at least benefit from continuous improvement. This chapter provides a six-step methodology with application suggestions to guide a team through a continuous improvement project.

DISCUSSION QUESTIONS

1. Pick one process in your organization that requires improvement. Describe how you would do the following:

   a. Define its performance gaps in terms of effectiveness and efficiency.

   b. Determine priorities for reducing, cycle time, variation, and cost.

2. Answer either a, b, or c for the process selected in question 1:

   a. For *cycle-time* reduction prepare a worksheet showing real value-added, business value-added, and non-value-added activities, and explain where you would begin to reduce cycle time.

   b. For *variation* reduction explain whether you first need to eliminate special causes of variation, or reduce common causes.

   c. For *cost* reduction prepare a worksheet showing costs attributable to each activity, and explain where you would begin to reduce costs.

3. Describe how you would do the following for the improvement project described in question 2:

a. Identify the most important factors that limit performance.

b. Identify the root causes underlying each factor.

c. Design an experiment to confirm each root cause.

REFERENCES

Leitnaker, M., R. Sanders, and C. Hild. 1996. *The Power of Statistical Thinking*. Reading, MA: Addison-Wesley.

Hicks, D. T. 1992. *Activity-Based Costing for Small- and Medium-Sized Businesses and an Implementation Guide*. New York: John Wiley.

Nolan, T. W., and L. P. Provost. 1990. "Understanding Variation." *Quality Progress* (May), 70.

Tenner, A. R., and I. J. DeToro. 1992. *Total Quality Management: Three Steps to Continuous Improvement*. Reading, MA: Addison-Wesley.

14 | Process Benchmarking

BENCHMARKING ORIGINS

The practice of comparing one's products and services to those of competitors has been used for decades. Extension of the concept to encompass a comparison of processes represented a breakthrough by Dr. Robert Camp in a project conducted at Xerox in 1983. Camp (1989) documented his experience in his book *Benchmarking: The Search for Industry Best Practices That Lead to Superior Performance*. Camp was the first to describe the concept and its application, thereby enabling others to dramatically improve their business performance. His contributions to this chapter are gratefully acknowledged.

Benchmarking's roots can be traced back to *reverse engineering*, where competitors' products were purchased and compared. These samples were literally torn apart to determine the technology employed, methods of construction, component costs, and performance features. This is still a common practice for understanding differences between products, as is its companion technique the *mystery shopper*, which samples and compares competitors' services.

Chrysler used reverse engineering to develop their world-class LH cars in the early 1990s by targeting the best features in competing vehicles and incorporating those best features in its LH models. "Recognizing that no single car does everything the best, the Chrysler team picked the best in each category and tried to make the LH at least as good" ("Chrysler Targets Best," 1992, 1).

Chrysler emulated the Acura Legend's smooth and powerful 200-horsepower engine, the tight and quiet body of Nissan's Maxima, the interior roominess of the Ford Taurus, Pontiac Bonneville, and Lexus LS 400, and the ride and handling of the Ford Taurus, Chevy Lumina, Nissan Maxima, BMW 5-series, Audi 100, and Mercedes S-class. Chrysler emulated the BMW 7-series air conditioning and heating systems to provide "airy comfort in any weather" ("Chrysler Targets Best," 1992, 1).

Their new LH models offered the best competitive features and were successfully launched, but was Chrysler shooting behind the duck? If the features it emulated in the design phase were already in the marketplace, how could they know if its competitors would not advance beyond Chrysler when its LH models finally hit the market?

Reverse engineering alone is insufficient to provide the information needed to significantly improve performance. It misses the more important issue of understanding the means by which competitors developed superior features and capabilities in the first place. After all, the competitors had already launched models with these better features. It might be better to understand and develop a process to produce these superior features, as opposed to simply emulating the features themselves.

COMPETITIVE BENCHMARKING

This time-lag deficiency of reverse engineering pushed firms to compare themselves to their competitors not by reverse engineering alone but also by comparing a broad range of performance measurements. Thus, firms compared their new product-development cycle times to their competitors' times. When a competitor had shorter new-product-development times, the shorter time became the "benchmark" the firm adopted. When firms compared their use of assets and discovered their chief competitor had a higher return on assets (ROA), the competitor's higher return became the new target.

This formal concept of *competitive benchmarking* was developed and used extensively by Xerox Corporation in the early 1980s. At that time, Xerox faced a serious threat from competent foreign competitors that were offering the same products at much lower prices. In the late 1970s, Xerox was stunned to learn that the market they had created and dominated for two decades was suddenly being satisfied by others. The leases on copiers Xerox had placed in customers' offices were being canceled in such large numbers that the very survival of Xerox was in question.

To its credit, Xerox mustered a task force of their best and brightest specialists to verify the threat as something other than a case of dumping or a violation of their patents. Once verified with the help of its Japanese affiliate, Fuji-Xerox, Xerox conducted a series of studies on the performance secured by competition across a broad spectrum of business activities. These superior performance attributes became benchmarks that Xerox challenged themselves to achieve.

As Xerox progressed in redesigning its business to meet the competitive threat, it made two important discoveries:

- Competitors were not superior to Xerox in every facet of their business operations. Even when competition had superior performance, it was not sufficient for Xerox to simply emulate that performance. Xerox, having been surprised once by competition, wanted to surpass its competitors and achieve even higher levels of performance.

- Simply knowing the levels—benchmarks—others had attained in key business activities was insufficient to drive improvement. This knowledge helped to identify gaps but didn't offer insight into how to close them.

PROCESS BENCHMARKING

Xerox learned that giving people demanding targets without providing an understanding how to achieve that target was not constructive. This became apparent in one of the earliest studies at Xerox. Dr. Camp, working in the logistical and distribution organization, conducted a study of the best practices of the picking and packing operations at Xerox. His study uncovered a highly unlikely but profoundly significant benchmarking partner—L. L. Bean.

Although in a completely different industry, Camp found that Xerox and L. L. Bean were identical in the picking and packing functions they performed. Both had a variety of sizes and configurations of their merchandise. Xerox handled small electronic components and machines the size of a desk, and L. L. Bean picked and packed knives and canoes. Both firms had manual inventory systems, and both workforces were unionized. Xerox and Camp (1989, 285) concluded that L. L. Bean was approximately 300 percent more productive than Xerox in picking and packing and that their practices were transferable to Xerox. But Camp didn't leave it there. He went on to study and document the work steps and practices that L. L. Bean used that resulted in its superior performance.

This understanding of the picking and packing *process* enabled Xerox to compare its processes to L. L. Bean's and identify differences. These superior techniques discovered by Camp were incorporated in the revised Xerox process with a dramatically beneficial effect. This experience taught Xerox that benchmarks are important to understand what is possible but insufficient to change performance. Process understanding is also required to fundamentally alter an organization's work practices. Thus, Camp (1995) made an important distinction between benchmarks and benchmark*ing* and has further elaborated this point in his more recent book on *Business Process Benchmarking*.

BENCHMARKING DEFINED

Process benchmarking is defined as "finding and implementing best practices that lead to superior performance" (Camp, 1995). This deceptively simple definition may cause management to underestimate the effort required to successfully complete a study. Consider that a benchmarking study first requires that you know and document the current methods by which you perform the work targeted for improvement, that you define the specific products or services produced by this work, that you know your customers and their specific requirements, and that measures have been defined that describe the work. This process understanding rarely exists, and a team of five people working one-third of their time may require four months to complete a typical benchmarking project—not a trivial exercise.

TABLE 14.1	Ten-Step Benchmarking Model

PLANNING

1. Identify the benchmark subject.
2. Identify benchmark partners.
3. Collect data.

ANALYSIS

4. Determine the gap.
5. Project future performance.

INTEGRATION

6. Communicate results.
7. Establish goals.

ACTION

8. Develop action plans.
9. Implement plans and monitor results.
10. Recalibrate benchmarks.

SOURCE: Adapted from Camp (1995, 20).

To maximize the likelihood for a successful study, Camp provides a ten-step benchmarking road map (Table 14.1). Other benchmarking proponents have combined the original ten steps differently—in four-, six-, seven-, or eight-step models—but they all cover Camp's steps in one fashion or another (Camp, 1995, 9). We will use Camp's approach, since it is the most widely accepted.

PLANNING

STEP 1: IDENTIFY THE BENCHMARK SUBJECT

Considering the time and resources required to complete a typical benchmarking project, an organization is limited in the number of projects that it can afford. The challenge is to select those improvement opportunities for which benchmarking can provide the most significant advantage. Chapters 11 and 12 provided tools and techniques for identifying the benchmarking subject and documenting it in a project description.

Once the processes have been selected for the improvement study, the team needs to describe how the work is currently performed by preparing detailed flowcharts. This documentation helps the team to build consensus on how the work is actually performed, cycle time, costs, and errors created in the current workflow. This understanding is essential, since a comparison to a superior system will not reveal deficiencies in the current system unless such understanding and documentation exists.

Various techniques can be used to graphically describe work. Methods range from a pictorial representation of the steps captured in a manner similar to the way a comic strip develops a story line or with one of the more common flowcharting tools described in Chapter 10. Using common flowcharting symbols makes inter-company comparisons easier, since many firms use these conventions. Conventional flowcharting can also help to overcome language problems when comparing organizations on a worldwide basis.

STEP 2: IDENTIFY BENCHMARK PARTNERS

Once the scope of the benchmarking project has been defined, the next step is to identify the comparative organizations with which the team should benchmark. Which organizations have the best practices that the team can emulate? Although the answer to this question varies for each individual benchmarking study, four sources are common to all studies and should be examined in sequence:

1. *Internal:* Most organizations include other departments that perform identical or similar work to the benchmarking team. In these cases, the first benchmarking partners should be internal. Technical training, for example, is usually only one of many types of training provided by an organization. Other training programs might cover management, sales, computer use, communications, and specific job skills. If our benchmarking project is directed at improving the technical training curriculum development process, then all of these other types of training must be included in our study, since they may employ some practices that the benchmarking team could adopt.

   Corporations comprised of many separate companies—like Asea Brown Bavaria (1,400), Johnson and Johnson (168), or General Electric (78)—will find even richer opportunities to benchmark internally, since another group within the corporate family will likely have a best practice that may be useful to the benchmarking team.

2. *Competitive:* Benchmarking competitors is an essential part of any comparison. Recognize that benchmarking is not industrial espionage but industrial information gathering. Anticipating a few caution signs will allow pursuit of information in an ethical and legal manner. In fact, public-domain information is so extensive that a competitor's best practices can sometimes be determined without direct contact. Some of these public sources are listed in Step 3, Collect Data. Detailed searching techniques are beyond the scope of this book but are explained in other books, including those written by benchmarking's leading authority, R. C. Camp.

   The difficulties of benchmarking competitors are eliminated by participating in joint studies conducted by a third party. A consultant or industry trade association may be retained to collect, analyze, and publish industry-wide information. This approach protects the individual sources.

The key to avoiding legal and ethical problems when engaging a direct benchmarking exchange with competitors is to focus on *process* information and not *business* data. For example, discuss the rate of billing errors, cost, or cycle time per thousand invoices, or compare process steps or computer technology employed. On the other hand, don't ask for the number of products sold per invoice, the revenue value of each invoice, or the number of invoices per accounting period. *Don't ask for information that you're unwilling to provide.*

The Benchmarking Code of Conduct developed by the International Benchmarking Clearing House (n.d.) has facilitated benchmarking studies. This code describes the nature of a benchmarking exchange that should take place between partners and covers such items as the legality, confidentially, and use of information collected. A copy of *The Benchmarking Code of Conduct* is provided in Appendix D.

3. *Functional and world-class leaders:* The internal and competitive sources of best practices are useful and important but may not yield sufficient information to assist an organization in becoming world-class. That is not to say that internal and competitive studies should be skipped. Instead, experience teaches that those studies must be augmented by looking outside one's own industry to organizations that are performing similar work and achieving world-class performance. After all, why restrict a benchmarking study to one's own industry when someone performing the same application is achieving superior results?

   We have already cited the study of L. L. Bean conducted by Xerox in 1983 as a dramatic example of improving performance by studying an organization that is achieving superior performance in the same practice but in a different industry (Tucker, Zivan, and Camp, 1987). Examples of such comparisons have spread since the Xerox/L. L. Bean study and include defense contractors benchmarking distribution systems with cosmetic companies, and copier manufacturers benchmarking invoicing systems with financial services firms to improve billing accuracy.

4. *Generic or innovative:* This last source of best practices is an extension of functional benchmarking and again offers the prospect of achieving large gains. This technique differs from functional benchmarking in that the search is not restricted to a common application. Instead, it looks to adopt or adapt a method or practice that someone employs for doing something often completely different.

A medical appliance manufacturer that produces titanium hip replacements serves as an example of generic or innovative benchmarking. Such medical appliances are produced by an artisan in about six weeks. The technique is at least 2,000 years old and begins with a wax replica that is placed in a sand mold and heated until the wax evaporates. Molten titanium is poured into the resulting cavity. After it cools, the artisan polishes the completed appliance.

The firm tries to shorten delivery time by maintaining an inventory of replacement joints, but none can fit a patient as well as a custom-made appliance. In a benchmarking project to improve their foundry operation, the medical appliance firm discovered a technique used in the auto industry to produce prototype parts with a computer-driven device that lays down one micron of metal at a time and builds a unique auto part in hours. The medical appliance firm has commissioned the building of a prototype device that should produce a custom hip replacement in six hours instead of six weeks. The application of a methodology used in one business to another can have a dramatic impact on performance.

A second example is a low-cost airline in southwest Texas that undertook a project to maximize its revenue by benchmarking the time a plane wastes on the ground. After all, airline revenues are generated only when planes are in the air carrying passengers between destinations. The project team needed to learn how ground crews could service aircraft—including refueling, tire changes, catering, and cleaning—to minimize ground time and comply with safety regulations. The team met with teams that had perfected such techniques—race-pit crews at the Indianapolis Speedway. Racing professionals are expert at these very practices and complete similar tasks in periods of time that are measured in seconds.

Having identified the four types of comparisons, we now need to apply this approach to the team's specific project. The team needs to identify comparative organizations internally, competitively, functionally, and generically that they should benchmark for each major portion of the targeted process. Typically, a team can brainstorm about twenty internal and competitive organizations it may be able to benchmark. The last two groups—functional and generic—require more work to identify, and part of this work will be completed in Step 3.

The key learning point here is that the team should identify at least 100 prospective benchmarking partners from which they will select three or four for in-depth study. Limiting or constraining the identification of candidates at the outset may result in the improper selection of benchmarking partners later. An example of a beginning list of benchmarking partners developed by the Technical Training Group is shown in Table 14.2.

TABLE 14.2	Comparative Organizations: Curriculum Development			
WORK STEPS	**INTERNAL ORGANIZATIONS**	**DIRECT COMPETITORS**	**FUNCTIONAL LEADERS**	**GENERIC LEADERS**
Analyze needs	Sales training	Amalgamated Shelby	TRW	
Analyze tasks	Data processing Engineering	Marshall Shelby		Boeing
Design programs	Management training	Shelby Western	Forum	Danbury Flying School
Write materials	Management training	Universal		
Evaluate results	Sales training	Marshall	Xerox	
Train instructors	Human resources	Shelby		

STEP 3: COLLECT DATA

Find Data Sources

The benchmarking team can expand the search for comparative organizations by tapping the following sources of information:

- *Internal:* Some organizations have a company library or information center. Other companies have online information systems. Materials acquisition or purchasing groups represent an information window that can reveal organizations with whom to benchmark. Internal market research or competitive studies represent another source to glean names of organizations that may be world-class or that employ techniques that may have a bearing on the team's project.

- *External:* The public domain contains so much information about organizations and their best practices that the problem is one of sifting through mountains of data as opposed to finding data. Sources such as professional associations, public seminars, lectures, and trade shows are all available through an organized search. A librarian who is familiar with the benchmarking project is an invaluable resource in identifying organizations with best practices.

  A search can tap the World Wide Web or online capabilities of many libraries to find everything published on the team's topic, anywhere in the world. The search will yield files containing the titles, authors, and abstract, which can be used to retrieve the publication. If the team believes that a particular article has application to their project, it might consider contacting the authors directly to discuss their research, experience, and findings.

- *Original:* Another approach—the most costly—is to contact potential benchmarking partners directly through phone or mail surveys. This approach uses a series of increasingly detailed questionnaires about the benchmarking topic. For example, if 100 organizations have been identified as potential candidates, then the benchmarking team would send a simple questionnaire to each one, asking about the performance of the subject process and their willingness to benchmark.

  Since response rates to surveys are usually low, the team could look to enhance the rate of returns by including their own performance data on the same questions as part of the request. Providing such data sets a tone of openness, sharing, and possible collaboration.

  When the responses to the initial questionnaire are received, more detailed questions can be directed to promising respondents until the team finds the select few it wants to meet with directly to compare process information.

Prepare Data Collection

Conducting a site visit requires extensive preparation to ensure the visit is mutually useful and productive. Simply visiting another organization may be socially pleasing but is not apt to yield any significant learning. In addition, world-class organizations that are overwhelmed with requests for benchmarking visits will not welcome visits that are not likely to be productive. To ensure success, careful preparation is required.

Preparing questions in advance also ensures consistency. Asking different partners different questions impedes correlating and summarizing results. Test the questions on internal benchmarking partners to reveal deficiencies in their design. Revise the set of questions as needed before use on site visits.

Forward the completed questions to benchmarking partners before the site visit. This is usually the first test the prospective benchmarking partner uses to understand the degree to which the requesting team is prepared.

Preparation of penetrating questions takes thought. A suggested approach is to first list the topics on which the team would like to secure information and then prioritize this list. For example, on a first pass, the team may be interested in the following items for the major sections of their process:

Labor content	Asset utilization	Support tools
Defect rate	Required skill	Customer requirements
Material content	Technology	Warranty experience
Inspection procedures	Employee training	
Cycle time	Data collection	

This list can be prioritized to identify the "vital few," resulting in either a shorter list or a ranked order of topics. The team now can begin to develop questions to extract information on each important topic.

Take advantage of the different forms of questions, such as open-ended, multiple-choice, and scaled. Open-ended questions may be useful to begin a discussion but don't lend themselves to quantitative analysis later. Conversely, multiple-choice, forced-choice, and scaled questions force responses into specific categories but inhibit diverging into related information that may be of critical importance. Consider both the content of the question and its form to extract the required information. See Table 14.3 for examples of different types of questions.

Visit Sites

CONTACT BENCHMARKING PARTNERS   Arrange site visits with selected benchmarking partners after completing and testing the questions. If phone or mail questionnaires were used to collect information from selected partners, you may already know who can arrange the visit. Alternatively the partner's quality or benchmarking office may be appropriate starting points.

TABLE 14.3	Four Types of Questions
TYPE	**EXAMPLE**
Open-ended	How did you choose the order-entry process and computer system you have?
Multiple-choice	Why did you select the material-handling equipment used for order picking? ❑ Vendor reputation ❑ Cost ❑ Ongoing maintenance support
Forced-choice	Would you buy again from your ASRS vendor? ❑ Yes ❑ No
Scaled	How important was maintenance support in your choice of ASRS vendor? ❑ Very important ❑ Somewhat important ❑ Important ❑ Not important

We have consistently referred to organizations with whom one benchmarks as *partners*. The term is deliberately chosen to convey the need for gain by both parties. There may be common interest in a particular process, or the benchmarking partner may ask for assistance in arranging a benchmarking visit with another department of the requesting organization. Without mutual benefit, the likelihood of a successful exchange is low.

PREPARE AN AGENDA   Prepare an agenda and list of attendees to share with your benchmarking partners in advance of each visit. As part of this preparation, a protocol should be agreed to that defines what information will be exchanged and what documents will be made available. It is embarrassing for one team to make a request of another team that is denied. Topics to be discussed and information and documents to be exchanged should be approved prior to the meeting.

ASSIGN ROLES TO SITE-VISIT TEAM   A typical site-visit team includes three to four members, each of whom plays a specific role. One member should be designated as the presenter, and he or she should be prepared to professionally present the project team's current flowcharts and related process information. Another team member should be prepared to ask the questions that have been forwarded to the partner. A third member should be the scribe and have a notebook computer to record responses. The team members should organize, rehearse, and prepare themselves thoroughly to conduct a productive site visit.

A fourth member can fill any number of supporting roles. If certain specialized knowledge is required to understand the information presented, the team may invite such a specialist. Some teams regularly invite a senior manager, since this gives the manager the opportunity to see a world-class performer in action. This exposure enables the participating manager to rethink what his or her organization needs to accomplish.

In turn, the benchmarking host will likely have a team of two to four participants and will likely designate the same roles just described. Depending on the scope of the project, each team might take a half day to describe its process and respond to questions.

Some will argue that the burden of merely planning a benchmarking study cannot be handled on top of a normal workload and that an outside consultant should be hired. When time pressures are extreme, when external sources have high creditability, or when specialized skills are required in designing the study, hiring an outside consultant may be appropriate. However, relying on consultants diminishes organizational learning and potentially reduces ownership in the findings.

Balance represents another approach to moderate the magnitude of work involved in benchmarking. Don't think that everything must be done with external sources. Instead follow the 70-30 rule of thumb employed by many organizations familiar with benchmarking—conduct 70 percent of the studies with internal personnel and 30 percent with external consultants.

PREPARE A SITE-VISIT REPORT   Prepare a Site-Visit Report on the *same* day as the visit to ensure that you capture impressions that may not have been documented by the scribe. Do whatever is needed—use the hotel lobby, airport lounge, or wherever—to debrief each team member's impressions while they are still fresh in their memories. Consolidate each Site-Visit Report into an overall Best Practices Report, on which the team will base its recommendations.

ANALYSIS

STEP 4: DETERMINE THE GAP

In the three steps of the planning phase just completed, we accomplished three things: the team selected a benchmarking topic, identified those organizations that employ industry best practices and possible world-class practitioners, and collected data from a number of sources.

The fourth step is to analyze the data collected from site visits, literature searches, professional association contacts, and any of the other sources used. Analyze the data to determine which processes and practices are at parity with, ahead of, or behind others. Identify gaps or differences between your organization's performance and the best-in-class or world-class organizations. This analysis should identify which inputs are superior, which practices are superior, which outputs are superior, and by what measure each component is superior.

Define the Key Performance Indicator

It is often useful to develop a summary statistic—key performance indicator—that represents overall bottom-line results (see Chapter 7). This statistic simplifies making comparisons between organizations and projecting future performance, as we will do in Step 5. Calculating a summary statistic may be as simple as dividing an organization's output by the number of people involved. In warehousing, for example, dividing the number of orders picked and packed by the number of employees offers a rough measure of efficiency that can be used to compare organizations and identify those organizations that are superior.

In our example of the Technical Training Group, we are interested in the speed of the service technicians as they repair equipment malfunctions. A summary statistic—1.4 hours mean time to repair (MTTR)—is the average time taken by all technicians in a specific training class to repair equipment in which the instructors had introduced faults. This summary statistic can be used to compare performance with other training organizations and as a baseline from which the team can project the impact of improvements in their training programs.

Be careful when selecting key indicators or comparing quantitative measures because data that seem the same can be quite different when examined in detail. Erroneous conclusions can result if different elements are included in the calculations or if different assumptions are used. Our experience shows that the analysis of quantitative measures must be supplemented with qualitative information.

Analyze Performance Gaps

Compare the results achieved by your benchmarking partners in an array of dimensions. Determine the value, performance, or cost advantage that you could achieve by adopting the best practices of the firms studied. An example of the performance gaps identified by our Technical Training Group—including their key performance indicator—is given in Table 14.4.

TABLE 14.4 Performance Gap Analysis

PERFORMANCE MEASURE	OWN	COMPANY A	+/– %	COMPANY B	+/– %
Time to train (avg.)	5 days	6 days	+20	4 days	–20
Cost to train (avg.)	$1,800	$1,200	–33	$1,000	–44
Time for course development (avg.)	12 weeks	12 weeks	parity	13 weeks	+9
Cost of course development (avg.)	$35k	$25k	–29	$20k	–43
Technicians trained	15%	10%	–33	5%	–67
Average test score (MTTR)	1.4 hrs.	1.1 hrs.	–22	0.9 hrs.	–36

TABLE 14.5	Advantage of Adopting Best Practices			
INTERNAL PRACTICES	**BENCHMARKING PARTNERS**			**ADVANTAGE OF BEST PRACTICES**
	A	**B**	**C**	
1. Practice 1	Best	Better	Same	3%
2. Practice 2	Better	Best	Better	6%
3. Practice 3	Same	Worst	Not as Good	—
4. Practice 4	Not as Good	Same	Best	4%
5. Not Performed	Better	Best	Worst	1%
6. Practice 6	Not as Good	Same	Best	4%
Advantage	**6%**	**11%**	**15%**	**18%**

In addition to analyzing differences between the team's own performance and those of each benchmarking partner, we also can examine how the targeted operation would perform if all of the best practices were adopted. Our experience reveals that implementing the combination of best practices from all partners may allow the benchmarking team to leapfrog the performance of every partner studied.

This idea is illustrated in Table 14.5, in which each practice in our internal process is compared to the corresponding practice used by three other firms. An assessment as to the extent of superiority is also shown. The overall performance advantage of each firm is noted at the bottom of each column. In this example, companies A, B, and C are superior to our internal process by 6, 11, and 15 percent, respectively.

Comparing each practice across all firms shows (theoretically at least) that the benchmarking team could combine all of the best practices to achieve the 18 percent performance advantage shown in the last column. The benchmarking project could enable the team not only to improve but to become superior to every other firm studied. A more compelling case for dramatic process improvement and change is hard to make.

This leapfrogging phenomenon offers a fundamental reason for benchmarking and explains why firms that are already considered to be world-class are willing to benchmark with organizations that are not. World-class organizations know that no one is best at everything, including themselves, so they are always interested in discovering superior work steps that they can incorporate into their processes.

Analyze Process Differences

A side-by-side comparison of flowcharts describing the processes used by each of the benchmarked partners offers another approach to find improvement opportunities. Typical observations and implications are listed in Table 14.6. Figure 14.1 illustrates significant differences in processes among the three training organizations benchmarked. These differences may reveal clues as to how a process may be achieving superior performance.

TABLE 14.6	Observations by Comparing Flowcharts	
OBSERVATIONS	**IMPLICATIONS**
Fewer steps	Fewer people, lower cost
Different sequences	Better workflow, reduced cycle time
Fewer hand-offs	Shortcuts, reduced errors
Fewer inspections	Higher-quality work and less rework
Steps outsourced	Utilizing specialized skills, lower cost

FIGURE 14.1   Flowchart Comparisons

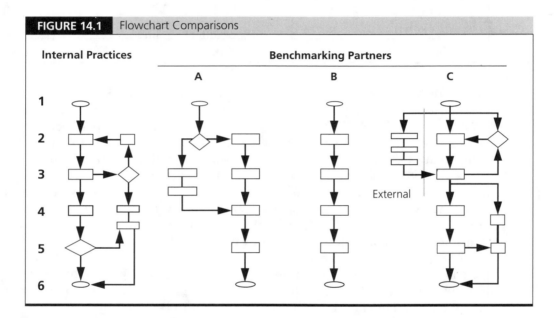

Best of Best

As a result of these analyses, it is now possible to compile a list of best practices for the benchmarked process. This list describes each step in the targeted process, the best practice, the performance advantage of that best practice, and the value expected if each best practice was employed. Compilation of this information forms the basis on which recommendations will be made later in Step 6. An example list of best practices for the Technical Training Group is shown in Table 14.7.

It may also be useful to sketch a "best-of-best" flowchart, at least to the extent that preliminary assumptions can be tested. This preliminary sketch will be revised later after each step in the process is analyzed in depth.

STEP 5: PROJECT FUTURE PERFORMANCE

At this point in the project, the management sponsor might ask the team the following questions:

TABLE 14.7	Sample Best Practices for Curriculum Development Process		
CURRENT PRACTICE	**BEST PRACTICE**	**PERFORMANCE ADVANTAGE**	**VALUE GAIN**
1. Analyze needs			
• Discuss deficiencies with trainers	• Survey the client to identify requirements, current performance deficiencies, and set program goals.	• Saves 1 day in field observations of incumbents	$350
	• Observe top and average performers on the job to measure performance differences and calculate improvement potential.	• Sets measurable targets for improvement against which to assess success	1 day
2. Analyze tasks			
• Observe incumbents on the job	• Conduct task analysis to identify job duties and create a task map.	• Improves the accuracy of learner objectives and saves 0.5 days of rewrites	$175
• Create learner objectives	• Convert the task map into learner objectives.	• Same	0
3. Design programs			
4. Write materials			
5. Evaluate results			
6. Train instructors			

- How do you compare today with industry best?
- How will you gain a performance advantage?
- What will it mean to your operation? to the company?
- What will it cost us to convert?

To answer these questions, the benchmarking team needs to know the answers to these questions:

- What were performance trends in recent years?
- What is the current performance gap?
- How will industry performance change in the coming years?
- Will the gap widen, narrow, or remain the same?
- What implications does this have for our business?
- How can we gain a significant performance advantage?

Quantify Advantages

The team often can simplify presentation of quantitative data through use of its summary statistic—key performance indicator. Using mean time to repair (MTTR) to represent the performance of the Technical Training Group, we can compare performance among our benchmarking partners to understand the magnitude of improvement that is needed. We can examine historical data to show previous trends. Ideally, during data acquisition in Step 3 we looked for information on improvements that the industry is expecting to achieve in the future. In Figure 14.2 we display past trends along with a projection of industry gains and the improvements the team expects to be able to secure over the same time frame. Note that projections of future performance of our own practices excludes improvements gained through benchmarking.

The team should develop a second projection as well, one showing the effects of implementing the best practices discovered through benchmarking. Again using the Technical Training Group as an example, Figure 14.3 projects future performance with all of the best practices discovered through benchmarking incorporated. Instead of allowing the MTTR performance gap to widen, implementation of best practices is expected to offer a performance advantage.

In addition to projecting improvements in terms of its summary statistic, the team also should quantify how the changes will affect other performance indicators. One way to capture the hearts and minds of senior managers is to translate benefits into the contributions they will make in the firm's goals and objectives. An example for the Technical Training Group is provided in Table 14.8. This table compares the performance gaps of current practices to the advantages projected with best practices implemented.

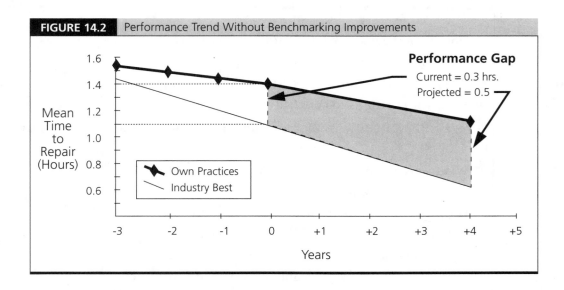

FIGURE 14.2 Performance Trend Without Benchmarking Improvements

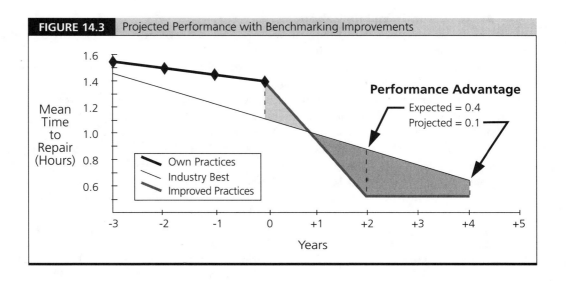

FIGURE 14.3 Projected Performance with Benchmarking Improvements

TABLE 14.8 Summary of Projected Performance Improvements

		OWN CURRENT PRACTICE			OWN WITH BENCHMARKS		
PERFORMANCE	**COMPETITION**	**ACTUAL**	**GAP**	**%**	**PROJECTED**	**ADVANTAGE**	**%**
Average test score (MTTR)	1.1 hrs.	1.4 hrs.	0.3 hr.	22	0.5 hr.	0.4 hr.	27
Time to train (avg.)	6 days	5 days	1 day	20	4 days	1 day	20
Cost to train (avg.)	$1,200	$1,800	$600	33	$1,000	$200	17
Time for course development (avg.)	12 weeks	12 weeks	parity	parity	8 weeks	4 weeks	33
Cost of course development (avg.)	$25,000	$35,000	$10,000	29	$20,000	$15,000	43

SUMMARY OF KEY RESULTS FROM IMPLEMENTING BEST PRACTICES

MTTR will improve from a 0.3 hr. gap to a 0.4 hr. advantage, which will translate to repairs in the field that are 27 percent more effective than the competition.

Reducing classroom time from six to four days will enable technicians to spend more time in the field.

Reducing program development time from twelve to eight weeks and from $35,000 to $20,000 will allow the development of three additional programs per year with no additions to staff.

Assess Operational Implications

The last activity in Step 5 is to assess the operational implications for implementing the proposed changes—implications that typically offset the gains from closing gaps. Financial impacts need to be calculated so that the net value of implementing the best practices is understood.

Changes are not implemented in a vacuum and will reverberate across the organization. Groups affected normally include customers, suppliers, management, staff, and operational or online personnel. All impacts need to be identified and shared with the affected groups to provide ample opportunity to adjust. For example, Xerox ignored downstream operations when it benchmarked and emulated L. L. Bean's picking and packing operation. Xerox failed to consider how improved productivity would affect the shipping department, which was unprepared to handle the increased volume.

Table 14.9 lists some of the types of changes that might be considered. Failure to find all implications can undermine an otherwise excellent improvement project through loss of credibility. The team needs to explain how its recommended changes affect the work unit, its department, and the organization as a whole. A sample of the impacts that the Technical Training Group identified are listed in Table 14.10.

TABLE 14.9   Sampling of Possible Significant Impacts

• Staff reductions	• New job descriptions	• Revised reporting relationships
• Staff redeployment	• Reorganization	• Supplier changes
• Changed priorities	• Budget reductions	• New input requirements

---

TABLE 14.10   Sample Technical Training Impacts on Other Groups

SUPPLIERS

- Engineers will have to provide operating manuals and hands-on training to curriculum designers.
- The Graphics Department will have to create artwork on PCs.

STAFF

- Technical illustrations used in printed materials and classroom will have to be created on PCs and embedded into documents.
- The Production Group will no longer paste up artwork but will position on PCs.

INTERNAL ORGANIZATIONS

- Fewer recycles will reduce the field operation's training budget.
- The cafeteria will need to support fifty additional students per week.
- The Corporate Travel Department must book twenty-five additional rooms to accommodate larger classes.
- Regional training centers will be closed.

CUSTOMERS

- Field technicians will have to complete a self-study program prior to attending classroom training.
- Field managers will need to verify the technicians' preschool preparation.
- Technicians will have to travel to the Corporate Training Center, and their travel budgets need to be increased by 10 percent.

INTEGRATION AND ACTION: STEPS 6 THROUGH 10

The action required in Steps 6 through 10 is common to all process improvement efforts—continuous improvement, benchmarking, and reengineering—and is covered in Chapter 16. Key activities pertinent to benchmarking are described below.

INTEGRATION

- *Communicate results*. Share the information gained through the planning and analysis phases with your team's sponsor to ensure support for implementing recommended changes. Some organizations have established formal structures for sharing their planning and analysis information, so that new teams can benefit from the experience gained in prior benchmarking projects. Appendix E describes the infrastructure installed at Texas Instruments to facilitate corporatewide communication of best practices.
- *Establish goals*. Revise the organization's goals and objectives to capture the competitive advantage you expect to gain by implementing recommended changes.

ACTION

- *Develop action plans*. Test the new process in a scaled-down pilot version to identify unanticipated problems. Establish priorities for implementation, develop definitive plans, and revise performance projections to incorporate lessons learned from the pilot tests.
- *Implement plans*. Install the improved process, manage the changeover, and update documentation.
- *Monitor results*. Establish systems to track progress and to alert the team when corrective action is required. Reward and recognize successful team contributions.
- *Recalibrate benchmarks*. Set new targets, and define where and how the next increment of improvement will be obtained.

SUMMARY

Benchmarking is a powerful process improvement approach that has the effect of reenergizing improvement options through external comparisons with industry and world-class leaders. While the concept is not difficult to understand, completing a benchmarking project requires a disciplined, methodical approach and an in-depth commitment. This chapter provides a ten-step approach that should enable any team to successfully complete a benchmarking project.

DISCUSSION QUESTIONS

1. How would you select the most important area to benchmark in your organization? What tools or techniques would you use?

2. What internal resources does your organization have to help identify comparative organizations?

3. Are you prepared to organize a data search or a site visit?

4. Can you define a single measure that best represents how well your process performs?

5. Can you plot the historic trends and project future levels for your key performance measure?

REFERENCES

Camp, R. C. 1989. *Benchmarking: The Search for Industry Best Practices That Lead to Superior Performance*. Milwaukee, WI: Quality Press.

Camp, R. C. 1995. *Business Process Benchmarking: Finding and Implementing Best Practices*. Milwaukee, WI: Quality Press.

"Chrysler Targets Best." 1992. *USA Today*, October 26, 1.

International Benchmarking Clearing House. n.d. *The Benchmarking Code of Conduct*. American Productivity & Quality Center, 123 North Post Oak Lane, Houston, TX 77024-7797.

Tucker, G., S. M. Zivan, and R. C. Camp. 1987. "How to Measure Against the Best." *Harvard Business Review* (Reprint 87112) (January/February).

15 | Reengineering

OVERVIEW OF REENGINEERING

From a brief article published in 1989, "Reengineering Work: Don't Automate, Obliterate" (Hammer, 1990) and a book published in 1993, *Reengineering the Corporation: A Manifesto for Business Revolution* (Hammer and Champy, 1993), reengineering has burst onto the contemporary business scene as arguably the most popular management intervention of the 1990s (Cole, 1994, 77). However, the early literature left much to be desired, since no guidance or methodology was provided for effective implementation. Instead, reengineering became mainly a rallying cry for change, due in large measure to dissatisfaction with the lack of results in existing quality programs and the appeal of a "clean sheet" approach.

Early proponents labored to differentiate reengineering from total quality management (TQM) by explaining that TQM occasionally worked on improving existing processes even though they should have been eliminated altogether. Reengineering guru Michael Hammer explains, "Quality stresses continuous improvement of existing processes, while reengineering, by contrast, discards existing processes and replaces them with entirely new ones" (Cole, 1994, 79).

TQM practitioners looked to fit reengineering into their ever-expanding tool kit to address the shortcoming of previous quality efforts. They reasoned that just as surely as organizations need continuous improvement of existing processes, they also need reengineering in order to leapfrog competitions. They concluded that both could be accommodated under the TQM umbrella. Table 15.1 summarizes differences between continuous improvement and reengineering.

TABLE 15.1	Reengineering Compared to Continuous Improvement	
	REENGINEERING	**CONTINUOUS IMPROVEMENT**
Source of leadership	Often managed by outsiders	Usually run by managers or associates close to the business
Orientation	Top down	Includes associate level input
Improvement objective	Breakthrough	Incremental
Duration	Project-oriented	Long-term

SOURCE: Adapted from "After Reengineering" (1994, 40).

REENGINEERING DEFINED

Michael Hammer and James Champy's (1993, 31) definition of reengineering begins with a simple statement of "starting over" and is subsequently expanded to a more formal explanation (1993, 32): "Reengineering is the fundamental rethinking and radical redesign of business processes to achieve dramatic improvements in critical measures of performance, such as cost, quality, service and speed."

Three key terms in Hammer and Champy's definition—fundamental, radical, and dramatic—serve to differentiate reengineering from the other improvement paths (continuous improvement and benchmarking) that were covered in Chapters 13 and 14. These terms deserve clarification:

- *Fundamental:* Fundamental implies that everything—every assumption, every reason, every activity—is challenged by asking why it should be continued. The implication is that nothing should be accepted as sacred. Over time, practices that were once required become obsolete and need to be removed.

- *Radical:* The major difference between continuous improvement and reengineering is the latter is not about improvement at all, but about "reinvention, . . . disregarding all existing structures and procedures, and inventing completely new ways of accomplishing work" (Hammer and Champy, 1993, 33).

- *Dramatic:* The intent in reengineering is to seek an order of magnitude improvement (ten times), not a slight tuning of performance. If marginal gains—5 to 10 percent—are the goal, then continuous improvement is a more appropriate path than reengineering.

BENEFIT FROM EXPERIENCE

The failure rate of early reengineering projects was alarmingly high, in the range of 50 to 70 percent according to Hammer and Champy (1993, 200). In spite of the high failure rate, there seems to be little to dissuade managers from pressing ahead to reengineer, however. One estimate shows that U.S. spending on reengineering will grow 20 percent annually from a 1994 level of $32 billion to $52 billion by 1997

(Christofferson, 1994, 50). The failure rate is too high to be attributable to chance and implies that something was inherently wrong with the approaches used in early projects. Analysis of these pioneering projects offers valuable lessons, both in terms of things to avoid and things to make essential.

Avoid Repeating Mistakes from the Past

Deloitte & Touche surveyed 400 U.S. and Canadian chief information officers (CIOs) in 1993 and found a half dozen prime obstacles to reengineering (see Figure 15.1). Similarly, CSC Index, Inc. surveyed 600 large North American and European firms in 1994 and found information to dispel four myths that had impeded early projects (see Table 15.2).

Critical Success Factors

The CSC Index, Inc. survey also found six factors that correlate with successful reengineering projects. Of the North American firms surveyed, 33 percent had exceeded all goals, 39 percent had met most goals, 24 percent had met some goals, and 2 percent had not met their goals. Of the European firms, 10 percent exceeded their goals, 19 percent met their goals, 48 percent met most goals, 17 percent met some goals, 3 percent had not met any goals ("Reengineering," 1994, 25). When reasons for the successes and failures were diagnosed, eight critical success factors emerged (see Table 15.3). An additional six keys to success were identified for the first factor—effective project management.

Manganelli and Klein offer a seventh critical success factor—speed. The span of attention that most organizations have for a major project is as short as the time between crises. Since timing of the next major problem is not predictable, there is a need to complete reengineering projects as rapidly as possible to avoid

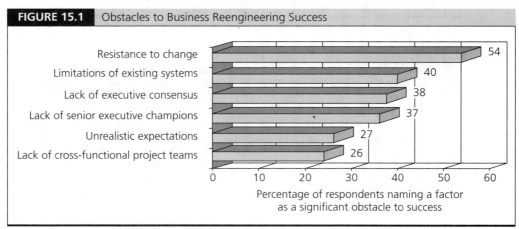

FIGURE 15.1 Obstacles to Business Reengineering Success

Resistance to change — 54
Limitations of existing systems — 40
Lack of executive consensus — 38
Lack of senior executive champions — 37
Unrealistic expectations — 27
Lack of cross-functional project teams — 26

Percentage of respondents naming a factor
as a significant obstacle to success

SOURCE: Adapted from Maglitta (1994, 96).

TABLE 15.2 Dispelling Four Common Myths

MYTH #1: REENGINEERING ALWAYS INVOLVES DOWNSIZING.

Survey findings: While downsizing is one of the outcomes of reengineering, the bulk of the cuts will not come through layoffs. Job reductions from reengineering pale beside the pink slips of the major downsizing and restructuring of the 1990s.
Comment: While labor is a major cost component of most processes and reengineering diminshes the need for staff, opportunities exist to reinvest labor in other resource poor processes or in increasing capacity for more volume.

MYTH #2: IT'S SAFER TO SET MODEST GOALS THAN AMBITIOUS ONES.

Survey findings: Setting one's sights lower, in fact, does not appear to be a safe strategy.
Comment: Lower goals result, apparently, in lower performance, whereas those who aim higher have a better record of attaining their goals. This is contrary to popular thought but is an important consideration for senior managers who are establishing reengineering mandates.

MYTH #3: MOST REENGINEERING EFFORTS FAIL TO GENERATE ANY RESULTS.

Survey findings: Results appear to be mixed. Those pursuing cost reductions seem to have met their targets, and nearly three-quarters of those pursuing cycle-time reductions and productivity increases have achieved their goals.
Comment: The track record on results seems to be improving, and expectations are that disciplined approaches will enable the trend to continue.

MYTH #4: REENGINEERING IS A FAD THAT'S ON THE WAY OUT.

Survey findings: What the fad myth misses is that reengineering is the result of a fundamental economic restructuring in the United States and Europe—the decline of product-based competiton in mature, saturated markets—and is a shift from competing on what we make to competing on how we make it.
Comment: Enormous improvements in quality and productivity have been secured in the industrialized nations in the last twenty years, and they were secured through the application of a variety of techniques, one of which is reengineering. This trend is unlikely to change, except that reengineering success will increase.

SOURCE: Adapted from CSC Index (1994, 9).

TABLE 15.3 Critical Success Factors

REENGINEERING	PROJECT MANAGEMENT EFFECTIVENESS
1. Project management	1.1 Effective use of teams
2. Senior management commitment	1.2 Commitment of time and resources by reengineering team members
3. Corporate culture	1.3 Clarity of scope and purpose
4. Case for action	1.4 Establishment of strong communications
5. Early project success	1.5 Realistic planning and schedules
6. Information systems	1.6 Effective training and communications
7. Speed	
8. Experience	

SOURCE: Adapted from CSC Index (1994, 5–6).

being overtaken by events. "Reengineering must be done rapidly because senior executives require results in shorter time frames than ever before and . . . because reengineering programs fail if they take too long to produce any results" (Managelli and Klein, 1994, 11).

Experience represents an eighth critical success factor. While the reasons for failure vary, a consensus has emerged that success rates are lowest for an organization's initial project. After experience is gained, success rates climb. This view has been extended to attribute experience to be even more important than methodology. "Experience, more than possession of the right approach or methodology is the key to a reengineering triumph. It works like this: if you make a mistake, spend more time and money, and try again" (Christofferson, 1994, 52).

Readers can profit from the experience of others through two examples. Appendix F shares a work in progress of how Xerox Corporation intends to become more responsive to customers' requirements, and quicker at bringing new technology to market. Appendix G describes a reengineering project at Praxair, Inc., to reduce the time to commercialize new products by 50 percent.

REENGINEERING APPROACHES

Approaches to reengineering projects can follow any of three routes. Select the route for your own organization that will minimize exposure to the extraordinary failure rates experienced by early practitioners. In selecting the best route, consider your tolerance for risk and the frequency with which your organization will likely apply reengineering in the future:

- *Just do it.* Reading anecdotes about how others were able to save millions of dollars provides the motivation to jump into a reengineering project but doesn't offer either the requisite methodology or experience. The high failure rate experienced by early practitioners should be expected by those who select this route.

- *Hire a consultant.* Certainly less risky than the first route, hiring a consultant can provide the required expertise but suffers from two of its own limitations. First, retaining an experienced consulting firm is expensive. If improvement is urgently needed and specialized knowledge required, then hiring a consultant will likely be justified. The second limitation is the lost opportunity for organizational learning. Relying on a consultant to direct the entire reengineering effort eliminates the need for the organization to build its own expertise. The success of subsequent reengineering projects will hinge on bringing back the same consulting expertise. If the likelihood of future projects is low, then hiring a consultant is probably the best path.

- *Develop internal capability*. A third route is for an organization to become self-reliant and build its own internal capabilities. While initially difficult, this path becomes easier as experience is built through subsequent projects. If there is a need to relieve specific "pain points," then a consultant might be retained to assist in that specific area. This targeted approach of using specialized skills minimizes expense and enables an organization to strengthen its own capabilities without jeopardizing the project's success.

In our experience, the third route is most frequently the preferred choice. To maximize success along this path, a road map is offered in the form of a six-step model. Using this methodology reduces the potential for failure while an organization builds it own expertise.

REENGINEERING PROJECT MODEL

OVERVIEW

The remainder of this chapter describes a six-step road map for reengineering (Figure 15.2). The first two steps—organize and launch—represent the planning phase. These steps are similar to their counterparts in continuous improvement

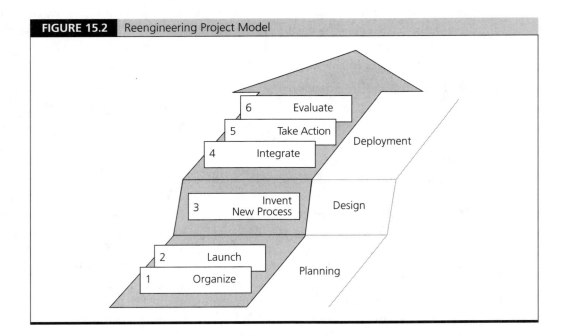

FIGURE 15.2 Reengineering Project Model

and benchmarking but are more intensive. Step three—invent a new process—is the heart of the project, where a team will labor full-time for up to six months to design a new process from a clean sheet of paper. The last three steps—integration, action, and evaluation—form the deployment (or installation) phase. As was the case with planning, steps in the deployment phase are similar to their counterparts in continuous improvement and benchmarking. The following is an overview of the reengineering methodology.

1. *Organize the reengineering project.* Begin by examining the organization's health and its ability to accept the drastic changes that should be expected from a successful reengineering project. Construct an inventory of the organization's processes and determine which are the critically important core processes. Assess the effectiveness and efficiency of existing processes in order to determine improvement priorities. Base decisions for launching improvement efforts on three factors—importance, opportunity, and feasibility. Reserve reengineering for use on only those few processes offering the combination of both greatest importance and opportunity.

2. *Launch the reengineering project.* Appoint full-time members to the project team who have the needed skills and knowledge of both reengineering and the process that is the subject of the project. Examine both external and internal environmental forces that could have a bearing on the project's success. Document the project's plan in a charter with clearly defined scope, expectations, measures of success, and estimated resource requirements.

3. *Invent a new process.* Starting with a clean sheet of paper, break all the rules and define what an ideal process might look like. Develop several alternatives, and use process benchmarking to find the best practices currently employed by others. Test the conseqences of adopting radical designs and trim them back step-by-step as little as possible to eliminate the most severe consequences in order to arrive at the best solution.

4. *Integration.* Communicate recommended plans to all stakesholders and sponsors to ensure acceptance. Reflect the improvements anticipated through the reengineering project in the organization's goals and objectives.

5. *Action.* Pilot test the new process to find and eliminate unanticipated problems. Establish implementation priorities, set schedules, and assign responsibilities. Develop a transition plan and coordinate staffing, training, roll-out, and ramp-up to full deployment. Manage the changeover, and update documentation.

6. *Evaluation.* Monitor implementation, correcting problems as they occur. Reward and recognize successful team contributions, and launch continuous improvement to sustain and extend gains.

Step 1: Organize the Reengineering Project

For reengineering to be successful, top management must not only be involved, but their involvement must be intense. Order-of-magnitude improvements frequently entail structural changes, uncertainty, large expenditures, reassignment of key personnel, career changes, and some degree of business risk. Reengineering efforts are not to be undertaken lightly but only after careful analysis. The first tasks in organizing the project are to ensure that the organization's culture is geared for the anticipated changes and that the current condition of the process warrants investment in reengineering.

1.1 ANALYZE THE ORGANIZATION'S CULTURE   Review the health of the organization's culture with respect to process-oriented thinking, direction-setting, and its tolerance to accept change (refer to Chapters 2, 3, and 4). Recall from Figure 15.1, that resistance to change was identified as the single most common obstacle to successful reeningeering projects.

1.2 IDENTIFY CORE PROCESSES   Construct an inventory of the organization's processes, and determine which are the critically important core processes—both operational and supporting (see Chapter 6). Map the subprocesses that form the building blocks of each core process.

1.3 MEASURE EFFECTIVENESS AND EFFICIENCY   Measure the performance of each process in terms of both effectiveness and efficiency (see Chapters 7, 8, and 9).

1.4 UNDERSTAND THE PROCESS   Draw a block diagram (refer to Chapter 10) that identifies core processes, subprocesses, and their interactions. Detailed flowcharts of tasks and activities are generally not required for reengineeering, since the objective of the project is to obliterate these processes. *Caveat:* Don't confuse the absence of a requirement for details as an excuse to skip flowcharting your processes. The overall understanding gained through drawing the "big picture" is absolutely essential.

1.5 RATE PROCESS CONDITION   Assess the health of your organization's processes (Chapter 11) to determine the size of performance gaps. The size of each gap will be indicative of the magnitude of its improvement opportunity.

1.6 SET PRIORITIES FOR IMPROVEMENT   Base decisions for improvement on a combination of three factors—importance, opportunity, and feasibility (Chapter 12). Rating process condition helped to define the opportunity. The organization's business drivers, goals, and objectives will help to establish the relative importance of improvement efforts. Reengineering is the most difficult, resource intensive, and risky of the three alternative paths—continuous improvement, benchmarking, and reengineering. Select reengineering only for those processes offering the greatest opportunity *and* having the greatest importance.

1.7 REPORT FINDINGS AND OBTAIN BUY-IN   Prepare a written report that describes the scope and expectations of the reengineering project to gain executive support, sponsorship, and required resources. No reengineering project should proceed beyond this point without complete endorsement. Recall from Figure 15.1 that the lack of executive consensus and champions are two major obstacles to successful reengineering projects.

Step 2: Launch the Reengineering Project

2.1 APPOINT THE REENGINEERING TEAM   Reengineering is too complex and time consuming to be assigned on a part-time basis to people who must also operate the process. Rather, reengineering typically requires a dedicated, full-time project team. When commissioned, members should possess skills and knowledge in the subject process and in reengineering. Expertise in reengineering usually involves prior experience and process modeling or computer simulation skills.

If a core process is the target of the project, expertise can be provided by either inviting employees familiar with its various subprocesses to join the team, or by asking them to supplement the core team as part-time contributors. The decision on their membership will likely hinge on controlling the size of the team. Representation from a member of the information systems (IS) staff is also common. The project team is typically headed by the process owner (see Chapter 12 for additional guidance on selecting members). Recall from Figure 15.1, that 26 percent of the respondents to Deloitte & Touche's survey indicated that the lack of cross-functional teams was a major obstacle to successful reengineering.

The team should schedule to complete the design phase (Step 3) within six months. If this does not appear likely, either increase the size of the team, or reduce the scope of the project.

2.2 TRAIN THE TEAM   The team should include at least one member with experience in reengineering (or supplement the team with a qualified consultant). Consider providing a short training course to members who are not familiar with reengineering, so that the entire team has common understanding, expectations, approach, and language.

2.3 ANALYZE THE ENVIRONMENT   Scan the environment to determine potential external threats and opportunities to the organization's objectives for the performance of the subject process. These may take the form of changes in regulations, in the economy, or from competitors. Also consider changes in demographics, markets, and trends in technology.

Even though the new process will likely be designed within six months, full deployment for a large project could span over two years. The amount of effort invested in an environmental scan should be proportionate to the size, complexity, importance, and duration of the project.

2.4 DETERMINE DIRECTION   In parallel with analyzing the external environment, assess the organization's strengths and weaknesses, and identify the internal "pain points." Review long-range plans and changes required. Determine or reconfirm the direction of the firm with regard to its mission, vision, values, goals, and objectives.

2.5 DRAFT PROJECT CHARTER   Draft a charter—also known as a *project description*—to clarify roles, responsibilities, and expectations. The document should explain the desired state that the team hopes to achieve. In doing so, it will explain why members have been asked to join the team, define the scope of work proposed to be undertaken, and show the impact that the project will make in achieving specific business objectives. The team will periodically update its charter as the project progresses. Refer back to Chapter 12 for additional information on preparing charters.

Table 15.4 provides a sample document that one team used to gain support for a project to reengineer its company's new product development process. Referred to as a *mandate for change*, this document ties the project to the organization's goals and objectives, and spells out measures of success. Unlike continuous improvement or benchmarking—where prompt and easy approval should be expected—significant effort might be required merely to launch a reengineering project. A mandate for change may be included within the project description.

2.6 REASSESS THE ORGANIZATION'S READINESS FOR CHANGE   With the completed charter, the process owner should reaffirm management's support for the project and test the organization's readiness for change. Progress may require dealing with potential resistance, including moving individuals to other positions, providing orientation, training, or specific personal counseling. If support or readiness is only marginal, perhaps the project should be deferred, rather than squander significant resources on an ill-fated venture. Recall from Figure 15.1, that resistance to change was identified as the single most common obstacle to successful reeningeering projects.

TABLE 15.4	Sample Mandate for Change

MANDATE FOR CHANGE—ABC OFFICE PRODUCTS COMPANY

Process: Product Development

CURRENT MARKETPLACE

Industry technology has changed dramatically in recent years.
* Product market life is now limited to 3 to 4 years.
* Customers upgrade equipment every 36 to 48 months.
Market is now 50% rental.
* Our installed base of customers is highly susceptible to cancellations.
* We must upgrade our own equipment before competition.

PROBLEM STATEMENT

* Current time-to-market for new products requires 26 months.
    - Best competitors require only 18 months.
        * Competitive products reach the market sooner,
        * Gain name recognition, and
        * Capture market share before our introduction.
    - Short product life cycle (3 to 4 years) gives us little time to recover our investment and show profit.
    - Late entry requires more advertising and promotion, reducing revenues and margins over the product life cycle.
        * Our cost for development is 10 percent higher than our competitors', which necessitates either higher prices to customers or lower profit margins.

MARKET NEEDS

* State-of-the-art processing power
* Networking capability
* 24-month payback for customers

COST OF INACTION *(PENALTY FOR DOING NOTHING)*

* Without dramatic gains:
    - Could lose 20% market share
    - Risk losing 50% installed base
* Unlikely that parent corporation will continue supporting division with less than 8% return on assets

PROJECT RESOURCES *(TIME, STAFF, COSTS)*

* Design phase—6 months
* Deployment—12 months from approval of design
* Project team
    - 6 full-time through design phase
    - $1,200,000

DIAGNOSTICS *(WHAT'S WRONG)*

* Product development process is too slow and costly.
* Automation has produced only modest time-to-market gains.
* Competitors have reduced their time-to-market 10% annually.
* We are currently 30% behind the market.
* Incremental gains (3 to 5% annually) will leave us further behind.

THE PRIZE *(MEASURES OF SUCCESS)*

* Reduce product development time-to-market from 26 to 11 months.
* Increase new product releases from 2 to 5 per year.
* Improve gross margins from 17 to 43%.
* Increase market share from 13 to 30% within 3 years.
* Reduce head count by 50 to 80 people. All displaced staff will be reassigned to comparable positions in other divisions.

Step 3: Invent a New Process

The term *invent* is deliberately chosen for Step 3, instead of alternatives like design or develop. The term was chosen to reinforce the intentions of reengineering—the fundamental rethinking and radical redesign of processes to achieve dramatic improvements. If you are merely looking to tune a process, you are applying continuous improvement and should refer to Chapter 13. If you are merely looking to emulate best practices of others, you are benchmarking and should refer to Chapter 14. The remainder of Chapter 15 is reserved for those seeking serious change.

Inventing a new and clearly superior process from a clean sheet of paper proceeds in two distinct stages. The first uses divergent thinking to expand the realm of possibilities to find idealized designs. The second uses convergent thinking to narrow the possibilities to the single best candidate.

> *Corporate visions are frequently illusions or delusions. To be effective, a vision should consist of an operationally meaningful description of the organization its stakeholders would have if they could have any organization they wanted—without constraints. It should be a consensus formulation in which all the stakeholders or their representatives have had a hand*
>
> **—R. L. ACKOFF (1993, 401).**

3.1 INVENT AN IDEALIZED DESIGN   Any number of approaches can be used to find an idealized design, but all are based on one thing—creative thinking. R. L. Ackoff offers an approach to creative thinking that fits nicely with the objectives of inventing a new process.

Begin by recognizing two types of idealized designs, constrained and unconstrained. A *constrained idealized design* begins with the assumption that the organization was destroyed last night. It no longer exists, but its environment is assumed to be untouched. By contrast, an *unconstrained idealized design* removes all shackles of corporate and regulatory requirements (Ackoff, 1993, 401).

In reality, the reengineering of processes will face constraints, and the constraints will generally tighten as one progresses down from core processes to subprocesses. Why then did we mention *unconstrained* designs? The answer is to open team members' minds to creative thinking. Ackoff (1993, 403) recommends doing the following:

> *PREPARE TWO SEPARATE visions of an idealized design, one constrained by its containing system(s) and the other not. The constrained design assumes no changes in any of the organization's relevant containing systems. Even under this assumption, however, most organizations can be radically redesigned.*
>
> *It is preferable to prepare the constrained design first. Surprisingly, the unconstrained design is seldom very different from the one that is constrained. This reveals that most of the obstructions between the current organization and where its redesigners would ideally like to be lie within the designers and the organization, not in its environment.*

3.2 EXPAND POSSIBILITIES   Don't limit your thinking to merely two designs. Instead, develop several scenarios that yield various design options. Use *process benchmarking* (Chapter 14) as an exercise to find still other possibilities. Compare your alternative designs with your competitors' best practices. Combine the best-of-the-best into your designs to develop world-class processes that can deliver the performance promised in the project's mandate. At this stage, these processes may not be feasible for a variety of reasons—culture, cost, skill mix, or technical limitations. Nonetheless, they represent a starting point of what might be possible.

When looking to create a dramatically improved process, remember to eliminate hand-offs and organizational barriers in your current process. Also look to creatively use information technology: capture the rapid advances in electronic documents and data interchange that were not even dreams when your current process was conceived. Refer to Table 15.5 as a checklist for evaluating idealized designs.

3.3 SELECT BEST DESIGN   Having identified both constrained and unconstrained versions of an idealized design, find the best solution through three substeps: (a) identification of self-imposed constraints, (b) their removal, and (c) exploration of the consequences of having done so.

Continuing with the creative process advocated by Ackoff (1993, 407), "Self-imposed constraints take the form of assumptions made about what can or cannot be done. Most of them are assumed to be imposed by external sources. In my experience, this is not true; most are self-imposed."

By working through constraints and differentiating those that are self-imposed from those that are truly part of the external environment, the reengineering team should push their constrained design to closely approximate their unconstrained one. The provision for exploring the consequences of removing constraints serves as a lubricant for this step. As Ackoff (1993, 407–408) has said,

TABLE 15.5	Checklist for Evaluating Idealized Designs

ALTERNATIVE SCENARIOS HAVE BEEN GENERATED THAT:

- ❑ Challenged the status quo.
- ❑ Broken rules.
- ❑ Disrupted organizational boundaries.
- ❑ Employed information technology.

IDEALIZED DESIGNS HAVE BEEN DEVELOPED THAT:

- ❑ Equal or exceed competitors' capabilities.
- ❑ Combined several jobs into one.
- ❑ Located and sequenced work so it makes the most sense.
- ❑ Reduced checks and controls.
- ❑ Reduced the number of hand-offs.
- ❑ Simplified decision making.

IT IS DIFFICULT to identify self-imposed constraints. This is reflected in the difficulty of solving puzzles because a puzzle is a problem that is difficult to solve precisely because of a self-imposed constraint. This explains why we are usually surprised when we are shown a solution to a puzzle that we were unable to solve. Unfortunately, knowing that creativity and puzzle-solving require identification and removal of self-imposed constraints does not, by itself, make identifying such constraints one bit easier.

DEPLOYMENT

The new process is deployed (or installed) in the last three steps. These steps are common to all improvement efforts—continuous improvement, bench-marking, and reengineering—and are covered in Chapter 16. Each is summarized below.

Step 4: Integration

- *Communicate results.* Communicate recommended plans to all stakeholders and sponsors to ensure acceptance. Document the team's findings in a written report. A Best Practices Report is provided as a sample in Appendix H.

- *Revise goals and objectives.* Reflect the improvements anticipated through the reengineering project in the organization's goals and objectives. In all likelihood, six months have elapsed since the reengineering team began its project. Regardless of the frequency with which your organization reviews its goals and objectives—quarterly, semi-annually, or annually—it is timely to examine the positive impact expected for your project.

Step 5: Action

- *Pilot the improved process.* Test the new process in a scaled-down version or test critical facets to identify unanticipated problems. Make appropriate adjustments after evaluating results of the pilot test.

- *Develop action plans.* Establish implementation priorities, set schedules, and assign responsibilities. At this stage of the project, it is not uncommon to replace some team members whose skills were needed during the design phase with others who might fit better with the needs of a deployment team. Unlike continuous improvement where small changes are discovered and imple-mented on an ongoing basis, reengineering is more like a project—and often a very large one. The team that was best suited for the design phase may not be the same as the one needed for effective deployment. To ensure continuity, retain at least half of the original members through to completion.

- *Implement plans.* Develop a transition plan and brief all involved parties. Develop the necessary training or acquire human resources with required skills. Coordinate site development, staffing, training, roll-out, and ramp-up to full deployment. Manage the changeover, and update documentation.

Step 6: Evaluation

- *Monitor results.* Monitor implementation, correcting problems as they occur.
- *Reward participants.* Reward and recognize successful team contributions.
- *Identify next steps.* Launch continuous improvement to sustain and extend gains.

SUMMARY

Reengineering is the most dramatic, expensive, risky, rewarding process redesign option available, yet every organization has to consider this improvement option when faced with the need for significant organizational improvement. This chapter points out the mistakes of other reengineering projects, dispels several reengineering myths, and provides a six-step method to lead reengineering teams to a successful conclusion.

DISCUSSION QUESTIONS

1. Is there a need in your organization to reengineer a core process or subprocess?
   a. What is the technique to confirm your selection?
   b. How would you gain management support for it?
   c. Is your organization prepared for the challenge?
2. What approach would you use to guide the reengineering project? Does one method appear to fit your needs better than another?

REFERENCES

Ackoff, R. L. 1993. "Idealized Design: Creating Corporate Visioning." *OMEGA International Journal of Management Science*, 21, no. 4, 401.

"After Reengineering: Taking Care of Business." 1994. *Datamation* (October 15), 40.

Christofferson, R. 1994. "Reengineering Missteps, Miscues." *Information Week* (June 20), 50.

Cole, R. E. 1994. "Reengineering the Corporation: A Review Essay." *Quality Management Journal* (July), 77.

CSC Index. 1994. *Executive Summary: State of Reengineering Report—North America and Europe*. Cambridge, MA: CSC Index.

Hammer, M. H. 1990. "Reengineering Work: Don't Automate, Obliterate." *Harvard Business Review* (July/August), 104–112.

Hammer, M. H., and J. Champy. 1993. *Reengineering the Corporation: A Manifesto for Business Revolution.* New York: Harper Business.

Maglitta, J. 1994. "Reengineering the Workplace: Rocks in the Gears." *Computerworld* (October 3), 96.

Manganelli, R. M., and M. M. Klien. 1994. *The Reengineering Handbook.* New York: American Management Association.

"Reengineering: Critical Success Factors." 1994. *Information Week* (September 12), 25.

16 Installing the Improved Process

Regardless of the improvement path taken—continuous improvement, benchmarking, or reengineering—all roads lead to implementation. Planning, analysis, and design have no value if the improved systems are not implemented. This last chapter describes implementation in three phases—integration, action, and evaluation.

INTEGRATION

COMMUNICATE RESULTS

If the improvement team is not empowered to act on its own recommendations, it will need to secure management's approval before progressing further. Any number of excuses can get in the way of accepting recommended changes. Typical barriers include transition costs, natural resistance to change, and the not-invented-here syndrome. Skepticism might be encountered in some cases, and outright hostility may be found in others. The team must communicate its findings in a manner to ensure acceptance. This can be accomplished by being clear and credible. Four suggestions are offered:

1. *Decide who needs to know.* Both formal and informal decision makers can be found in every organization. Additional groups needing to know the team's findings often include customers, suppliers, staff, and line or operating personnel with whom the team works. The team needs to decide who (by name) among these constituencies needs to know their findings, what they need to know, and why they need to know it.

2. *Select the best presentation vehicle.* Cultures vary, and what is accepted in one organization may not be viable in another. In some cultures, written reports are required with detailed supporting documentation. In other cultures, verbal presentations with overhead transparencies, prebriefings, and handouts are required. In still other organizations, a one-page executive summary and

informal discussion are all that is needed. The point is that the team must tailor its delivery to the recipients.

3. *Organize your findings.* Our experience shows that findings should be captured in a Best Practices Report. An example from one benchmarking team is provided in Appendix H. This document summarizes the work the team has completed and forms an integral part of the communication package. The report also may be useful to other improvement teams. Lastly, the discipline of documenting recommendations in a Best Practices Report ensures that findings will be thoroughly prepared. Tips for preparing a Best Practices Report include being descriptive as well as quantitative, presenting facts not opinions, stressing performance gains not methods of investigation, and including a preliminary estimate of the cost to implement the recommendations.

4. *Share the spotlight.* The recommendations should be presented by the complete team. Portions should be divided, so that every member shares the opportunity to present to management—an approach that offers both developmental opportunities and a form of recognition. Sharing the presentation among all members also reinforces the appearance that the recommendations are the consensus of the entire group.

In corporate cultures where management shuns surprises, the team should ascertain management's acceptance of its recommendations in advance of formal presentations. That is not to say that every recommendation should be accepted automatically without challenge. However, questions should be raised and answered and issues identified and resolved before a formal presentation. If the team keeps its sponsor informed throughout the project, and if the sponsor understands and endorses each step, acceptance should be certain.

Sometimes a team's recommendations will be rejected. When this happens, the next item on the management agenda should be to determine what went wrong with their management process that allowed a team to develop recommendations that were "off the mark" and rejected.

REVISE GOALS AND OBJECTIVES

Every organization should have clear direction regarding its short-term objectives and longer-term goals. Any substantive recommendation will affect these direction-setting statements. Therefore, anticipated changes should be reflected in revised goals and objectives. Failure to revise direction-setting statements after accepting a project team's recommendations indicates that the organization is not serious in following through. The Technical Training Group's goals and objectives are presented in Table 16.1, along with revisions resulting from their improvement project. Once again, management must endorse, support, and approve the proposed changes.

TABLE 16.1	Sample Revised Goals and Objectives	
MISSION		**REVISED**
Provide training to all technical personnel and continually improve their skills and productivity, so that they achieve their job targets and satisfy all end-user service requirements.		No change
GOAL		
Achieve the industry's best technical training.		No change
OBJECTIVES		
Improve mean-time-to-repair (MTTR) test scores from 1.4 to 1.2 hrs.		Reduce MTTR to 0.5 hrs.
Reduce program development time and costs by 10%.		Reduce program development time and costs by 25%.
Increase interest level in class by 20%.		No change

ACTION

PILOT THE IMPROVED PROCESS

Pilot new practices before full-scale implementation. The pilot may be as simple as passing a few pieces of paper around the room to symbolize a new workflow. In a more complex process or in one undergoing significant changes, an actual trial run should be conducted. The pilot might be a small-scale version of the complete process, or it might be a full-scale test of a segment.

The size and scope of the pilot depend on the type of process undergoing improvement and the magnitude of the change. Small changes resulting from continuous improvement will likely not require piloting. The information that would be learned through piloting may already have been obtained through experimenting (see Chapter 13). On the other hand, step changes resulting from benchmarking or reengineering will usually justify the time and effort required to design and operate a pilot test.

When designing the pilot, include plans to push the pilot to its limits to determine operating boundaries. Be certain to allow time and resources for revising plans to capture changes dictated by surprises that cannot be anticipated. After all, this is why you undertook a pilot study in the first place.

Plan-do-study-act: Remember to include time and resources for modifying your plans *after* piloting. Why bother wasting time with the pilot if you don't intend to learn from it?

DEVELOP ACTION PLANS

The Technical Training Group has secured management approval, goals have been revised, and performance targets adjusted. The new process has been pilot tested, and changes made to reflect results of these tests. The challenge before the Technical Training Group is how to implement their recommendations. Required tasks are to (1) establish priorities, (2) develop a definitive plan, and (3) revise performance projections.

Establish Priorities

Not all opportunities will yield the same payoffs. Some will offer bigger savings, some will be more difficult to implement, some will be more costly, others will require staff changes, and still others will have significant impacts upstream (suppliers) or downstream (customers). Implementation will be prioritized through the same three factors that were described for improvement efforts in Chapter 11—importance, opportunity, and feasibility.

Given these considerations, changes will likely be implemented in stages. More important than choosing the first one to be implemented is the development of criteria by which changes should be staged. Once the criteria have been defined, determining the implementation sequence will be relatively straightforward. A sample of the criteria by which priorities can be determined is listed in Table 16.2.

These criteria will enable a team to prepare a worksheet to assess the positive (+) and negative (−) factors for implementing each proposed change. Table 16.3 illustrates an example that the Technical Training Group completed for one of the

TABLE 16.2	Implementation Priority Criteria	
CRITERIA	**CONSIDERATIONS**	
Choose the criteria by which priorities will be determined for each proposed change in practice.		
• **Performance improvement**	How much will this new practice contribute to improve the work unit's effectiveness and/or efficiency?	(Importance)
• **Timing**	How soon can this process be installed and show results?	(Opportunity)
• **Success probability**	What are the risks and certainty of results?	(Feasibility)
• **Costs**	How many people, specialists, equipment, and tools are needed to make it happen? What are their costs?	(Feasibility)
• **Facilities**	Do facilities have to be enlarged? Do we need to relocate?	(Feasibility)
• **Staffing**	What changes in personnel are required?	(Feasibility)
• **Training**	Who needs training on what, where, when, and for how long?	(Feasibility)
• **Controls**	What inspectors, measurements, and monitoring systems are needed?	(Feasibility)

TABLE 16.3	Sample Implementation Priority Analysis		
CRITERIA	**+/− FACTORS**	**CRITERIA**	**+/− FACTORS**
Performance improvement	+ Saves several weeks + Improves test scores − No negative performance impacts	**Facilities**	+ No direct impact
Timing	+ 3 weeks + No impact on current work − First quarter too busy	**Staffing**	− Hire curriculum design specialist + Promote one editor to designer
Success probability	+ Very high, no new technology involved + Staff likes new approach	**Training**	− Five designers attend 2 weeks of training, $8,000
Costs	− New publishing software, $4,500 − New laser printer, $1,000	**Controls**	− Monitor retraining

NOTE: Not all criteria are pertinent every time. Perhaps only two or three apply to any individual practice.

TABLE 16.4	Sample Technical Training Implementation Schedule
WORK PRACTICE	**SCHEDULE**
1. Needs analysis	Implement immediately.
2. Task analysis	Implement within 30 days.
3. Program design	Implement immediately.
4. Materials preparation	Implement 30 days after designers are retrained.
5. Evaluate results	Initiate when all new practices are installed.
6. Instructor training	Initiate after first pilot is conducted.

improvements that they intend to implement. After establishing priorities, an implementation schedule can be prepared, and an example of the Technical Training Group's schedule is illustrated in Table 16.4.

Develop Definitive Plans

Prepare a definitive action plan for full-scale implementation. Be sure to include the four critical factors—who, what, how, and when. An example of an action plan is illustrated in Table 16.5.

- *What:* List specific action items—tasks that must be completed.

- *How:* Estimate resources required, including personnel, equipment, and materials.

TABLE 16.5	Sample Technical Training Action Plan		
ACTION ITEM	**RESOURCES REQUIRED**	**RESPONSIBILITY**	**COMPLETION DATE**
1. Write new procedures manual analysis method.	Process manual	Kelley	Oct. 6
2. Set approval points.	Scheduling calendar	Estevez	Oct. 6
3. Create a progress chart.	PERT chart	Estevez	Oct. 30
4. Train designers.	Procedures manual	Peterson	Jan.
5. Explain procedures to suppliers.	Procedures manual	Peterson	March
6. Complete instructor training.	$10,000	Jenkins	June

- *Who:* Assign responsibilities for each action item. The team that launched the improvement process might not include the right people for implementation. Recognize the tasks ahead and assign appropriate resources.

- *When:* Establish expected completion dates for each task.

Revise Performance Projection

Having prepared an implementation schedule, the Technical Training Group now needs to show the impact that the latest plans have on closing their performance gap. Revise earlier performance projections to reflect actual implementation plans. Figure 16.1 shows the gains in the team's key performance indicator—mean time to repair (MTTR)—resulting from a benchmarking project.

Figure 16.1 shows the trend in MTTR three ways. It first shows the slow improvement expected if the original training development practices were continued. It also shows the improvement that was projected when the team completed its analysis (Chapter 14). Finally, it shows the pace of improvements currently expected, now that definitive plans have been developed. This latest projection will serve as the target for monitoring progress during full-scale implementation.

This figure illustrates two common problems. First, rather than jumping to a 67 percent reduction in MTTR in two years as originally projected, definitive planning shows two-and-one-half years are needed, 25 percent longer. Second, rather than gaining benefits evenly during the implementation period, results are not reaped until the end. In this example, only 50 percent of the anticipated gains will be realized by the original two-year completion point. Our experience shows that initial projections tend to understate both the time and effort required, often by 50 or even 100 percent.

IMPLEMENT PLANS

Finally it's time to capture the benefits promised by the improvement team by changing over to the new and better process. Don't forget two often overlooked points:

- *Manage the changeover.* Some organizations have formal procedures for changing the design or operation of their processes. Other organizations rely on systems that can be termed informal at best. Follow the procedures appropriate for your own organization. Note, however, that if your current process is described as informal, it may be a candidate for improvement itself.

- *Document new process.* New flowcharts, designs, or operating procedures were likely drafted in earlier steps in the improvement process. Update your documentation to show the new process that is being installed.

EVALUATION

MONITOR RESULTS

Establish a monitoring system to track progress and alert the team when corrective action is required. Also, develop a reporting mechanism to inform the sponsor of progress. Use the updated performance projection as the target and a chart similar to Figure 16.1 to map progress.

In addition to setting up a system to track progress, step back and evaluate the process used by the team to identify, analyze, and implement improvements. Are changes needed in your process for continuous improvement, benchmarking, or reengineering? No evaluation would be complete without identifying the cause. Was the improvement effort poorly planned, misguided, or understaffed? Were process performance problems incorrectly analyzed at the outset, or were certain cultural requirements missing?

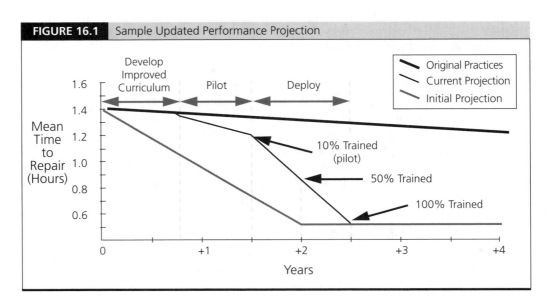

FIGURE 16.1   Sample Updated Performance Projection

TABLE 16.6	Criteria for Evaluating Team Performance
GOALS	• Were goals understood and supported by all members and by management? • Were goals realistic—ambitious but achievable? • Were goals within the scope of ownership of team members or the sponsoring manager? • Did the goals contribute to the mission, vision, and objectives of the organization?
ROLES	• Did all members know and fulfill their responsibilities? Members' responsibilities may include allocating time to team meetings, performing specific roles, as well as working outside of meetings. Members also are responsible for coaching other members. If one member is not supporting the team, others have the responsibility of asking that individual to step off the team.
PROCESS	• Was a structured, defined, disciplined process followed by the team in pursuit of its goal? Which path was followed—continuous improvement, benchmarking, or reengineering?
DEVELOPMENT	• As a result of involvement on the team, have all members learned new concepts, tools, or techniques that they can apply to their own work outside of the team?
INNOVATION	• Did the team question conventional wisdom and traditional approaches? • Did the team find new ways to attack old problems? • Did the team recommend an entirely new approach that both improves customer satisfaction and reduces costs?
RESULTS	• Did the team achieve its goal? • Does the solution permanently improve the underlying work process?

NOTE: *Results usually arrive incrementally and rarely as dramatic breakthroughs. Don't debate which is more important because both are needed. In our opinion, breakthroughs come only when a lot of incremental improvements have already been secured and when processes are under control. The danger of looking for only one major breakthrough and not the incremental improvements, as well, is that you may get neither.*

SOURCE: Adapted from Tenner and DeToro (1992, 186–188).

REWARD PARTICIPANTS

True teams succeed or fail together. Members of successful teams should be recognized and rewarded in a fashion consistent with your organization's culture. One form of recognition is for teams to present their success stories to others in publicized events. This not only serves to recognize the contributions of the team but provides a learning experience for others who may be struggling with similar issues.

We advocate teamwork to get results. However, the process of building teams provides value by itself. To keep sight of this, six criteria are offered in Table 16.6 for evaluating the performance of teams. Evaluate a team's success by considering how well it performs in each of the areas outlined in the table.

IDENTIFY THE NEXT STEPS

Successful benchmarking or reengineering initiatives will likely lead to continuous improvement. Similarly, successful continuous improvement initiatives will likely lead to recycling for further gains. In these happy instances, next steps should be obvious.

However, what if the project fell short of its objectives or was abandoned? Diagnose the cause of the problem before setting yourself up to reenact your failures.

- If the improvement effort was poorly planned, misguided, or understaffed, then your next step would be to correct the deficiencies and resume the failed project (Chapters 12 through 15).
- If problems are attributable to an incorrect analysis of the process at the outset, then your next step would be to go back and reexamine your organization's view of processes and performance measurements (Chapters 5 through 11).
- If failure was caused by a nonsupportive organizational culture, then your next step must be to rebuild this faulty foundation (Chapters 2 through 4).

The step-by-step procedures explained in this book have been applied by organizations around the world to obtain significant improvements in business performance. You should expect to achieve similar success. After installing improvements, you should be prepared to set even more ambitious targets and launch new projects to bring your processes to world-class performance levels.

SUMMARY

The culmination of all process improvement efforts is in their implementation. This chapter explains the need for piloting and planning as well as communicating and evaluating the changeover to a redesigned process. The suggestions and guidelines in this chapter should help to ensure success.

DISCUSSION QUESTIONS

1. Select a project that is nearly ready for implementation or one that has recently been completed. How would you determine the size and scope of a pilot to test the new process before full-scale deployment?
2. For the project used in question 1, compare the rate and magnitude of performance improvement now expected to the levels originally projected when the project was launched. Are they bigger, smaller, or about the same?
3. What should be done to reward or recognize members of the improvement team?
4. What are the next steps for improvement after the conclusion of this project?

REFERENCE

Tenner, A. R., and I. J. DeToro. 1992. *Total Quality Management: Three Steps to Continuous Improvement*. Reading, MA: Addison-Wesley.

APPENDIXES

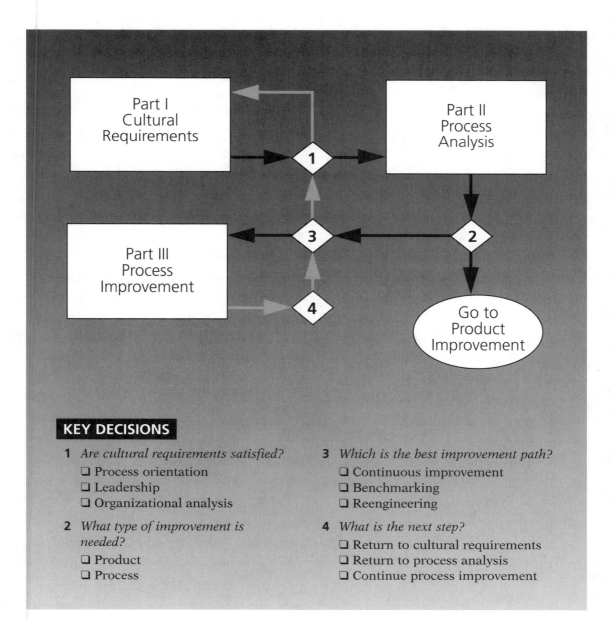

Part I
Cultural
Requirements

1

Part II
Process
Analysis

2

3

Part III
Process
Improvement

4

Go to
Product
Improvement

KEY DECISIONS

1 *Are cultural requirements satisfied?*
- ❑ Process orientation
- ❑ Leadership
- ❑ Organizational analysis

2 *What type of improvement is needed?*
- ❑ Product
- ❑ Process

3 *Which is the best improvement path?*
- ❑ Continuous improvement
- ❑ Benchmarking
- ❑ Reengineering

4 *What is the next step?*
- ❑ Return to cultural requirements
- ❑ Return to process analysis
- ❑ Continue process improvement

APPENDIX A

APQC Process Classification System

Chapter 5 defined processes and described various techniques for their classification, one of which is a decimal numbering system. The International Benchmarking Clearinghouse at the American Productivity and Quality Center (APQC) provides a comprehensive system covering thirteen categories of operational, management, and supporting processes that can be found in most organizations. This system serves as a checklist against which organizations can compare their own processes to ensure that none have been overlooked. The contribution of this information from the International Benchmarking Clearinghouse is gratefully acknowledged.

1. UNDERSTAND MARKETS AND CUSTOMERS

1.1 Determine customer needs and wants
  1.1.1 Conduct qualitative assessments
    1.1.1.1 Conduct customer interviews
    1.1.1.2 Conduct focus groups
  1.1.2 Conduct quantitative assessments
    1.1.2.1 Develop and implement surveys
  1.1.3 Predict customer purchasing behavior
1.2 Measure customer satisfaction
  1.2.1 Monitor satisfaction with products and services
  1.2.2 Monitor satisfaction with complaint resolution
  1.2.3 Monitor satisfaction with communication
1.3 Monitor changes in market or customer expectations
  1.3.1 Determine weaknesses of product/service offerings
  1.3.2 Identify new innovations that are meeting customers' needs
  1.3.3 Determine customer reactions to competitive offerings

2. DEVELOP VISION AND STRATEGY

2.1 Monitor the external environment
  2.1.1 Analyze and understand competition
  2.1.2 Identify economic trends
  2.1.3 Identify political and regulatory issues
  2.1.4 Assess new technology innovations
  2.1.5 Understand demographics
  2.1.6 Identify social and cultural changes
  2.1.7 Understand ecological concerns

2.2 Define the business concept and organizational strategy
- 2.2.1 Select relevant markets
- 2.2.2 Develop long-term vision
- 2.2.3 Formulate business unit strategy
- 2.2.4 Develop overall mission statement

2.3 Design the organizational structure and relationships between organizational units

2.4 Develop and set organizational goals

3. DESIGN PRODUCTS AND SERVICES

3.1 Develop new product/service concept and plans
- 3.1.1 Translate customer wants and needs into product and/or service requirements
- 3.1.2 Plan and deploy quality targets
- 3.1.3 Plan and deploy cost targets
- 3.1.4 Develop product life cycle and development timing targets
- 3.1.5 Develop and integrate leading technology into product/service concept

3.2 Design, build, and evaluate prototype products and services
- 3.2.1 Develop product/service specifications
- 3.2.2 Conduct concurrent engineering
- 3.2.3 Implement value engineering
- 3.2.4 Document design specifications
- 3.2.5 Develop prototypes
- 3.2.6 Apply for patents

3.3 Refine existing products/services
- 3.3.1 Develop product/service enhancements
- 3.3.2 Eliminate quality/reliability problems
- 3.3.3 Eliminate outdated products/services

3.4 Test effectiveness of new or revised products or services

3.5 Prepare for production
- 3.5.1 Develop and test prototype production process

- 3.5.2 Design and obtain necessary materials and equipment
- 3.5.3 Install and verify process or methodology

3.6 Manage the product/service development process

4. MARKET AND SELL

4.1 Market products or services to relevant customer segments
- 4.1.1 Develop pricing strategy
- 4.1.2 Develop advertising strategy
- 4.1.3 Develop marketing messages to communicate benefits
- 4.1.4 Estimate advertising resource and capital requirements
- 4.1.5 Identify specific target customers and their needs
- 4.1.6 Develop sales forecast
- 4.1.7 Sell products and services
- 4.1.8 Negotiate terms

4.2 Process customer orders
- 4.2.1 Accept orders from customers
- 4.2.2 Enter orders into production and delivery process

5. PRODUCE AND DELIVER FOR MANUFACTURING-ORIENTED ORGANIZATION

5.1 Plan for and acquire necessary resources
- 5.1.1 Select and certify suppliers
- 5.1.2 Purchase capital goods
- 5.1.3 Purchase materials and supplies
- 5.1.4 Acquire appropriate technology

5.2 Convert resources or inputs into products
- 5.2.1 Develop and adjust production delivery process (for existing process)
- 5.2.2 Schedule production
- 5.2.3 Move materials and resources
- 5.2.4 Make product
- 5.2.5 Package product
- 5.2.6 Warehouse or store product
- 5.2.7 Stage products for delivery

5.3 Deliver products
- 5.3.1 Arrange product shipment
- 5.3.2 Deliver products to customers
- 5.3.3 Install product
- 5.3.4 Confirm specific service requirements for individual customers
- 5.3.5 Identify and schedule resources to meet service requirements
- 5.3.6 Provide the service to specific customers

5.4 Manage production and delivery process
- 5.4.1 Document and monitor order status
- 5.4.2 Manage inventories
- 5.4.3 Assure product quality
- 5.4.4 Schedule and perform maintenance
- 5.4.5 Monitor environmental constraints

6. PRODUCE AND DELIVER FOR SERVICE-ORIENTED ORGANIZATION

6.1 Plan for and acquire necessary resources
- 6.1.1 Select and certify suppliers
- 6.1.2 Purchase materials and supplies
- 6.1.3 Acquire appropriate technology

6.2 Develop human resource skills
- 6.2.1 Define skill requirements
- 6.2.2 Identify and implement training
- 6.2.3 Monitor and manage skill development

6.3 Deliver service to the customer
- 6.3.1 Confirm specific service requirements for individual customer
- 6.3.2 Identify and schedule resources to meet service requirements
- 6.3.3 Provide the service to specific customers

6.4 Ensure quality of service

7. INVOICE AND SERVICE CUSTOMERS

7.1 Bill the customer
- 7.1.1 Develop, deliver, and maintain customer billing
- 7.1.2 Invoice the customer
- 7.1.3 Respond to billing inquiries

7.2 Provide after-sales service
- 7.2.1 Provide post-sales service
- 7.2.2 Handle warranties and claims

7.3 Respond to customer inquiries
- 7.3.1 Respond to information requests
- 7.3.2 Manage customer complaints

8. DEVELOP AND MANAGE HUMAN RESOURCES

8.1 Create and manage human resource strategies
- 8.1.1 Identify organizational strategic demands
- 8.1.2 Determine human resource costs
- 8.1.3 Define human resource requirements
- 8.1.4 Define human resource's organizational role

8.2 Cascade strategy to work level
- 8.2.1 Analyze, design, or redesign work
- 8.2.2 Define and align work outputs and metrics
- 8.2.3 Define work competencies

8.3 Manage deployment of personnel
- 8.3.1 Plan and forecast workforce requirements
- 8.3.2 Develop succession and career plans
- 8.3.3 Recruit, select and hire employees
- 8.3.4 Create and deploy teams
- 8.3.5 Relocate employees
- 8.3.6 Restructure and rightsize workforce
- 8.3.7 Manage employee retirement
- 8.3.8 Provide outplacement support

8.4 Develop and train employees
  8.4.1 Align employee and organization development needs
  8.4.2 Develop and manage training programs
  8.4.3 Develop and manage employee orientation programs
  8.4.4 Develop functional/process competencies
  8.4.5 Develop management/leadership competencies
  8.4.6 Develop team competencies
8.5 Manage employee performance, reward and recognition
  8.5.1 Define performance measures
  8.5.2 Develop performance management approaches and feedback
  8.5.3 Manage team performance
  8.5.4 Evaluate work for market value and internal equity
  8.5.5 Develop and manage base and variable compensation
  8.5.6 Manage reward and recognition programs
8.6 Ensure employee well-being and satisfaction
  8.6.1 Manage employee satisfaction
  8.6.2 Develop work and family support systems
  8.6.3 Manage and administer employee benefits
  8.6.4 Manage workplace health and safety
  8.6.5 Manage internal communications
  8.6.6 Manage and support workforce diversity
8.7 Ensure employee involvement
8.8 Manage labor-management relationships
  8.8.1 Manage collective bargaining process
  8.8.2 Manage labor-management partnerships
8.9 Develop Human Resource Information Systems (HRIS)

9. MANAGE INFORMATION RESOURCES

9.1 Plan for information resource management
  9.1.1 Derive requirements from business strategies
  9.1.2 Define enterprise system architectures
  9.1.3 Plan and forecast information technologies & methodologies
  9.1.4 Establish enterprise data standards
  9.1.5 Establish quality standards and controls
9.2 Develop and deploy enterprise support systems
  9.2.1 Conduct specific needs assessments
  9.2.2 Select information technologies
  9.2.3 Define data life cycles
  9.2.4 Develop enterprise support systems
  9.2.5 Test, evaluate, and deploy enterprise support systems
9.3 Implement systems security and controls
  9.3.1 Establish systems security strategies and levels
  9.3.2 Test, evaluate, and deploy systems security and controls
9.4 Manage information storage & retrieval
  9.4.1 Establish information repositories (data bases)
  9.4.2 Acquire & collect information
  9.4.3 Store information
  9.4.4 Modify and update information
  9.4.5 Enable retrieval of information
  9.4.6 Delete information
9.5 Manage facilities and network operations
  9.5.1 Manage centralized facilities
  9.5.2 Manage distributed facilities
  9.5.3 Manage network operations
9.6 Manage information services

9.6.1 Manage libraries and information centers
9.6.2 Manage business records and documents
9.7 Facilitate information sharing and communication
9.7.1 Manage external communications systems
9.7.2 Manage internal communications systems
9.7.3 Prepare and distribute publications
9.8 Evaluate and audit information quality

10. MANAGE FINANCIAL AND PHYSICAL RESOURCES

10.1 Manage financial resources
10.1.1 Develop budgets
10.1.2 Manage resource allocation
10.1.3 Design capital structure
10.1.4 Manage cash flow
10.1.5 Manage financial risk
10.2 Process finance and accounting transactions
10.2.1 Process accounts payable
10.2.2 Process payroll
10.2.3 Process accounts receivable, credit and collections
10.2.4 Close the books
10.2.5 Process benefits and retiree information
10.2.6 Manage travel and entertainment expenses
10.3 Report information
10.3.1 Provide external financial information
10.3.2 Provide internal financial information
10.4 Conduct internal audits
10.5 Manage the tax function
10.5.1 Ensure tax compliance
10.5.2 Plan tax strategy
10.5.3 Employ effective technology
10.5.4 Manage tax controversies
10.5.5 Communicate tax issues to management
10.5.6 Manage tax administration
10.6 Manage physical resources
10.6.1 Manage capital planning
10.6.2 Acquire and redeploy fixed assets
10.6.3 Manage facilities
10.6.4 Manage physical risk

11. EXECUTE ENVIRONMENTAL MANAGEMENT PROGRAM

11.1 Formulate environmental management strategy
11.2 Ensure compliance with regulations
11.3 Train and educate employees
11.4 Implement pollution prevention program
11.5 Manage remediation efforts
11.6 Implement emergency response programs
11.7 Manage government agency and public relations
11.8 Manage acquisition/divestiture environmental issues
11.9 Develop and manage environmental information system
11.10 Monitor environmental management program

12. MANAGE EXTERNAL RELATIONSHIPS

12.1 Communicate with shareholders
12.2 Manage government relationships
12.3 Build lender relationships
12.4 Develop public relations program
12.5 Interface with board of directors
12.6 Develop community relations
12.7 Manage legal and ethical issues

13. MANAGE IMPROVEMENT AND CHANGE

13.1 Measure organizational performance
13.1.1 Create measurement systems
13.1.2 Measure product and service quality

13.1.3 Measure cost of quality

13.1.4 Measure costs

13.1.5 Measure cycle time

13.1.6 Measure productivity

13.2 Conduct quality assessments

13.2.1 Conduct quality assessments based on external criteria

13.2.2 Conduct quality assessments based on internal criteria

13.3 Benchmark performance

13.3.1 Develop benchmarking capabilities

13.3.2 Conduct process benchmarking

13.3.3 Conduct competitive benchmarking

13.4 Improve processes and systems

13.4.1 Create commitment for improvement

13.4.2 Implement continuous process improvement

13.4.3 Reengineer business processes and systems

13.4.4 Manage transition to change

13.5 Implement TQM

13.5.1 Create commitment for TQM

13.5.2 Design and implement TQM systems

13.5.3 Manage TQM life cycle

SOURCE: Courtesy of the International Benchmarking Clearinghouse at the American Productivity and Quality Center, 123 North Post Oak Lane, Houston, TX, August 1995.

APPENDIX B | Six-Sigma Analysis

This appendix provides additional technical information on Motorola's six-sigma analysis that was introduced in Chapter 8 for characterizing the capability of processes to operate without errors. Recall from Chapter 8 that the ability of a process to deliver products within their specifications can be characterized by a term called the *capability index* (either C_p or C_{pk}). Motorola's six-sigma approach provides a simplified alternative that eliminates the need for statistical analysis.

A six-sigma value can be assigned to a process simply by looking up a number on a table or on a chart like Figure B.1. The performance number is assigned on the basis of how many errors were detected in the outputs as a ratio or percentage of the opportunities to produce those errors. Readers can use Figure B.1 directly or read this appendix for background and clarification.

DEFINING TERMINOLOGY

First let's clarify how Motorola calculates values for its six-sigma analysis. Motorola based its performance metric on the normal curve but with the mean shifted by 1.5σ. The rationale for this shift is explained later in this appendix in the section titled "Protecting Against Shifting of the Mean." For now, let's concentrate on its construction with the aid of the two curves in Figure B.1.

Values for Motorola's six-sigma analysis are depicted in the mean-shifted curve shown in Figure B.1. These are the same as the chart presented in Chapter 8. Figure B.1 also displays a mean-centered curve, and the relationship of each curve to C_p or C_{pk}.

> **MEAN CENTERED:** This curve represents the area in the "tails" (both upper and lower) of the normal curve beyond the referenced point as measured in standard deviations. For example, looking up the area in the tail beyond $\sigma = 3.0$

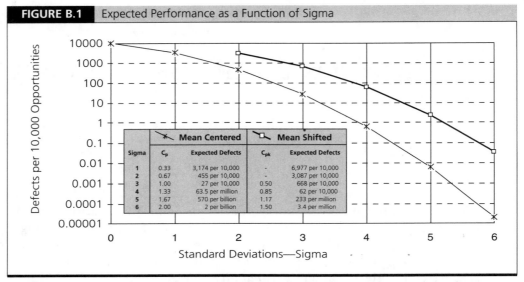

| FIGURE B.1 | Expected Performance as a Function of Sigma |

SOURCE: Adopted from M. J. Harry, and J. R. Lawson, *Six Sigma Producibility Analysis and Process Characterization* (Reading, MA: Addison-Wesley, 1992), 5-6–5-7.

in a statistics textbook will show 1.35×10^{-3}, which is equivalent to 1350 ppm, or 13.5 out of 10,000. This is the area under the "upper tail." The mean-centered curve in Figure B.1 includes both tails, so this figure is doubled to 2.70×10^{-3}.

MEAN SHIFTED: This curve represents the area in the "upper tail" of the normal curve beyond the referenced point as measured in Motorola's deviation units, which correspond to normal standard deviations plus 1.5. For example, the area in the tail beyond $\sigma = 3.0$ is 1350 ppm, or 13.5 out of 10,000. This point is plotted at 4.5 deviation units in Motorola's mean-shifted curve in Figure B.1 $(4.5 = 3.0 + 1.5)$.

VISUALIZING SIX-SIGMA

Motorola's six-sigma represents an error rate of merely 0.00034 percent (3.4 ppm), and one might ask, "How much is enough?" Recall this value is determined by the area under the normal beyond 4.5σ above the mean $(6.0 = 4.5 + 1.5)$. This performance level is so good that it is difficult to visualize. Ponder the following examples that are equivalent to 3.4 ppm:

- Measuring the circumference of the earth to within 300 feet and
- Consuming 1 extra automobile gasoline tank fill-up (15 gallons) from a large (100,000 barrels per day) petroleum refinery.

On the surface, the six-sigma goal would seem to be absurd. It extends beyond practical limits and the expectations of normal variation. Digging deeper, however, two factors emerge to make six-sigma a sound goal: the concept of joint events and shifting of the mean.

PROTECTING AGAINST JOINT EVENTS

The concept of joint events impacts goods and services that are comprised of numerous individual components or produced through multiple sequential steps. The probability of finding defects in the output can be estimated by multiplying by the proportion of defects for each component or from each step. The concept is illustrated through the following examples.

Suppose that a product was manufactured through four steps and each step produced acceptable results 83 percent of the time. This percentage was selected because it corresponds to producing defects one-sixth of the time (17 percent) and can be modeled by the tossing of dice. Assume for the purpose of explanation that the numbers 1 through 5 on the dice represent acceptable performance and the number 6 represents a defect. The task becomes one of predicting the probability of throwing a die four times in succession without having a six appear.

The probability of success for this combination of dice throws is calculated as 0.83^4 or can be written as the following equation:

$$P \text{ (Probability)} \quad = 0.83 \times 0.83 \times 0.83 \times 0.83$$
$$= 0.48$$

Even though each step in the process is 83 percent reliable, the result from their combination is expected to be acceptable merely 48 percent of the time.

As a second example, the yield of each step is increased from 83 to 90 percent. Again assuming four steps, what is the expected success rate?

$$P \text{ (Probability)} \quad = 0.90 \times 0.90 \times 0.90 \times 0.90$$
$$= 0.66$$

Achieving 66 percent success is not particularly exciting either, so even 90 percent defect-free results from each of four steps will disappoint most organizations. Table B.1 illustrates the expected results of multistep processes with various performance levels for each step. Notice in Table B.1 how rapidly defects increase as the number of steps increases, when each individual step is performing at the level equivalent

TABLE B.1	Predicting Performance for Various Example Processes							
	INDIVIDUAL PERFORMANCE: EACH STEP OR COMPONENT			RESULTING PERFORMANCE: PPM DEFECTS AS A FUNCTION OF NUMBER OF STEPS OR COMPONENTS				
SIGMA	C_{pk}	% ACCEPT	DEFECTS (PPM)	4	8	16	32
4	0.85	99.38	6,200	24,600	48,500	95,000	180,000
5	1.17	99.998	23	92	184	368	736
6	1.50	99.9997	3.4	14	27	54	109

to a four-sigma standard. Even though each step is 99 percent perfect, when combined as a four-step process, the resultant yield is reduced to 97.54 percent (defect rate equivalent to 24,600 ppm). If used in a thirty-two-step process, the yield would be reduced to merely 82 percent.

It therefore should not be surprising that organizations like Motorola are pursuing six-sigma performance. Delivering complex products or services demands high levels of performance from each component, step, or subprocess.

PROTECTING AGAINST SHIFTING OF THE MEAN

In addition to protecting against joint events, the increased capability afforded by the six-sigma goal also protects against a problem that has the technical name of *shifting of the mean*. In fact, protecting against this problem is so important that Motorola built their six-sigma model on mean-shifted performance.

An example will serve to show the impact of shifting of the mean. Take a mean-centered process that is performing with a capability index of 1.0. The upper and lower specification limits will each be 3σ from the mean. The likelihood that random variation will produce a result more than 3σ from the mean of a stable process is merely twenty-seven chances out of 10,000 opportunities, or 0.27 percent. But what happens if the process changes?

The answer is shown in Figure B.2, where this example process is upset and begins yielding products with their mean shifted by one standard deviation. The shifted process now produces ten times the number of defects, 2.72 percent. Alternatively, had the process been performing at the six-sigma goal, the same shift of one standard deviation would have merely increased defects from the immeasurably low 3.4 ppm to a nearly immeasurable 233 ppm.

FIGURE B.2   Example Impact of Shifting of the Mean

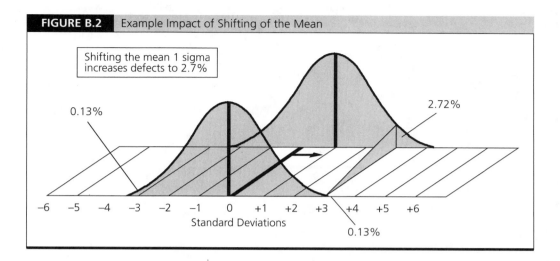

Shifting the mean 1 sigma increases defects to 2.7%

0.13%

2.72%

0.13%

Standard Deviations

−6 −5 −4 −3 −2 −1 0 +1 +2 +3 +4 +5 +6

APPENDIX C

Sample Project Description

Basic Products Corporation
Technical Service Group

Project Description

PROJECT TEAM MEMBERS

Thomas McKay
Bernice Lyons
Robb Campbell
Ira DeTorre

Contents

> ### Note to readers
>
> *This sample document was prepared for launching a benchmarking team. Similar project descriptions might be prepared for teams following other improvement paths. The description for a continuous improvement team might be somewhat abbreviated. By contrast, one for a reengineering project would likely be more extensive.*

Team Charter

The Technical Training Group proposes to improve its *curriculum development* subprocesses because it offers the largest opportunity to lower training costs, reduce training time, and improve test scores—objectives that are consistent with current business priorities. Process benchmarking has been selected as the improvement path.

Project Triggers

The impetus for this project comes from six sources—competitive analysis, independent study, field engineer management reports, student polls (internal customers), instructors polled (suppliers), and customer satisfaction surveys (external customers).

Competitive Analysis

One hundred customers were polled or interviewed to determine what their requirements are and how satisfied they are with our company's service and that of our competitors. Their expectations are displayed in Table C.1.

TABLE C.1 *Customer Analysis*

Customer Requirements	Basic Products	Shelby Industries	Amalgamated Products
Average response time	6 hrs.	4 hrs.	3.5 hrs.
Time to repair equipment	1.4 hrs.	1.1 hrs.	1.2 hrs.
Cost of repairs	$100	$125	$112
Frequency of breakdown	1.3 per mo.	1.2 per mo.	1.4 per mo.
Average downtime per month	6.8 hrs.	5.4 hrs.	6.1 hrs.

Independent Study

The most recent *Field Operations Report*, an independent third-party study, compared equipment repair times for the top ten companies in our industry. In that report, Basic Products ranked seventh in average equipment repair time (see Table C.2).

TABLE C.2 *Average Time to Repair Equipment*

Company	Rank	Hours
Shelby Industries	1	1.11
Amalgamated Products	2	1.28
Marshall Corporation	3	1.39
Benson Enterprises, Ltd.	4	1.41
Western Systems, Inc.	5	1.43
Universal Widgets Corp.	6	1.44
Basic Products	7	1.45
Triple Edge Gadgets	8	1.48
Widgets	9	1.49
Gizmo Products Co.	10	1.51

Field Engineer Management Reports

All field engineers are given quarterly performance reviews. The results are tabulated in a report that summarizes the most frequent reasons cited by field managers for engineers' performance deficiencies. The three problems cited most frequently for poor technical performance are

- Insufficient training,
- Not enough time with management, and
- Poor hiring.

This project will address the issue of *insufficient training*.

Student Polls (Internal Customers)

Questionnaires given to field engineers trained in the Education Center revealed several opportunities to improve technical training. Recently trained technicians ranked their suggestions for improvement as shown in Table C.3.

TABLE C.3   *Technicians' Suggestions for Improvement*

Improvements	Percentage of Technicians Responding
1. More hands-on time	87%
2. More visuals	75
3. Use of video for self-paced remediation	62
4. More diagnostics	47
5. Make learning more experiential	43

Instructors Polled (Suppliers)

Instructors expressed levels of satisfaction with the curriculum as shown in Table C.4.

TABLE C.4   *Instructors' Satisfaction with the Curriculum*

Requirements	Rating (1–10)
1. Percentage of trainees needing retraining	5.4
2. Average test scores after training	5.8
3. Program development time	7.1
4. Program technical content accuracy	8.8
5. Course teachability	9.5

Customer Satisfaction Surveys (External Customers)

Recent surveys indicate that external customers rank equipment downtime and service response time as their highest priorities (see Table C.5).

TABLE C.5   *Customers' Satisfaction*

Requirement	Priority	Rank
Equipment downtime	7.3	1
Service response time	7.8	2
Customer service	9.1	3
Equipment speed	9.2	4
Equipment cost	9.5	5
Safety features	9.6	6

The primary measure of the effectiveness of training will be "average time for trained service technicians to troubleshoot and repair defective equipment." This measure ties most closely with the customer's top priorities.

Project Goals

In assessing the current process, we determined the critical performance metrics that are used to measure training effectiveness and efficiency (see Table C.6). Although specific targets will be set as the analysis proceeds, we expect several important outcomes from this study:

- Reduce time to develop new curriculum,
- Reduce curriculum development costs,
- Improve average test scores,
- Reduce the percentage of students requiring retraining, and
- Improve teamwork within and between training work units.

TABLE C.6   *Performance Metrics and Industry Benchmarks*

Measure of Results	Internal Methods	Industry Leader	Benchmark
Average time to train	5 days	4 days	3 days
Average time to develop courses	12 wks.	8 wks.	6 wks.
Percentage retrained	15%	10%	5%
Average cost of course development	$35,000	TBD[a]	$20,000
Average test result (time to repair widget)	1.4 hrs.	1.1 hrs.	0.7 hrs.
Average cost to train	$1,800	TBD[a]	TBD[a]

a. To be determined through benchmarking.

Project Scope

The six-step curriculum development process spans four work groups. A complete end-to-end study of the entire training process is not justified (see Figure C.1). Instead, we will focus on *curriculum development*. Reasons for choosing this subprocess include the following:

- Curriculum development takes the longest and is the highest-budget item;
- It has the biggest impact on training outcomes (test scores); and
- Recent innovations in curriculum development techniques indicate that 50 percent cycle-time gains are attainable with dramatically improved test scores after training.

On completion, this project will reduce the time and cost for developing technical training courses. More important, it will reduce equipment downtime and enable us to leapfrog competitors in customer satisfaction. This improved performance will decrease the rate at which leases are cancelled and stabilize the current installed population of equipment.

It is expected that implementation of improvements will affect the timeliness of input provided to curriculum designers from engineers and field operations. It will also affect turnover and hiring of service representatives.

FIGURE C.1   *Process Map: Technical Training*

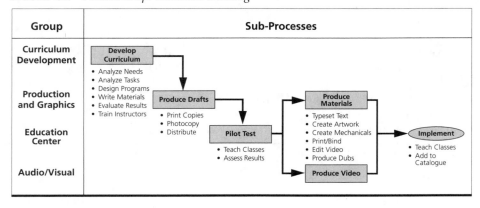

Methodology

A step-change in performance will be secured through process benchmarking. We expect to identify companies that are achieving superior results and emulate the specific practices enabling them to attain these highest performance levels.

Work will begin with a three-week literature search of trade journals. This will be followed by contacting several internal training organizations, at least two leading competitors, and one or two other companies known to be leaders in curriculum development. This work will lead to the identification of industry-best companies and practices.

Duration and Resources

Until industry-best companies and work practices are known, it is difficult to estimate the time and costs to conduct a thorough investigation and convert to best methods. On a preliminary basis, we estimate that four staff members working four months each can complete the project. Pending approval to continue with preliminary investigations, we anticipate costs as follows:

Item	Estimated cost
Salaries	$79,200
Travel	3,800
Consultant fees	1,200
Library search fees	450
Total	**$84,650**

Team Membership

Sy Ventura,	executive owner
Thomas McKay,	sponsor
Bernice Lyons,	literature researcher
Robb Campbell,	data collector
Ira DeTorre,	librarian

APPENDIX D | The Benchmarking Code of Conduct

International Benchmarking Clearinghouse

INTERNATIONAL
BENCHMARKING
CLEARINGHOUSE

The Benchmarking
Code of Conduct

- KEEP IT LEGAL
- BE WILLING TO GIVE WHAT YOU GET
- RESPECT CONFIDENTIALITY
- KEEP INFORMATION INTERNAL
- USE BENCHMARKING CONTACTS
- DON'T REFER WITHOUT PERMISSION
- BE PREPARED FROM THE START
- UNDERSTAND EXPECTATIONS
- ACT IN ACCORD WITH EXPECTATIONS
- BE HONEST
- FOLLOW THROUGH WITH COMMITMENTS

A Service of the
American Productivity
& Quality Center

THE BENCHMARKING CODE OF CONDUCT

■ PREAMBLE:

Benchmarking – the process of identifying and learning from best practices anywhere in the world – is a powerful tool in the quest for continuous improvement.

To guide benchmarking encounters and to advance the professionalism and effectiveness of benchmarking, the International Benchmarking Clearinghouse, a service of the American Productivity & Quality Center, and the Strategic Planning Institute Council on Benchmarking have adopted this common Code of Conduct. We encourage all organizations and individuals involved in benchmarking to abide by this Code of Conduct. Adherence to these principles will contribute to efficient, effective, and ethical benchmarking. This edition of the Code of Conduct has been expanded to provide greater guidance on the protocol of benchmarking for beginners.

■ BENCHMARKING CODE OF CONDUCT:

Individuals agree for themselves and their company to abide by the following principles for benchmarking with other organizations.

1. Principle of Legality.

1.1 If there is any potential question on the legality of an activity, don't do it.

1.2 Avoid discussions of actions that could lead to or imply an interest in restraint of trade, market and/or customer allocation schemes, price fixing, dealing arrangements, bid rigging, or bribery. Don't discuss costs with competitors if costs are an element of pricing.

1.3 Refrain from the acquisition of trade secrets from any means that could be interpreted as improper, including the breach or inducement of a breach of any duty to maintain secrecy. Do not disclose or use any trade secret that may have been obtained through improper means or that was disclosed by another in violation of a duty to maintain its secrecy or limit its use.

1.4 Do not, as a consultant or client, extend one benchmarking study's findings to another company without first obtaining the permission of the parties to the first study.

2. Principle of Exchange.

2.1 Be willing to provide the same type and level of information that you request from your benchmarking partner to your benchmarking partner.

2.2 Communicate fully and early in the relationship to clarify expectations, avoid misunderstanding and establish mutual interest in the benchmarking exchange.

2.3 Be honest and complete.

3. Principle of Confidentiality.

3.1 Treat benchmarking interchange as confidential to the individuals and companies involved. Information must not be communicated outside the partnering organizations without the prior consent of the benchmarking partner who shared the information.

3.2 A company's participation in a study is confidential and should not be communicated externally without their prior permission.

4. Principle of Use.

4.1 Use information obtained through benchmarking only for purposes of formulating improvement of operations of processes within the companies participating in the benchmarking study.

4.2 The use or communication of a benchmarking partner's name with the data obtained or practices observed requires the prior permission of that partner.

4.3 Do not use benchmarking information or any information resulting from a benchmarking exchange, or benchmarking-related networking as a means to market or sell.

4.4 Contact lists or other contact information provided by the International Benchmarking Clearinghouse in any form may not be used for marketing in any way.

5. Principle of First Party Contact.

5.1 Initiate benchmarking contacts, whenever possible, through a benchmarking contact designated by the partner company.

5.2 Respect the corporate culture of partner companies and work within mutually agreed procedures.

5.3 Obtain mutual agreement with the designated benchmarking contact on any hand-off of communication or responsibility to other parties.

BENCHMARKING PROTOCOL
Benchmarkers:

1. Know and abide by the Benchmarking Code of Conduct.

2. Have basic knowledge of benchmarking and follow a benchmarking process.

3. Prior to initiating contact with potential benchmarking partners, have determined what to benchmark, identified key performance variables to study, recognized superior performing companies, and completed a rigorous self-assessment.

4. Have developed a questionnaire and interview guide, and will share these in advance if requested.

5. Possess the authority to share and be willing to share information with benchmarking partners.

6. Work through a specified host and mutually agree on scheduling and meeting arrangements.

When the benchmarking process proceeds to a face-to-face site visit, the following behaviors are encouraged:

- Provide meeting agenda in advance
- Be professional, honest, courteous and prompt
- Introduce all attendees and explain why they are present
- Adhere to the agenda
- Use language that is universal, not one's own jargon
- Be sure that neither party is sharing proprietary information unless prior approval has been obtained by both parties, from the proper authority
- Share information about your own process, and, if asked, consider sharing study results
- Offer to facilitate a future reciprocal visit
- Conclude meetings and visits on schedule
- Thank your benchmarking partner for sharing their process

---

6. Principle of Third Party Contact.

6.1 Obtain an individual's permission before providing his or her name in response to a contact request.

6.2 Avoid communicating a contact's name in an open forum without the contact's prior permission.

7. Principle of **Preparation**.

7.1 Demonstrate commitment to the efficiency and effectiveness of benchmarking by being prepared prior to making an initial benchmarking contact.

7.2 Make the most of your benchmarking partner's time by being fully prepared for each exchange.

7.3 Help your benchmarking partners prepare by providing them with a questionnaire and agenda prior to benchmarking visits.

8. Principle of **Completion**.

8.1 Follow through with each commitment made to your benchmarking partner in a timely manner.

8.2 Complete each benchmarking study to the satisfaction of all benchmarking partners as mutually agreed.

9. Principle of the **Understanding and Action**.

9.1 Understand how your benchmarking partner would like to be treated.

9.2 Treat your benchmarking partner in the way that your benchmarking partner would want to be treated.

9.3 Understand how your benchmarking partner would like to have the information he or she provides handled and used, and handle and use it in that manner.

ETIQUETTE AND ETHICS

The following guidelines apply to both partners in a benchmarking encounter with competitors or potential competitors:

- In benchmarking with competitors, establish specific ground rules up-front, e.g., "We don't want to talk about things that will give either of us a competitive advantage, but rather we want to see where we both can mutually improve or gain benefit."

- Do not ask competitors for sensitive data or cause the benchmarking partner to feel they must provide data to keep the process going.

- Use an ethical third party to assemble and "blind" competitive data, with inputs from legal counsel in direct competitor sharing. (Note: When cost is closely linked to price, sharing cost data can be considered to be the same as price sharing.)

- Benchmarkers should check with legal counsel if any information-gathering procedure is in doubt, e.g., before contacting a direct competitor. If uncomfortable, do not proceed, or sign a security/non-disclosure agreement. Instead, negotiate a specific non-disclosure agreement which will satisfy the attorneys from both companies.

- Any information obtained from a benchmarking partner should be treated as internal, privileged communication. If "confidential" or proprietary material is to be exchanged, then a specific agreement should be executed to indicate the content of the material which needs to be protected, the duration of the period of protection, the conditions for permitting access to the material, and the specific handling requirements that are necessary for that material.

For further information call or write:
International Benchmarking Clearinghouse,
American Productivity & Quality Center,
123 North Post Oak Lane, Houston, TX 77024-7797,
713/685-4666, FAX: 713/681-5321.

Texas Instruments Benchmarking Core Team

Bill Baker
TEXAS INSTRUMENTS SYSTEMS GROUP, BENCHMARKING OFFICE

INTRODUCTION

Many American companies strive to win the Malcolm Baldrige National Quality Award and believe it to be their ultimate professional goal and reward. Texas Instruments (TI), Defense Systems and Electronics (DS&E), began the journey to improve the company in the 1980s. In 1988 the Malcolm Baldrige National Quality Award criteria were judged to be an excellent blueprint for achieving business excellence and used to drive continuous improvement.

> *Bill Baker* provides the following description of the infrastructure built at Texas Instruments to share their award-winning benchmarking expertise corporatewide. His contribution is gratefully acknowledged.

In 1990 the Baldrige examiner's feedback indicated benchmarking was an area that could be improved. The company created its strategy based on total quality management principles and identified benchmarking as one of the key thrusts to improve operations as shown in Figure E.1. With executive sponsorship, a fulltime benchmarking champion led the benchmarking process definition, training, and initial deployment.

Significant progress was substantiated when TI's DS&E won the 1992 Baldrige Award, and benchmarking was identified as one of the strengths in the site-visit examiner's report. Also in 1992, the company was recognized in *Business Week* (November 30, 1992, 74–75) as one of seven leading companies in America in the benchmarking process. In 1994, DS&E won two awards from the International Benchmarking Clearinghouse for excellence in benchmarking—the only companywide award and an award for one team's individual study.

ORGANIZATIONAL ALIGNMENT

This background was necessary to begin the main story—the evolution of the benchmarking deployment process. A singular benchmarking champion, assisted

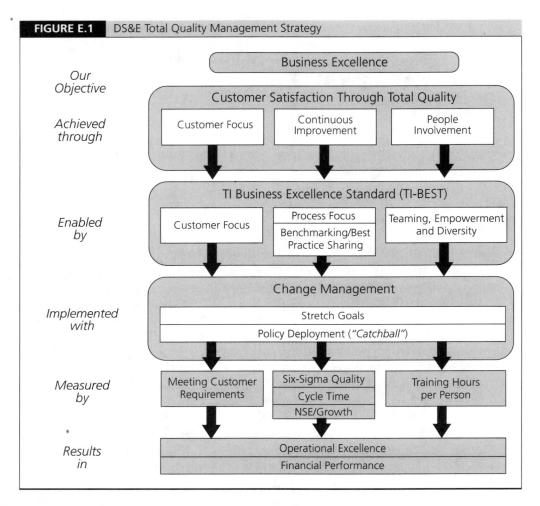

FIGURE E.1 DS&E Total Quality Management Strategy

Business Excellence

Our Objective

Customer Satisfaction Through Total Quality

Achieved through

| Customer Focus | Continuous Improvement | People Involvement |

TI Business Excellence Standard (TI-BEST)

Enabled by

| Customer Focus | Process Focus / Benchmarking/Best Practice Sharing | Teaming, Empowerment and Diversity |

Change Management

Implemented with

Stretch Goals
Policy Deployment ("*Catchball*")

Measured by

| Meeting Customer Requirements | Six-Sigma Quality / Cycle Time / NSE/Growth | Training Hours per Person |

Results in

Operational Excellence
Financial Performance

by part-time champions throughout the group, had served TI well up to this point. Following the Baldrige win, however, the company looked to further deploy and institutionalize the process improvements within their various site locations and to make benchmarking expertise available to all business managers.

The result was to create a *benchmarking core team* (BCT) from the most qualified benchmarking champions. The design criteria for the BCT was twofold—to have a BCT member resident at each of the nine major plant locations and, since DS&E was going to manage by process, to align a BCT member with each core process and process owner. This gave most team members dual roles—both plant and core process responsibility.

DS&E aligns its business processes with the customer's processes (see Figure E.2). Its eleven processes are comprised of six customer-related processes and five enabling processes, all of which cross previous functional boundaries.

All **BCT** members had a role in determining how the team would operate through participation in the development of its charter and operating guidelines. A full-time BCT team leader and administrative assistant serve as regular members, as well as coordinators of team activities. Example BCT outputs included the following:

- Standard benchmarking overview presentations were developed to convey the ten-step process.
- Lessons learned through four years of active benchmarking were documented.
- Summary presentations of high-profile success stories were prepared.

The BCT adapted to two organizational changes in 1995. From a strategic company viewpoint, the Defense Systems and Electronics Group expanded to

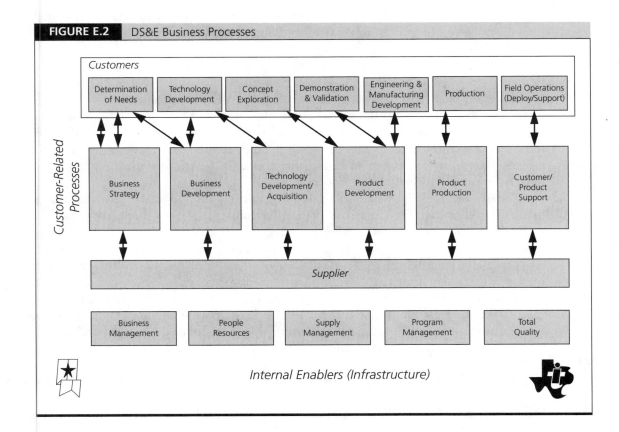

FIGURE E.2   DS&E Business Processes

include Communications and Electronics Systems and Defense Systems and Electronics under the new name of Texas Instruments Systems Group. BCT's responsibilities now encompasses both the defense and commercial sides of the systems business.

The second change was the new emphasis on sharing internal best practices in the Systems Group, as well as across other TI groups, including Semiconductors, Personal Productivity Products, Software, and Materials and Controls. Motivation for this *best-practice sharing process* came from TI's CEO, Jerry Junkins, who said, "If we only knew what we know at TI." Therefore, the benchmarking core team's role was extended to include responsibility for being *best-practice sharing facilitators*, TI's job title for a knowledge broker.

COMMUNICATIONS

The Systems Group benchmarking core team established a number of mechanisms for communicating with one another and with TI's Corporate Office of Best Practices. The main challenge was to cover nine sites in five Texas cities separated by a few to several hundred miles (Dallas, Plano, Lewisville, Sherman, and Austin). In teaming relationships, this could be called a "virtual team."

The BCT meets monthly to discuss plans, strategies, and any outstanding action items supporting the benchmarking and best-practice sharing processes. Meetings rotate among the major sites to promote learning and equalize travel.

A spreadsheet of team members' phone, fax, and pager numbers, internal mail drops, and e-mail addresses is maintained to ease communication. Any of these modes of communication is used depending on the urgency. A group e-mail ID was created that allows e-mail to be sent to the entire BCT with one address, including mail from other individuals or groups.

The *inquiry tracking system* was developed in early 1995 to enable team members to record calls or inquiries from customers and electronically track them on a real-time, online basis until the customer's needs have been satisfied. This tool is a modified Lotus Notes™ application and allows any team member to pick up where another has left off.

This system allows the BCT coordinators to determine responsibility for a given inquiry and assign that responsibility to the appropriate BCT member. Any BCT member can input status and view progress of a given call electronically. The inquiry tracking system is also utilized by the TI Corporate Office of Best Practices to communicate electronically and transmit assignments to the other benchmarking champions within the company.

To promote the benchmarking process within the Systems Group and to share successes, the *Benchmarking Success Stories* booklet covering thirty-one studies was published and distributed to key managers and teams in late 1994. Since benchmarking is primarily a process improvement tool, the booklet is organized

TABLE E.1	DS&E Example Study Profile

Business Process:	Product Production	**Subprocess**	
Study Name:	Product Production Reengineering	**(if Applicable):**	NA
Date Study Begun		**Contact Person:**	Howard Esslinger
(MM/YY):	03/92	**Date Study**	
		Completed (MM/YY):	12/94

Study Description

A literature search of 100 companies was conducted. A written survey was sent to 50 companies of which 28 responded. A total of 15 companies were visited. The benchmarking study included defense electronics companies but also included automotive and aircraft, commercial electronics, pharmaceuticals, mechanical equipment, household consumables, insurance, construction, and medical equipment.

Improvements and/or Savings Implemented

- Identified 150 "gems" that equated to 43 best practices.
- New product production process map will achieve 3- to 6-month cycle time versus today's cycle time of 7 to 28 months.
- Through benchmarking many ideas were validated as well as many others discovered.
- Have reviewed data with over 500 DS&E'ers representing QITs across all DS&E and at all levels of management
- Developed implementation plan for 1995–1996.

around the Systems Group business process model (refer back to Figure E.2). It is packaged as a loose-leaf notebook so that additional studies can be easily added.

Each BCT member identified success stories in his or her respective process. A benchmarking matrix was created that identified the business process owner, the BCT representative for that process, and then listed the studies that were either completed or in progress.

A standard template known as a *Study Profile* is used to summarize each benchmarking study. The template includes fields for the business process, subprocess (if applicable), study name, contact person, starting and completion dates, study description, and finally improvements and/or savings implemented. An example Study Profile is shown in Table E.1.

BENCHMARKING FROM A PLANT SITE PERSPECTIVE

A process was identified that allows each plant site to benefit from every benchmarking study. Studies are sponsored by the process owner. The BCT member takes an active role in each team's ten-step benchmarking process, ensuring that studies meet the business need and the goals of the sponsor. Site managers develop annual improvement plans that support their stretch goals and identify specific actions that will enable meeting these goals. Benchmarking plays a key role in this process, keeping the entire site focused on the annual plan.

This sitewide approach facilitates sharing successes and best practices across all disciplines, breaking down organizational boundaries, and concentrating on team building and process improvements. This approach captures the attention of the entire site population—from manufacturing, design, human resources, and facilities management—on a few key goals.

BCT COORDINATION

All requests for benchmarking support are routed to the BCT members so that resources can be checked for existing and subsequent activities that may benefit the requesting team.

The BCT member is also responsible for documenting and responding to external inquiries for benchmarking. These inquiries are recorded in the inquiry tracking system and forwarded to the process owner for a decision to participate or not. Once the process owner agrees to participate, the BCT member becomes responsible for supporting the study. Support includes providing any necessary training, ensuring that the Code of Conduct is adhered to, and ensuring that both companies reach a win-win conclusion.

Each BCT member reports key metrics for the benchmarking process, including the number of calls received, number of studies in progress, length of time to respond to an inquiry from either an internal or external customer, and best practices identified. In general, it is the responsibility of the benchmarking core team member to assist the owners in setting and attaining goals that yield a competitive business advantage.

EXAMPLE OF CYCLE-TIME REDUCTION IN PRODUCT PRODUCTION PROCESS

One example of a major effort is the improvement of the product production process, which starts with order activation and continues through the ship process. Extremely aggressive goals were set for cycle-time reduction based on input from a benchmarking study.

Individual process owners and sponsors are identified at the beginning of the year. Progress toward identifying and implementing best practices in each subprocess are reported to managers quarterly. The BCT member is responsible for coordination among subteams so that subprocesses are clearly defined and activities are communicated to prevent overlaps.

Step-change improvements achieved include these:

- The order-entry process had been taking six weeks. A target that was set for five days has been met and in some cases bettered.

- The printed circuit resources planning cycle had been operating on an eleven-day cycle and has been improved to require less than six hours.

Summary

The TI Systems Group benchmarking core team provides an infrastructure to help lead the way to gain a competitive advantage. The team is an integral part of the continuous improvement process. It is positioned to assist both core process owners and local site managers to make step-change improvements in the performance of their processes.

APPENDIX F

Process Redesign at Xerox Corporation

Wilbur I. Pittman
XEROX CORPORATE VICE PRESIDENT, PROCESS OWNER, MARKET-TO-COLLECTION

BACKGROUND

The Haloid Company was founded in 1906 in Rochester, New York, to produce large free-standing photographic equipment and related photographic paper and chemicals. The firm served local and state governments, attorneys, and large commercial organizations that needed to reproduce copies with archival quality. Haloid achieved mod-

> **Wilbur I. Pittman** *shares a work in progress at Xerox Corporation to redesign a core process. His contribution is gratefully acknowledged.*

erate success over the years but essentially remained a small, family-owned business.

In the late 1940s Haloid acquired the rights to a new dry-imaging process with the unique capability of copying onto plain paper, thereby eliminating the need for coated paper and wet chemicals. With the help of the Battel Memorial Institute, Haloid developed a new electrophotographic process called *xerography*. Several products were developed to capitalize on this new technology—one for the preparation of printing plates and a second as a high-volume, room-sized copier called a Copyflo® (a registered trademark of the Xerox Corporation).

TECHNICAL INNOVATION PROPELS SUCCESS

Haloid continued to refine the xerographic process and in 1959 introduced a new automatic copier for general office use. Their new 914 Copier® "was an instant success. *Fortune* magazine touted it as the single most successful commercial product ever introduced. In recognition of its new success, the Haloid Corporation changed its name to the Xerox Corporation, and a major new industry was born.

The new technology embodied in the 914 coupled with a novel leasing program propelled Xerox's annual growth of revenues and profits at 23 and 20 percent, respectively, throughout the 1960s. Xerox earned a 90 percent share of the office-copying market, and profit margins approached 70 percent, making Xerox the darling of Wall Street—truly, by any measure, a business success story.

Management Focuses on Quality

However, in the late 1970s Xerox was stunned by a foreign competitor that provided the same plain-paper copying capability but at much lower prices. Xerox customers canceled large numbers of leases on their machines with a devastating impact on Xerox. The company was plunged into a crisis of survival, and its future was in doubt.

In response to this business threat, Xerox adopted in 1983 a completely new management system called *Leadership Through Quality* that focused on improving the products and services sold to customers. This new approach marshaled the resources of the company in support of regaining lost market share and reversing the revenue and profit decline.

Leadership Through Quality enabled Xerox to emerge as a successful international player as measured by the positive acceptance of its products and services, increases in revenues and profits, as well as winning the Malcolm Baldrige National Quality Award in 1989. Revenues from business products and systems rose from $8.4 billion in 1983 to $12.4 million in 1989, and income rose from $348 million to $488 in the same period. Return on assets increased from 7.5 percent in the early 1980s to 12.5 percent in 1990. During this same period, customer satisfaction approached 90 percent, and product reliability improved as reflected by a 40 percent reduction in unscheduled maintenance calls from customers. Other achievements included the following:

1. Costs were reduced.
   - The supplier base was reduced from 4,000 to 400.
   - The cost of purchased parts was reduced by 45 percent.
   - Manufacturing costs were reduced by 20 percent.
   - Inventories were reduced to twenty days.

2. Productivity increased.
   - The manufacturing employee force was reduced from 12,000 to 6,000; production doubled.
   - Component lead time was reduced from thirty-nine weeks in 1980 to eight weeks in 1992.
   - Product development time was reduced by twelve months.

3. Quality improved.
   - Production-line defective parts were reduced by 73 percent.
   - Defects were reduced by 78 percent from 1981 to 1989.
   - Product reliability improved by 45 percent.
   - Defective components reduced from 10,000 parts per million in 1980 to 225 in 1993.

Management Focuses on Processes

Although Leadership Through Quality yielded substantial improvements in the quality of products and services, Xerox's senior managers were not satisfied. They determined that Xerox needed to become even more responsive to meeting customers' requirements and quicker at bringing new technology to market. Increased accountability and responsibility were identified as the keys, and creating smaller businesses was seen as the enabler.

In 1988 to 1989 Xerox moved to decentralize by dividing the monolithic corporation into nine business divisions, each built around a major product family. Each division included two to six business teams that had total product accountability and responsibility, beginning with the customer and extending all the way upstream to technology development. The structure is conceptually depicted in Figure F.1.

Prior to introducing the new organization, product-development teams would disband after a new product was brought to market. Responsibility would pass to others for follow-up even though these hand-offs impeded delivery of the new product. Issues would develop in coordinating the phase-in of new products with the phase-out of older ones. Functional conflicts developed in managing the associated trade-offs in product mix. The business team structure eliminated these cross-functional barriers.

When the establishment of the nine headquarters business divisions was complete, Xerox restructured the field organization by creating four customer operations divisions (CODs), each responsible for one region of the world:

- *Americas Operations* covers Central and South America, and Canada.
- *Fuji Xerox*, a business partner, covers Asia and the South Pacific.
- *Rank Xerox* covers United Kingdom, Europe, Russia, former East Block nations, Africa, and, through part ownership of Fuji-Xerox, Japan and the South Pacific.
- *Xerox US* covers the United States.

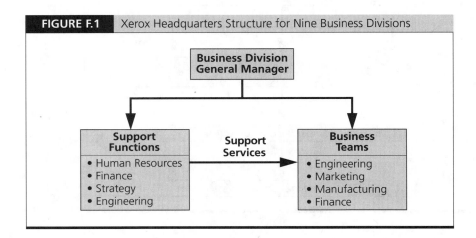

FIGURE F.1   Xerox Headquarters Structure for Nine Business Divisions

Organization of the customer operations divisions continues to evolve. In 1995 each customer operations division included subunits called *entities* (see Figure F.2), which in the case of Rank Xerox, constitute the various countries in its multinational region. For Xerox US, the entities consist of four geographic regions.

Reporting into the four U.S. regions are approximately forty customer business units (CBUs) that interact with the consumers who directly purchase Xerox products and services. This new structure moves accountability and responsibility away from the former headquarters functional groups to the CBUs—which have total responsibility for meeting the needs of their local customers.

To integrate the interests and needs of headquarters business teams in each business division with the field organization, business division representatives are placed in each of the four entities. This staff of business division representatives works with each of the CBUs to provide marketing and technical support.

MANAGEMENT FOCUS INCLUDES TIME

With the restructuring in place, Xerox acknowledged that *organizations don't get paid for functional excellence*. To illustrate this point, a function such as Real Estate Department can select geographically correct sites, design and construct buildings for world-class manufacturing, and tailor facilities to house the special needs of its inhabitants. The Real Estate Department can design and construct buildings so well that it may win design awards yet may have no positive impact on bottom-line profits.

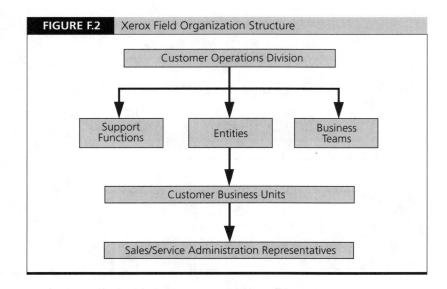

FIGURE F.2   Xerox Field Organization Structure

Using the same example in a process-focused organization, however, the Real Estate Department would be asked to provide facilities to specifically support cross-functional processes. This means designing facilities for teams comprised of engineers, information technology specialists, as well as marketing, production, human resource, materials management, and finance personnel. The site and resulting facility designed and constructed by the Real Estate Department could have a significant effect on the productivity of this cross-functional process-oriented team that could translate to the bottom line.

PROCESS ARCHITECTURE DEFINED

To deemphasize the role of functions and accelerate improvements, Xerox defined a *business process architecture* that is graphically illustrated in Figure F.3. In addition to selecting a few core processes for improvement, Xerox installed a specific governance process to oversee the overall effort. We have chosen to report on just one of these core processes, *market-to-collection* (MTC).

MARKET-TO-COLLECTION PROCESS MANAGEMENT

MTC Process Hierarchy

Six distinct levels have been defined within MTC, each offering greater detail (see Table F.1). The subdivision of the MTC core process culminates in hundreds

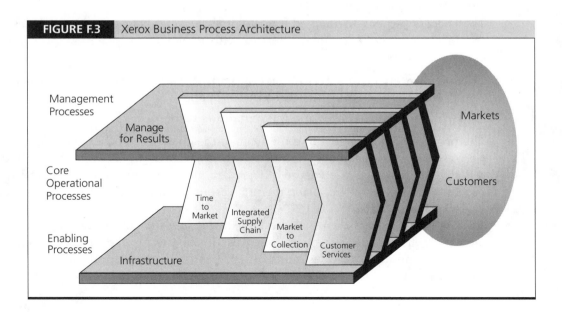

FIGURE F.3   Xerox Business Process Architecture

TABLE F.1	MTC Process Hierarchy	
LEVEL	**DESCRIPTION**	**COUNT**
1	Core process	1
1A	Process areas	3
2	Business processes	12
3	Subprocesses	40
4	Work processes	185
Task	Tasks	100's

of tasks, each of which is identified with a Xerox employee who might be located anywhere in the world. The ability to align processes to tasks and individuals provides the accountability and responsibility that Xerox is striving to instill throughout the corporation. This structured approach identifies every element that needs improvement and every employee who needs to be involved. All employees recognize how their work supports the MTC process.

The elements comprising the four highest levels of the MTC core process are shown in Table F.2. The relationships among the twelve business processes are graphically illustrated in Figure F.4. The MTC core process is number five within the Xerox architecture; hence all of its subordinate processes begin with the numeral five as their identifier.

Operational Management

The process owner is dedicated full-time for five years to the project of redesigning the MTC core process. He is charged with achieving sufficient improvement to enable the corporation to

- Function effectively and efficiently with less resources (Xerox downsized by 11,000 employees in 1993 through 1995) and
- Grow its revenue base with the remaining resources.

The process owners report to a member of the chairman's office meeting (COM)—Xerox's senior management committee that consists of the CEO and his eight direct reports. At this level, the senior officers are given the additional role and title of process champion—a supporter, mentor, resource, and confessor to their respective core-process owners.

The MTC process owner also established a steering committee of certain COM members who share major operational responsibilities around his core process. The steering committee provides more direct advice, counsel, and support than the champion alone, since the process owner can call meetings of his steering committee,

TABLE F.2	Elements of the Xerox Corporation MTC Core Process		
1	**Market-to-Collection**		
1A	**Market Management**	**Prospect-to-Implementation**	**Implementation-to-Collection/ Customer Relationship**
2–3	5.1 Market understanding • Evaluate business landscape • Analyze voice of the customer • Define markets and estimate size • Analyze competitive intelligence 5.2 Market modeling and strategies • Define market segments • Develop forecasts of market demand • Develop market strategies 5.3 Solutions management • Market solutions configuration • Benchmark competitive solutions • Manage solutions lifecycle • Establish solution contract guidelines • Define pricing strategies and guidelines • Define and implement pricing programs 5.4 Market communication • Create corporate image awareness • Create solution awareness • Define and manage marketing programs 5.5 Channel Strategy • Define channel mix • Define channel coverage • Establish channel contracts and guidelines	5.6 Sales operations planning and management • Implement direct and indirect channel strategy • Manage selling process 5.7 Selling process • Identify prospects • Make initial contact • Qualify customer interest • Identify customer requirements and translate into specifications • Determine potential solutions • Present proposal and justification • Negotiate to close order 5.8 Solution/order fulfillment management • Manage solution implementation • Evaluate solution implementation and monitor customer satisfaction • Recycle to expand solution	5.9 Invoicing • Create payment notice 5.10 Credit and collection management • Manage credit • Process customer payments • Manage collection 5.11 Customer relationship management • Manage customer relationship • Resolve complaint/ inquiry/request • Disseminate customer learnings 5.12 Contract management • Manage customer contracts • Manage third-party contracts

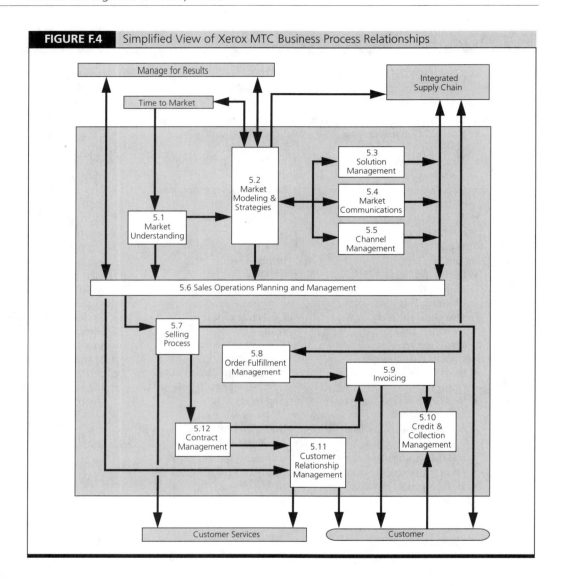

FIGURE F.4 Simplified View of Xerox MTC Business Process Relationships

a prerogative that only the CEO has with the COM. The steering committee provides coordination among the functions they manage as the market-to-collection process management team.

The MTC effort itself is managed by a staff of direct reports to the process owner. These managers are assigned full-time for a five-year period from functional organizations within Xerox. They are funded by their respective functional groups and will return to these same groups when their work on MTC is complete. The MTC staff includes a process implementation manager and representatives from finance and the business divisions, as well as an information technology specialist. The staff is supported by external process and systems consultants.

PROCESS REDESIGN PLAN

Launched in 1994, redesign of the MTC process is progressing in four phases: define, design, develop, and deploy (see Figure F.5). Worldwide deployment is scheduled for completion by the end of 1998. While its investment in redesigning the MTC process is proprietary information, Xerox is willing to say that net savings should approach $1,000,000 per business day following implementation.

FIGURE F.5	Xerox MTC Project Four-Phase Plan		
Phase 1	**Phase 2**	**Phase 3**	**Phase 4**
Define	Design	Develop	Deploy
• FormTeam • Create Vision • Identify Gaps			
1994	1995	1996	1997–98

PHASE 1: DEFINE

Phase 1 began with an assessment of the current performance of the MTC core process. Problems were identified and confirmed. The improvement team then drafted a vision of the desired state to be achieved by the year 2000 and built agreement for this statement across the corporation:

> *CUSTOMERS VALUE THE ease of doing business with Xerox, their Document Service Partner. Worldwide, our customer engagement processes are responsive, accessible, and simple to use. For both customers and Xerox, these processes add value to the range of Xerox Document Solutions and Services. Customers value Xerox people for their collectively superior knowledge and skills, and their mastery of leading edge document technology.*

The vision was translated into statements that the team expects customers will make when the improved MTC process is successfully installed. Examples of the vision translated into customer terms are found in Table F.3.

TABLE F.3	Our Vision of the View from the Customer

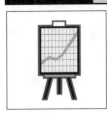				
MARKETING	**SELLING**	**ORDER MANAGEMENT AND IMPLEMENTATION**	**BILLING AND COLLECTION**	**RELATIONSHIP MANAGEMENT**
"I got a letter from Xerox one day asking if I knew how Andersen Consulting has reduced warehousing by 60%, is saving $1.3 million in reproduction costs, and is now preparing their student hand-outs on demand."	*"The Xerox salesperson was a polished professional and seemed to know a lot about my business. We spent our time on benefits rather than the usual haggling over price."*	*". . . And he took the order the same day! The machine arrived, and we were up and running when requested—in 6 locations! And they talked to my systems!"*	*"My computer paid their computer, and soon after I got a "Thank you" from my sales rep! I'm now printing on demand, <u>and</u> now I'm a Xerox success story."*	*"I continue to get great support from the Xerox team—everything from customized information to quick supplies ordering to changing my information. I can even enter an inquiry about my own orders."*
I got interested.	**I got hooked.**	**I placed an order.**	**I paid.**	**I'm elated!**

BEHIND THE SCENES: WHAT THE CUSTOMER WON'T SEE				
• Xerox Information Exchange • Marketing Databases • Smart Marketing	• Help for the salesforce • More time in the field • Simplified, flexible T&C	• Salesperson takes the order and feeds the Xerox Order Management System • No hand-offs • Tight coordination with equipment delivery and service	• Computer linkages	• Complete customer information • Customer order entry • Reduced workload for customer care

Gaps Identified

MTC senior managers reviewed performance data to identifying gaps between the current state and the desired future state. Their technique is shown conceptually in Figure F.6. This analysis helped the MTC leadership team to set priorities and focus efforts in eight of their twelve business processes (see Table F.4).

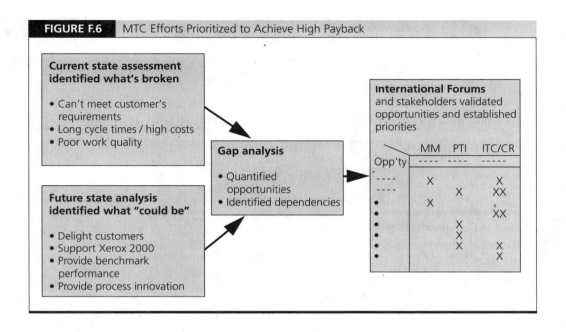

FIGURE F.6   MTC Efforts Prioritized to Achieve High Payback

Current state assessment identified what's broken

- Can't meet customer's requirements
- Long cycle times / high costs
- Poor work quality

Future state analysis identified what "could be"

- Delight customers
- Support Xerox 2000
- Provide benchmark performance
- Provide process innovation

Gap analysis

- Quantified opportunities
- Identified dependencies

International Forums and stakeholders validated opportunities and established priorities

Opp'ty	MM	PTI	ITC/CR
----	----	----	-----
----	X		X
----		X	XX
•	X		
•			XX
•		X	
•		X	
•		X	X
•			X

TABLE F.4   MTC Improvement Priorities

MARKET MANAGEMENT	PROSPECT-TO-IMPLEMENTATION	IMPLEMENTATION-TO-COLLECTION/ CUSTOMER RELATIONSHIP
5.1 Market Understanding	5.6 Sales Op's Planning & Management	5.9 Invoicing
5.2 Market Modeling & Strategies		5.10 Credit & Collection Management
5.3 Solutions Management	5.7 Selling Process	
	5.8 Solution/Order Fulfillment Management	5.11 Customer Relationship Management
5.4 Market Communication		
5.5 Channel Strategy		5.12 Contract Management

KEY TO BUSINESS PROCESS PRIORITIES

☐ Practice simplification to enable improved performance of other processes

▨ New productivity

▪ Critically broken—must be fixed

Others: Kaizen

Performance Measures Defined

The measure of how well MTC achieves its vision will be determined at three levels (see Table F.5). Revenue growth and profitability are measured at the corporate level. Business divisions and entities examine process effectiveness and efficiency in the three process areas. Finally, work groups look at quality and cycle time at the business and subprocess levels.

TABLE F.5	MTC Performance Measures Focus on Results

CORPORATE

- Cost to revenue (%)
- Days revenue outstanding
- Revenue growth

BUSINESS DIVISIONS/ENTITIES

- Performance by process area:
  - Cost to revenue (%)
  - Days revenue outstanding
- Market share
- Customer satisfaction post installation (%)
- Total revenue
- Customer retention
- Overall satisfaction index
- Revenue and profit (per customer business unit)

WORK GROUPS

QUALITY AND PROCESS CAPABILITY	CYCLE TIME
• Proposal hit rate • Customer required implementation date (% met) • Successful installations (%) • Invoice quality • Revenues uncollected (%) • Customer inquiry rate • Revenue achieved (% of target)	• Prospect-to-order • Order-to-invoice – Order-to-implementation – Implementation-to-invoice • Customer inquiry resolution time • Inquiries resolved in initial contact (%)

PHASE 2: DESIGN

The priority assessment led to preparation of a list of deliverables that the MTC improvement project is expected to provide between 1995 and 1998. These are displayed in Table F.6. Functional specifications have been defined and accepted worldwide. Detailed application specifications are being prepared.

Development of a *marketing communications database* (MCDB) is one example of efforts launched to improve the *market understanding business process*. This database will improve sales productivity by providing to sales representatives information they need to complete a sale. Xerox found that sales representatives spend up to 30 percent of their time collecting data they need to present to potential clients that already exists in one form or another somewhere in the corporation. The new MCDB will provide case studies on successful sales, territory coverage information, product configuration data, product pricing, product availability, customer data, and state and local tax rates—all in one easily accessible location.

TABLE F.6	MTC Deliverables	
MARKET MANAGEMENT	**PROSPECT-TO-IMPLEMENTATION**	**IMPLEMENTATION-TO-COLLECTION/ CUSTOMER RELATIONSHIP**
DOCUMENTS		
• Price list • Discount/promotions schedule • Standard terms and conditions	• Proposal • Customer agreements • Contract • Order agreement • Warranty registration form • Configuration specifications • Commission statement • Account establishment strategy	• Purchase order • Customer correspondence – Dunning – Contract renewal – Purchase order renewal • Invoice statement • Debit/credit memo • Meter cards • MTC report card • Customer report card
PRACTICES		
• Pricing • Standard terms and conditions • Contracts • Leasing/financing	• Role/job design • Product offerings • Configuration • Compensation • ISC coordination • Third-party coordination • Forecasting	• Billing/invoicing • Taxation • Payment processing • Renewals • Credit • Electronic data interchange • Customer inquiry management
SYSTEMS		
• Market information	• Sales force automation ("sales briefcase")	• Order processing ("backend systems") • Customer service

In providing sales representatives this readily accessible capability, MTC can potentially improve sales productivity by as much as 30 pecent, plus reduce the errors on sales orders, a benefit that ripples throughout all MTC processes. For example, sales orders entered correctly using the information provided by MCDB results in the correct equipment configuration being installed in the customer's office, correct invoices, fewer customer complaints, less need for customer help-desk personnel, prompt customer payments, and overall improved customer satisfaction.

Another example project is *sales force automation*, a new sales system expected to improve the rate of sales success by providing the sales representatives with a prescribed series of steps to follow in pursuit of a sale. The system provides sales personnel with product data such as pricing, configurations, and availability. The system also tracks where each sales representative is at each stage in the selling cycle with each prospect. This information assists in the scheduling of service personnel to install the products promised in the sale. In the future, this system will allow the salesperson to update customer records—previously a headquarters responsibility—and to schedule the product installation with transportation and installation teams.

Design work continues, with every expectation that the MTC project will be highly successful. One reason for optimism is that the MTC staff has invested heavily in bringing all individuals who have an interest in, or who are impacted by the MTC core process, to underwrite and support the effort. A second reason for optimism is the support from the highest levels in the corporation, not with acquiescence but with solid personal involvement, funding, and high exceptions of the outcome.

PHASES 3 AND 4: DEVELOP AND DEPLOY

Development will likely include creation of new information systems and supporting software. The skills and capabilities required to complete this phase have been identified and secured. Deployment includes testing of all systems, piloting of major components, and worldwide roll out. This phase is scheduled to be completed by the end of 1998.

SUMMARY

Many organizations looking to reengineer their key processes are concerned about the success of their projects and rightfully so. While they need to dramatically improve performance, they recognize the enormous challenges on their organization's culture, processes, and work procedures.

One response to these challenges is to invest time, money, and senior management attention on the reengineering project. The more resources and guidance provided, the more likely the project is to succeed.

Another response is to carefully balance the need for *speedy* solutions against the large amount of *detail* required to fully understand what needs to be reengineered. Spending too much time collecting too much data can explode the size of the project and threaten its success. Conversely, inadequate information gathering can mean ending up with redesigned processes that do not support the business.

Xerox Corporation's reengineering of their market-to-collection core process is offered as a model of a well-balanced approach.

APPENDIX G | Reengineering the Commercialization Process at Praxair

Using Analysis, Creativity, and External Learning to Achieve a Step Change Improvement

Donald D. Marple
QUALITY MANAGER, NORTH AMERICA ON-SITE GASES, PRAXAIR, INCORPORATED

Praxair Inc. is a worldwide—and North America's largest—producer of industrial gases and high-performance surface coatings, along with related services, materials, and systems. Praxair is a new company that was spun off from Union Carbide in 1992. Though new, it has a long heritage. The company was founded in 1907 by Karl von Linde, inventor of the cryogenic air separation process, and became a division of Union Carbide in 1917.

> **Donald D. Marple** provides the following success story on a project implemented to achieve a 50 percent reduction in the time to commercialize new products at Praxair. His contribution is gratefully acknowledged.

Praxair delivers value to customers by providing better methods of applying oxygen, nitrogen, argon, hydrogen, and other industrial gases to their processes, resulting in customers that can produce higher-quality, lower-cost products in an environmentally sound manner. In addition to applications, Praxair commercializes processes and systems for the production and distribution of these gases. These products bring value to customers through a reliable supply of low-cost product from plants located at the customer's site.

THE NEED FOR CHANGE

Praxair's commercialization process is owned by the vice president of technology. The process begins when a preliminary evaluation indicates that a new technology may be able to bring value to customers and ends when the application or process is in operation at the customer's site.

In early 1994, an evaluation by senior management of the commercialization process showed that a reduction in cycle time would offer a major opportunity to increase the value created by technology, both for Praxair and its customers. This analysis provided three goals for a step-change improvement in commercialization:

- Reduce the time to commercialization by 50 percent.
- Align the R&D organization with the restructured organizations of its internal clients. This will eliminate the disconnects that had been seen in the interfaces between R&D, the new business organizations, and customers. The new commercialization process is expected to eliminate these potential problem areas.
- Improve the contribution of technology to Praxair's business strategies by improving current business performance and providing more value to customers.

REENGINEERING PROJECT LAUNCHED

A *change team* was formed to reengineer the commercialization process, consisting of three technology directors, one key technology planning manager, and one internal business process improvement consultant. This team was chartered to meet the goals established by the process owner and by the president of Praxair Gases USA and to meet the needs of the stakeholders, including external customers.

The twenty stakeholders had an "open chair" at any of the change team meetings. They were kept informed of team activities by assigning one member of the change team to brief each stakeholder. In cases when the input of a stakeholder was required, he or she would fill the open chair at a team meeting. Commercialization process stakeholders also took part in the benchmarking site visits and were members of implementation subteams.

INTERNAL BENCHMARKING

Efforts to compress cycle time by 50 percent began in the summer of 1994 with a process benchmarking study. The change team analyzed a dozen past commercialization projects and developed listings of the factors that contributed to and impeded rapid commercialization. Factors the team found that contribute to rapid commercialization included

- A well thought-out proposal,
- General understanding at Praxair about the value of the technology,
- Management support,
- Business buy-in, and
- A perceived customer need.

Factors the team found that represent barriers to rapid commercialization included the following:

Internal to R&D:

- Time to get customer approval to proceed,
- Time to find potential customer test site or project,
- Time taken to get internal buy-in and support,
- Method of scheduling project reviews and approvals, and
- Number of hand-offs required in a project.

External to R&D:

- Customer reticence to be first,
- Tests require some shutdowns, with resultant losses,
- Difficulty in "killing" an ongoing project, and
- Changes in local business strategies.

The next step involved documenting and analyzing the effects of the commercialization process interactions with other parts of Praxair and with stakeholders. This analysis confirmed many of the previously identified factors that contributed to and impeded rapid commercialization.

PREPARATION FOR EXTERNAL BENCHMARKING

In preparation of a search to find best practices at other firms—including those that do the same work but in different industries—the team characterized their R&D process. A generic example of this characterization is shown in Table G.1. Its purpose is to identify the work that is done in the commercialization process without identifying it with the specific outcomes or products.

The change team also developed a high-level process flowchart and two sets of questions for benchmarking. One set of questions was a screening survey to determine if candidates for site visits did the same type of work, and if they did it well (Table G.2). The second set was a detailed list of questions to explore the best practices among those companies selected for site visits (Table G.3).

TABLE G.1	Characteristics of Praxair's Commercialization Process

- We commercialize applications and systems.
- Development and testing are required.
- Testing is done on customers' sites.
- We find ways to produce low-cost products.
- Customers are industrial companies.

TABLE G.2	Example Screening Questions

- What do you develop and commercialize?
- Do you consider technology development essential to your business?
- Are your customers industrial?
- What is the size of your R&D organization?
- How long does it take to commercialize technology?
- How much variation in this time?
- When do you consider technology to be commercialized?
- How is R&D performance measured?
- How many of your projects require pilot testing?
- What is your technical position in your industry?
- Is this position acceptable?

TABLE G.3	Example Site-Visit Questions

- Describe your development and commercialization process.
- What products or services do you commercialize?
- How do you manage the R&D process or projects?
- How is R&D performance measured?
- At what point do you consider technology to be commercialized?
- How long does it take to commercialize technology?
- How much variation in this time?
- What makes your firm successful in commercializing developments rapidly?
- Describe your budgeting process. What impact does it have on the speed of commercialization?
- What is your relationship with the approving authority, what is the process followed?

The change team was looking for companies that were known for their capabilities in innovation, that had recently made major changes in commercialization, and that had to deal with mature technologies. The team and the technology vice president made an initial list of forty-four potential best-performing companies. Sources of information were their own knowledge, information from the Industrial Research Institute, and lists of winners of the Malcolm Baldrige National Quality Award and the National Science Medal.

The list of candidates was quickly reduced to twenty-one companies. Initial contact with these companies was made by members of the change team. Contacts were made at the highest R&D levels to develop a good understanding of how each firm performed at commercialization. These contacts also helped establish a rapport that was valuable in securing agreement to site visits. In addition, the Praxair representatives offered to share knowledge in areas where Praxair is a potential best-performing company—cash application, logistics, project management and control, internal communication and employee newspapers, among others.

In August 1994, the screening survey was sent to twenty-one companies, and seventeen responded within two weeks. An evaluation of these seventeen companies showed that eleven were potential best-performing companies in commercialization. Ten of these firms were willing to entertain site visits, and seven of these sites were actually visited.

The list of site-visit questions was sent to each benchmarking partner several weeks before the visit to allow for the necessary preparation. The two parties then collaborated on an agenda. Each visit was scheduled to last most of the day.

BEST PRACTICES FOUND

Benchmarking partners' sites were visited in a seven-week period beginning mid-September 1994. Table G.4 summarizes ten areas of observations. Five of these observations were planned. The other five were unforeseen discoveries—technology planning, product line management, global management of technologies, marketing leadership, and the integration of engineering and quality. The site visits concluded the benchmarking phase of the project and provided the following outputs:

- A listing of the external best practices evaluated against the impediments and concerns of Praxair and
- A listing of Praxair's best practices, validated by discussions at the site visits.

EXTENDING BENCHMARKING INTO REENGINEERING

The change team wanted to improve everything they had seen so far. They wanted to "shoot ahead of the duck" and design a process that would be an improvement over the current best practices of Praxair, the external best practices, and their own new ideas. They began developing the attributes of the new process, an example of which is shown in Table G.5. These attributes, or features of the process, are characteristics that could lead to performance better than that seen internally and externally.

TABLE G.4	Site-Visit Observations
• Measures	• Technology planning
• Stage-gate process	• Product line management
• Technology reviews	• Global management of technologies
• Reward and recognition programs	• Marketing leadership
• Project classification	• Integration of research and engineering and quality

TABLE G.5	Attributes Commercialization Process Should Contain
• Multifunctional teams	
• Managed as a project	
• Continuity of team membership	
• Early involvement of stakeholders	
• External customer involvement	

COMMERCIALIZATION PROCESS REDESIGNED

The change team completed a high-level redesign of a new commercialization process based on

- Praxair's best practices,
- The external best practices, ranked against Praxair's impediments and concerns, and
- The change team's own new ideas.

The change team specified that the process should be carried out by cross-functional teams that had the skills and knowledge needed to complete commercialization. So that this work would be rewarding to the team members, they were to be given

- Requisite skills to execute the specific commercialization project,
- End-to-end accountability for the commercialization of the new product,
- Autonomy to do the work necessary for commercialization,
- Avenues of support and help if they were needed, and
- Feedback on their performance.

When this redesign of the commercialization process was concluded, the change team published

- A flowchart for the new commercialization process,
- The attributes of the process,
- The practices to be included in the redesign,
- A preliminary list of the new measures of process performance,
- A list of subteams to implement the high-level redesign.

SUBTEAMS LAUNCH IMPLEMENTATION

Each member of the original five-person change team became the leader of a six-person subteam, responsible for detailed specification and implementation of the new process. This structure leveraged the team to involve thirty people and increased buy-in from the R&D and stakeholder organizations.

Subteams were commissioned to flesh out the process in more detail, integrate the various parts of the process, finalize the measurement, and document the steps to be taken in the commercialization process. These subteams also completed a description of the new roles and responsibilities for organizations and functions dealing with commercialization.

Output from Subteams

Deliverables from the subteams included a documented process, a summary of the steps needed to integrate the new process with current practices and other organizations, and a plan for implementation. The subteams formulated the following list of measures to be followed for continuous improvement:

- The amount of top-line revenue growth from innovation through new technology,
- The cycle time to commercialize a new product versus the complexity of the commercialization project,
- The number of gate reviews held as originally scheduled, and
- The commercialization value realized by each *rapid commercialization project*.

The subteams also delivered procedures for the selection and composition of rapid commercialization teams. They developed and documented new roles and responsibilities for R&D managers, the senior technical staff, team members, team leaders in a scientific organization, and stakeholders.

A number of key technical people were uncomfortable leading groups, since this was not something they had done before. To overcome this problem, leaders and members of rapid commercialization teams participate in training before and during the operation.

Results

As a result of this change effort, all major commercialization projects now use the new rapid commercialization process. The high level of acceptance by the stakeholders' organizations is attributed to their involvement in the reengineering project and the responsiveness of the new process to their needs. The original change team is now a steering team that monitors implementation and evaluates ideas for continuous improvement. Intra- and interteam issues continue to be dealt with as part of the ongoing implementation plan.

What Worked Well?

In retrospect, certain elements led to the successful analysis, external learning, redesign, and ultimate implementation of the rapid commercialization process at Praxair:

- *Clear goals:* A clear set of goals regarding time, alignment, process improvement, and creating value drove the Praxair change strategy. These goals had the effect of focusing the change effort and keeping the team on track throughout the project.

- *Establishment of new measures:* Performance measures were introduced to evaluate the contribution of innovation to Praxair's revenue and profitability growth, as well as the speed with which the process was executed.

- *Clear and involved process ownership:* The technology vice president of Praxair was committed to achieving the goals of the change team and provided the direction and resources to do so.

- *Small core team made up of those who would implement change:* The original change team of five people consisted of those who would be responsible for implementing the new process. They did the analysis, benchmarking, and initial redesign. Praxair was able to avoid a situation where people had to sell upper management on the need for change. Those who determined what the change should be were the major force for implementation.

- *Analysis based on the key performance measure (cycle time):* The drive to improve time to commercialization provided a focus and a context for evaluation done during the analysis and external learning phases. The change team was constantly looking for ways to improve the speed of commercialization.

- *External learning:* Invaluable information on process design and implementation was learned from the seven companies that participated in benchmarking site visits. The change team had done a thorough job of selection, evaluation, and preparation for these visits. Quality tools were used to evaluate potential best practices for application to the rapid commercialization process and to overcome stakeholders' concerns identified during the analysis phase.

- *Subteam and stakeholder participation:* Proactive communication and active participation of stakeholders gave the change team the input and buy-in needed to affect change in the commercialization process and to deliver what the clients required and provided impetus for integration with the processes controlled by the stakeholders and customers of commercialization.

THE BOTTOM LINE

The rapid commercialization process at Praxair has put the company in a position to bring more value to its customers and its shareholders by reducing the time to bring new products to market and improving the quality of the products that are commercialized.

APPENDIX H | Sample Best Practices Report

Basic Products Corporation
Technical Services Group

Best Practices Report

PROJECT TEAM MEMBERS

Thomas McKay
Bernice Lyons
Robb Campbell
Ira DeTorre

Contents

> **Note to Readers**
>
> *This sample document was prepared by a benchmarking team. Similar best practices reports might be prepared by teams following other improvement paths. A continuous improvement team would likely skip preparing this type of report and launch directly into implementation. By contrast, a re-engineering team's report would likely be more extensive.*

Introduction

Project Purpose

The Technical Training Group undertook a project to improve its *curriculum development* subprocesses because it offers the largest opportunity to lower training costs, reduce training time, and improve test scores—objectives that are consistent with current business priorities. Process benchmarking was selected as the improvement path in order to achieve a step change in performance.

Project Triggers

The impetus for this study began one year ago when *Field Operations* published a report comparing equipment repair times for the top ten companies in our industry. In that report, Basic Products ranked seventh (Table H.1).

TABLE H.1   *Ranking of Equipment Repair Times*

Rank	Company	Average Hours to Repair Equipment
1.	Shelby Industries	1.11
2.	Amalgamated Products	1.28
3.	Marshall Corporation	1.39
4.	Benson Enterprises, Ltd.	1.41
5.	Western Systems, Inc.	1.43
6.	Universal Widgets Corp.	1.44
7.	Basic Products	1.45
8.	Triple Edge Gadgets	1.48
9.	Whammo Widgets	1.49
10.	Gizmo Products Co.	1.51

Insufficient training was one of the primary contributors to poor performance. In selecting what to improve within the jurisdiction of the Technical Training Group, estimates of improvement potential (see Table H.2) drove us to select the curriculum development subprocess as our highest priority.

Project Focus

Seven critical performance metrics (see Table H.3) were identified to gauge the effectiveness and efficiency of our technical training processes. The outcomes of training—superior job performance of the trained technicians and customer satisfaction—turned out to be many times more important than efficiency—reducing the cost of developing and delivering training. Therefore, *average time to repair equipment* serves as our primary measure of performance. This key statistic indicates how long it takes a service technician to troubleshoot and repair defective equipment and contributes directly to current business priorities.

TABLE H.2   *Estimates of Improvement Potential*

Training Function	Expected Impact on Improving Repair Time
Curriculum development	50%
Classroom instruction	30
Materials/video production	10
Organizational structure	10

TABLE H.3 *Critical Performance Metrics*

Measure of Results	Internal Methods	Industry Leader	Benchmark[a]
Average time to train	5 days	4 days	3 days
Cost per technician	$1,800	$1,200	$1,000
Average time to develop training courses	12 weeks	8 weeks	6
Percentage retrained	15%	10%	5%
Average cost of course development	$35,000	$25,000	$20,000
Average test result (time to repair equipment)	1.4 hrs.	1.1 hrs.	0.7 hr.

a. Achievable if all best-of-best practices are implemented.

Summary of Findings

Scope of Analysis

Our benchmarking study covered four internal groups, four competitors, and seven companies from other industries. This is broader than our initial plan, which only expected to cover two competitors and two companies from other industries.

Best Practices Descriptive Summary

Best practices found from the array of benchmarked organizations are summarized in Table H.4.

We reviewed and documented the work process and practices currently used internally to develop technical training curriculum and then compared them to the best of external processes and practices. The "best of the best" were selected and documented, which became the benchmark practices.

By combining the best-of-best methods from all organizations studied, we compiled the following system.

Step 1: Task Analysis

Considerable differences were observed among companies regarding how they analyzed training needs, ranging from extensive task analysis and flowcharting, to focus groups. The methods we plan to institute are a composite of best methods observed at five companies (Table H.5).

TABLE H.4 *World-Class Comparison Matrix*

Practice	Internal Organizations	Direct Competitors	World-Class Processes	Innovative Practices
Needs analysis	Sales training	Amalgamated Shelby	TRW	
Task analysis	Data processing	Shelby Amalgamated	AT&T	Boeing
Program design	Sales training	Marshall	Forum	
Writing materials	Sales training	Marshall	Xerox	U.S. Army
Evaluate results	Sales training	Shelby	Huthwaite	
Train instructors	Sales training	Shelby	AT&T	

TABLE H.5 *World-Class Task Analysis*

Current Method	Best Method	Performance Advantage	Value Gain
Not done	Survey client to identify current performance deficiencies, set program goals, and set customer requirements.	Saves one day in the field observing incumbents	$350
Not done	Conduct a task analysis to identify job duties and create a task map.	Improves accuracy of training objectives and saves one day of rewrites	$350
Observe incumbents perform on the job.	Same	No change	0
Survey managers and top performers.	Observe top and average performers on the job to measure performance differences to compute potential for improvement.	Sets measurable targets for improvement against which to assess success	Key[a]
Create performance objectives.	Same	No change	0

a. Key result that will lead to improved performance—reduced repair time—for trained technicians. Contribution of individual best practice cannot be determined.

Best practices for task analysis are $700 less expensive than our current methods, primarily because they are able to shorten the time by two days. The superior method determines the current skill deficiency by examining the skill level of top performers, and mapping the task to arrive at an outline of the training objectives.

More important is this method's impact on the effectiveness of the program. Since adopting these methods, one company reported that the average test scores of technicians trained improved by 12 percent. We expect to achieve similar improvements.

Step 2: Needs Analysis

Needs analysis is an important but neglected step in designing training programs. It has been our practice to bypass the important step of analyzing the target population. By assuming we knew the technician's demographics, we sometimes designed instructional programs that made learning more difficult than necessary (instructional level either too low or too high). One benchmarking partner estimates that target population analysis reduced the revisions required after pilot testing by 15 percent, which saved an average of three days of work.

Step 3: Program Design

We will be able to develop a program blueprint faster and less expensively than we presently can ($1,000 less), principally because our needs analysis data will be superior, and our methods for blueprinting will save several days of rewrites compared to our present method.

Step 4: Writing Materials

Writing training materials is the most time-consuming step in program development, consuming as much as 70 percent of the project's schedule. By adopting benchmark methods for task analysis, we expect to be able to reduce the writing time by two weeks, save about $3,500, and improve instructional design.

The impact on the technician's skill level is difficult to pinpoint, but our investigations of other companies revealed that test scores improve on average 15 percent with superior writing methods.

Step 5: Evaluate Results

No changes are proposed at this time for methods to evaluate results. Changes here may be part of a second phase of work.

Step 6: Train Instructors

No changes are proposed at this time for methods to train instructors. Changes here may be part of a second phase of work.

TABLE H.6 *Planning and Analysis Costs*

Item	Actual
Salaries	$102,200
Travel	3,500
Consultant fees	2,500
Library search fees	1,700
Purchase of sample training materials	1,100
Total	**$111,000**

Deployment Costs

Item	Estimated
Training curriculum designers	$30,000
PC software	1,500
Other	3,200
Total	**$34,700**

Duration and Resources

Four staff members completed the planning and analysis phases in five months at a total cost of $111,000 (compared to initial estimated costs of approximately $85,000). Costs for the deployment phase are estimated to total about $35,000 (Table H.6).

Analysis of Performance Gaps and Gains

Current Performance Gap

We estimate that we can reduce our curriculum development costs by $5,200 per course by adopting best practices. More important, adopting best practices should improve the effectiveness of our courses, as measured by technicians' average time to repair equipment, from an average test score of 1.4 hours per service call to 0.7 hour. In addition, we could reduce the time it takes to develop new courses, which would enable us to produce training courses for new equipment faster and allow for quicker revisions as changes are made to exiting equipment.

Historical Trends

We were able to improve the average test score of technicians trained from 1.5 hours to 1.4 hours, a 6.7 percent increase, primarily through a longer training program (five versus three days). This longer program, however, has led to complaints about technicians' time away from the job during training and added cost for training.

During the same period, our best competitor improved its average time to repair equipment from 1.3 hours to 1.1 hours, a 15 percent improvement. The competitor's advantage is attributed, in part, to more effective training methods and materials.

Impact of Superior Training

The current performance gap of 0.3 hour per repair places us at a competitive disadvantage, both in terms of cost and customer satisfaction. With our staff of 1,500 technicians, our competitor currently enjoys a cost advantage of $9,000 per day, which is equivalent to about $1,800,000 annually (see Table H.7).

Projected Performance Gap

Our investigations revealed that the competition is investing in computer-aided instruction materials, which would further reduce their training time from 3 days to 2.5 days and improve the average time to repair equipment to 0.8 hour within two years.

During the same period, we would expect our training methods to achieve only 1.2 hours per service call, which means that the current performance gap would widen. Without strategic changes, our competition would increase its advantage to 0.4 hour (0.8 versus 1.2) within two years (see Figure H.1). This trend indicates our competitor's advantage might increase to $2,400,000 annually.

TABLE H.7   *Impact of Current Performance Gap*

	Own	Competition	Net Advantage	Percentage of Advantage
Average repair time (hour)	1.4	1.1	– 0.3	– 21.5%
Number of calls per day	5.0	6.0	1.0	– 20.0%
Average labor cost per hour	$20.00	$20.00		
Average cost per call	$28.00	$22.00	– $6.00	– 21.5%

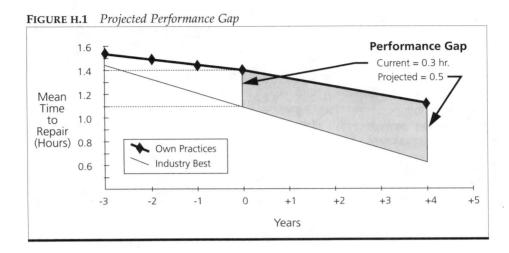

FIGURE H.1   *Projected Performance Gap*

Projected Performance Advantages

With the adoption of best practices, we could achieve an average test score of 0.7 hour in two years. Assuming our best competitor's technicians perform at 0.8 hour per repair, we will reverse a 0.3 hour *disadvantage* to a 0.1 hour *advantage*.

This has enormous implications for customer base stability and costs of service. With the adoption of best practices, we expect to become the industry leader in technical training as defined by our key performance metrics.

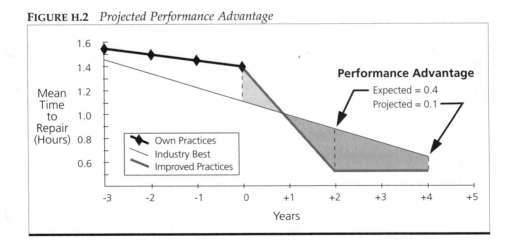

FIGURE H.2   *Projected Performance Advantage*

TABLE H.8 *Projected Performance Advantage in Two Years*

	Own Current Performance	Best Competitor		Own Future Performance
		Current	Outlook	
Average time to train	5 days	3 days	2.5 days	3 days
Cost per technician	$ 1,800	$ 1,600	Unknown	$ 1,200
Average time to develop training courses	12 weeks	10 weeks	Unknown	8 weeks
Percentage retrained	15%	10%	Unknown	5%
Average cost of course development	$ 35,000	$ 25,000	Unknown	$ 30,000
Average test score (time to repair equipment)	1.4 hrs.	1.1 hrs.	0.8 hr.	0.7 hr.

Index